Christmas Mumming in Newfoundland

Published for
Memorial University of Newfoundland
by University of Toronto Press

Christmas Mumming in Newfoundland

*Essays in Anthropology
Folklore, and History
Edited by
Herbert Halpert and
G. M. Story*

Copyright Canada 1969 by
University of Toronto Press
Printed in Canada
SBN 8020 3200 1

Preface

THE IMMEDIATE ORIGIN of this book was a seminar held at Memorial University in St. John's, Newfoundland, in January 1963 by the Department of Sociology and Anthropology. At this seminar one of the Fellows of the Institute of Social and Economic Research, Melvin Firestone, gave a paper on a Christmas custom, 'janneying,' he had observed in the Newfoundland community where he had been working. Frightening figures in folklore and patterns of masking had already been subjects of conversation and preliminary study by several of us, so that Dr. Firestone's paper, which appears in this volume as "Mummers and Strangers in Northern Newfoundland," was rich in interest not only to his fellow anthropologists but also to the linguists, folklorists, and other students of Newfoundland in the audience. It was obvious, ten minutes after the paper had been delivered, that at least seven people present had heard a paper on a subject they too wanted to write about. A conference was swiftly called by Herbert Halpert, the topics were agreed upon and the book was under way.

The essays were written, and may be read, as independent contributions; but most of them were circulated for comment among the group at different stages of composition. This process, as editors of similar collections will readily appreciate, was a necessarily protracted one, especially after most of the contributors left St. John's, some to do further fieldwork in Newfoundland, others to go to the United States, Great Britain, and elsewhere; and it was directed by the senior editor. The delay proved fruitful. First, it enabled James Faris (whose interest was aroused by sight of the early drafts) to join the original eight contributors. Secondly, it led to the expansion of the very short book first envisaged into a deeper and more closely articulated study of Christmas mumming in Newfoundland. In this final stage of preparation, both editors have worked side by side, and in continuous (if distant) touch with the by now scattered contributors.

In editing the volume, we have allowed repetition to stand when it involves independent description of parallel data in different communities. The method of reference and the form of bibliographical citation have been standardized as have been minor variations in spelling and punctuation. However, such variable terms as 'mumming' (or 'mummering') or 'janneying' follow the preference of the individual authors. The cross-references in parentheses to different sections of the book are editorial additions, and the editors (in addition to their signed contributions) are also responsible for the Introduction, the Bibliography, and the presentation of the data on the Newfoundland distribution of mumming and the mummers' play in appendix III.

We are indebted to the following libraries, institutes, and business firms for the use, and sometimes the photographing, of their collections: The Memorial University Library, the Gosling Memorial Library, the Provincial Archives, the F. M. O'Leary Co., Ltd., the *Evening Telegram* and the *Daily News* (all at St. John's); the University of Pennsylvania Library in Philadelphia; the Library of the British Museum, the Bodleian Library, Oxford, and the School of Scottish Studies at Edinburgh.

Expenses entailed by fieldwork were met by grants from the President and Regents of Memorial University, the Institute of Social and Economic Research, and the Canada Council. To the Canada Council we are also indebted for a grant in aid of publication.

Dr. L. Harris, Mr. Leo Moakler, Mr. M. O. Morgan, Dr. E. R. Seary, Dr. Ian Whitaker, and Mr. Carl Withers assisted us in a number of ways. To three of them, Dr. Harris, Dr. Seary, and Mr. Withers, we are further indebted for a careful reading of the completed manuscript. Two British folklorists, Dr. E. C. Cawte and Mr. Alex Helm, generously gave us access to the results of their extensive research on mumming in the British Isles.

To (Mrs.) Winnie Martin, Secretary in the Folklore and Language Archive of the Department of English, we are especially grateful. She kept expert control of the material as it was assembled, and – at home and at the University – deciphered and typed our varied and difficult scripts through what must have seemed an interminable series of drafts and revisions.

Finally, on behalf of all the contributors to this book, we must record our deep appreciation of the warm co-operation of hundreds of Newfoundlanders, fishermen, university students, and others, who have recorded their memories, answered our questions and questionnaires, and, by allowing us to witness and sometimes to participate in a living folk tradition, have made this book possible.

H.H./G.M.S.

The Memorial University of Newfoundland
St. John's, Newfoundland
September 1967

Contents

Preface   v

Note on the Contributors   xi

I Introduction   2

II Newfoundland: Fishermen, Hunters, Planters, and Merchants
BY G. M. STORY   7

III A Typology of Mumming
BY HERBERT HALPERT   34

IV Mummers and Strangers in Northern Newfoundland
BY MELVIN M. FIRESTONE   62

V Mumming in 'Deep Harbour':
Aspects of Social Organization in Mumming and Drinking
BY LOUIS J. CHIARAMONTE   76

VI The Mask of Friendship:
Mumming as a Ritual of Social Relations
BY JOHN F. SZWED   104

VII The 'Naluyuks' of Northern Labrador:
A Mechanism of Social Control
BY SHMUEL BEN-DOR   119

VIII Mumming in an Outport Fishing Settlement:
A Description and Suggestions on the Cognitive Complex
BY JAMES C. FARIS   128

IX The Disguises of Newfoundland Mummers
BY J. D. A. WIDDOWSON AND HERBERT HALPERT   145

x Mummers in Newfoundland History:
A Survey of the Printed Record
BY G. M. STORY   165

xi Newfoundland Mummers' Plays: Three Printed Texts
EDITED BY HERBERT HALPERT AND G. M. STORY   186

Appendices

i Janneying in 'Coughlin Cove'
BY CLYDE E. WILLIAMS   209

ii Mummering and Janneying: Some Explanatory Notes
BY J. D. A. WIDDOWSON   216

iii The Newfoundland Distribution of the
Mummers' Play and Christmas Disguising   222

Bibliography   231

Index   241

Note on the Contributors

SHMUEL BEN-DOR was born in Israel. He took his B.A. degree at the University of Jerusalem, and his M.A. and PH.D. at the University of Minnesota. He has done fieldwork in Israel and Labrador. At present he teaches anthropology at Wayne State University, Detroit, Michigan, and is conducting research in Jewish Shtetl culture. His interests are social anthropology and cultural change.

LOUIS J. CHIARAMONTE was born in Boston, Massachusetts. He received his B.A. degree from Brandeis University, and his M.A. from Columbia University. He has done fieldwork in the Caribbean and in Newfoundland. He is now at the University of Bergen, Norway, completing his PH.D. His interests include peasant fishing communities, nonverbal communication, and ethnophotography.

JAMES C. FARIS was born in Colorado. He took his B.S. degree at the University of New Mexico and his PH.D. at Cambridge University, England. At present he is conducting research among the Nuba in the Sudan. His interests include cognitive studies, methodology, and linguistic anthropology.

MELVIN M. FIRESTONE was born in Omaha, Nebraska. He received his B.A. degree from the University of New Mexico, and his M.A. and PH.D. from the University of Washington. He teaches anthropology at Arizona State University, Tempe, Arizona. His major interests are social anthropology, folklore, and culture and personality.

HERBERT HALPERT was born in New York City. He took his B.S. degree at New York University, his M.A. at Columbia University, and his PH.D. at Indiana University. He has taught English and folklore at universities in Indiana, Kentucky, Illinois, Arkansas, and New York, and since 1962 has taught at Memorial University of Newfoundland, where he is Head of the Department of Folklore. He has done extensive fieldwork in many parts of the United States, Western Canada, Alaska, and Newfoundland. His interests include all areas of folklore, with special emphasis on the British Isles and North America. He is a Fellow of both the American Folklore Society (and a Past President of the Society) and the American Anthropological Association, and has held several national awards.

G. M. STORY was born in St. John's, Newfoundland. He received his B.A. degree from McGill University, Montreal, and his D.PHIL. from Oxford University where he was a Rhodes Scholar. Since 1954 he has taught English at Memorial University of Newfoundland. His interests include Tudor and Renaissance literature, bibliography and textual criticism, and Newfoundland language and folklore.

JOHN F. SZWED was born in Eutaw, Alabama. He took his B.S. degree at Marietta University, and another B.S., M.A., and PH.D. at Ohio State University. He teaches anthropology at Temple University in Philadelphia, and has taught at the University of Cincinnati and Lehigh University. He has conducted fieldwork in Trinidad and Newfoundland. His major interests are ethnomusicology, folklore (especially myth and ritual), economic anthropology, and linguistics.

J. D. A. WIDDOWSON was born in Sheffield, England. He took his M.A. at Oxford University and his M.A. at Leeds University. He teaches mediaeval English literature, language, and linguistics at Sheffield University. He has done extensive fieldwork in East Yorkshire and Newfoundland, and is now completing work for a PH.D. in folklore and linguistics at Memorial University of Newfoundland. His interests are linguistics (especially dialectology and phonetics) and folklore.

CLYDE E. WILLIAMS was born in Tucson, Arizona. He studied as an undergraduate at the University of Arizona and Memorial University of Newfoundland. He is now completing graduate work at Indiana University in linguistics and folklore, and is employed in research at the Southwest Regional Laboratory, Inglewood, California.

Christmas Mumming in Newfoundland

Introduction

This book approaches a living folk tradition from three directions. First, it presents the intensive observations made in widely scattered areas of Newfoundland and Labrador by five social anthropologists, each of whom finds in Christmas mumming important insights into Newfoundland rural society. Second, it presents the results of folkloristic investigations conducted in a large number of communities both by fieldwork and by questionnaire, and attempts to examine the whole mumming complex. Finally, the historical essays provide an introduction both to the origin and growth of rural Newfoundland communities and elucidate the changing patterns of the folk custom in time by surveying the Newfoundland texts and documents.

Throughout the book, the fundamental emphasis is upon the Newfoundland custom. But that custom is not, of course, peculiar to the Island. Masking, with its frequently attendant costuming, is a worldwide phenomenon, connected with religion, ritual, and drama. The behaviour of the disguised figures bulks large in the ethnographic and folkloristic literature of a wide range of cultures throughout the world; indeed, so large and complex is the British and Irish material alone (from which we presume the Newfoundland customs to have been derived), that the task of systematic compilation and analysis has only been undertaken by scholars in recent years. To such analysis, the vitality of the Newfoundland mumming tradition offers a unique field for observation. It is the combination of trained observation of a still living tradition, together with fresh historical data, which, we believe, makes this book a contribution of particular value.

We believe, however, that the present study is of considerable interest for another reason as well. Most of the essays are not only descriptive but also speculative; they are concerned, that is, not only with the presentation of data but also with its interpretation. Though for historical and ecological reasons the folklorist will not find in Newfoundland the full range of British and Irish calendar customs, the material assembled seems sufficiently extensive and varied to permit generalization; and this the book attempts in a speculative typology which, advanced as one way of organizing a varied and complex body of material, may prove to be of interest when applied to the more complete array of evidence available to scholars elsewhere. The historical essays pose general questions on the origin and spread of folk custom in Newfoundland, the factors affecting its modification in time, and the social *milieu* which, in the past, affected its form and function. Of special theoretical significance of another kind are the contributions of the social anthropologists, who found in Newfoundland Christmas mumming an opportunity to test assumptions about the social mechanisms and nature of rural communities.

Individual Newfoundland 'outport' communities, by reason of their origin and the circumstances of their development, have scanty documentation. As one of the contributors to this volume has observed elsewhere, in many ways we know less about the small fishing settlements of Newfoundland than about portions of East and West Africa, which have for many years been subjected to intensive sociological and anthropological study. Since 1962, each of the social anthropologists represented in this volume has completed a study of a selected Newfoundland or Labrador community;[1] and though their essays in this book are focused on a limited subject, it is one which has enabled them to illuminate the structure and social dynamic of multiple rural societies. They have examined Christmas mumming, especially in the characteristic Newfoundland form of the "house-visit,"[2] both function-

---

1 / A number of these studies have appeared in multilithed editions for limited circulation by the Institute of Social and Economic Research: Shmuel Ben-Dor, *Makkovik: Eskimos and Settlers in a Labrador Community* (1966); James C. Faris, *Cat Harbour: A Newfoundland Fishing Settlement* (1966); Melvin Firestone, *Brothers and Rivals: Patrilocality in Savage Cove* (1967); and John Szwed, *Private Cultures and Public Imagery: Interpersonal Relations in a Newfoundland Peasant Society* (1966). To these should be added Tom Philbrook's *Fisherman, Logger, Merchant, Miner: Social Change and Industrialism in Three Newfoundland Communities* (1966). Some are now being prepared for more extended publication.

2 / Throughout this volume we have used single quotation marks for local words and phrases, and double quotation marks both for ordinary quotations and, as here, for certain technical terms.

ally as a mechanism of social control, and as a key to an understanding of the ordering of experience in rural Newfoundland. Christmas mumming in Newfoundland is, of course, part of relaxed, high-spirited holiday festivities. But most of the essays in this volume are primarily concerned with other aspects of mumming – an emphasis dictated by the historical, contemporary, and comparative data.

Newfoundland continues to offer a rich field for the anthropologist. As for the folklorist, so varied and copious has our material been on this custom alone that we have had to reserve for separate publication much that was originally intended for inclusion in this study, together with fresh material collected since the volume was substantially completed. This later material, which is still being organized for future publication, includes further descriptions of the "house-visit," costumes, behaviour, as well as texts, numerous fragments, and accounts of performances of the mummers' play, the latter recorded principally through fieldwork; a large body of data on the St. Stephen's Day custom of Hunting the Wren; and information on the hobby horse, the Christmas bull, and other related customs and traditions. An essay on frightening figures, at one time intended for the present volume, is being expanded into a book by itself. Newfoundland and Labrador, that is to say, are proving to be unusually rich as repositories of living folk custom and tradition, and the first fruits of our study of one such custom are here presented.

Most of the essays in this volume were originally written independently of one another and may therefore be read in any order. Nevertheless, the essays are arranged in deliberate order in an attempt to achieve a balance between the contemporary form, the historically documented past, and the perspective of the custom in other countries. The first essay (chapter II) sketches the curious history of the Newfoundland communities from their origins in the seventeenth and eighteenth centuries to the more fully documented nineteenth century, and draws attention to some of the historical and ecological factors which helped to mould the lives of the people. The second essay (chapter III) proposes a framework for the whole mumming complex, for we believe that only thus can the special features of the Newfoundland aspects of the custom be seen in proper relief. Chapters IV to IX treat mumming in its modern form, as seen from contemporary fieldwork and reports. Finally, chapters X and XI present the Newfoundland historical sources on the custom. The appendices bring together a purely descriptive account of mumming in an east coast fishing village, a note on some of the major terms for mumming and mummers, and

6 Introduction

a summary distribution study of Christmas disguising and the mummers' play in Newfoundland.

We emphasize again that the descriptions in chapters IV to VIII and in appendix 1 are of independent communities in widely separated areas of Newfoundland and Labrador, and that therefore we have allowed apparent repetition of material to stand as validating the similarity of the custom in different places. All the essays are self-sufficient and carry their own documentation, though the final form of most of them was achieved by a process of interchange of comment and criticism. Collectively, we believe, they illuminate the central subject of Christmas mumming in a way that demonstrates in more than a theoretical fashion the results of co-operation among scholars in different disciplines.

Newfoundland: Fishermen, Hunters, Planters, and Merchants

BY G. M. STORY

Hunters and fishermen are always the boldest of pioneers and often the homeliest of men, when their hunting and fishing season is over. .... The example of fishermen and hunters makes stay-at-homes stray from home; and most of those who follow this example are neither fishermen nor hunters, but settlers. Then comes a crisis. Hunters and fishermen oppose settlers – for settlers and wild beasts are incompatible; and there is war – as in Manitoba – in which wild beasts and hunters disappear; or there is absorption – even as the whalers of Cook Strait, New Zealand, were merged into the settlers, and the whales disappeared; or there is absorption of another kind and all the settlers are transformed into fishermen, and none of the fish disappear. This last process took place in Newfoundland, and nowhere else in the world.[1]

The Island of Newfoundland stands athwart the entrance to the Gulf of St. Lawrence, the principal waterway leading into the North American continent.[2] It is about the same size as Iceland (a little over 41,000 square miles), and triangular in shape: on the west, the Great Northern Peninsula juts northward to Labrador; the southwestern corner reaches towards Nova Scotia (sixty-five miles away) and New England; the eastern tip (the Avalon Peninsula), extends far out into the North Atlantic, only 1,700 sea miles from the British Isles and on nearly the same lines of latitude. This threefold orientation, towards

1 / J. D. Rogers, *Newfoundland* (1911), pp. vi–vii.
2 / I am indebted to Herbert Halpert, who teased this essay from me; to Dr. Leslie Harris for assistance with a number of historical problems; and to my brother, Mr. Colin Story, for information and insight gleaned from him over many years.

the Labrador Sea, across the Gulf to the Maritimes and the New England States, and east towards Europe, is a fundamental geographic fact of Newfoundland's economic, political, and cultural history.

From the north the Labrador Current, whose cold waters carry southwards the marine organisms of Arctic seas, sweeps past the coast of Labrador, a territory of which some 140,000 square miles belong to Newfoundland. The current brushes the northeast coast of the Island, and then turns in a gigantic clockwise motion around the eastern tip. As it turns, it meets the warm waters of the eastward-bound Gulf Stream, and their union occurs over the shoal waters of the Grand Banks; off the south and west coasts, it mingles with the Gaspé Current, laden with the effluvia of the St. Lawrence watershed, and here too the junction takes place over the shoal waters of offshore banks. The proximity, and particularly the mingling, of these great currents, rich in their varied marine organisms, gives Newfoundland its characteristic marine environment.

Inshore and offshore, Newfoundland waters are one of the great fishing grounds of the world. In a ceaseless cycle, the seals make their annual migration south through the Davis Strait to the winter feeding- and whelping-grounds in the Gulf, on the Grand Banks, and off the northeast coast of the Island; the whale and the tuna sport themselves in these waters, feeding seasonally on the herring, squid, mackerel, and other species. And the cod, in a unique phenomenon, detach enormous numbers of their deep-sea populations each spring and summer, turning in pursuit of the tiny silvery caplin and other 'bait-fish' on their annual roll, or 'scull,' towards the shore. "With the Greeks," an imaginative historian has observed, "ocean was a synonym for barrenness, land alone being lifegiving. To the Newfoundlander the land is a forest or a 'barren,' the ocean a mine or harvest-field, and on the foreshore the yield of the ocean is prepared for market."[3]

It was chiefly to reap this marine harvest that the maritime nations of Europe sailed to Newfoundland from pre-Columbian times. The voyages of the Norsemen were not sustained; but from the 1480s onwards, Portuguese, Spanish, Basque, French, and English fishermen made voyages to Newfoundland waters. They came, for the most part, to fish and not to settle; and when, a century after the period of Cabot's discovery, or rediscovery, settlement began, tension and conflict between the summer fishermen and settlers was a crucial factor in the development, or rather in the failure to develop normally, of the Island's English communities. Newfoundland became a unique example

3 / *Ibid.*, p. 190.

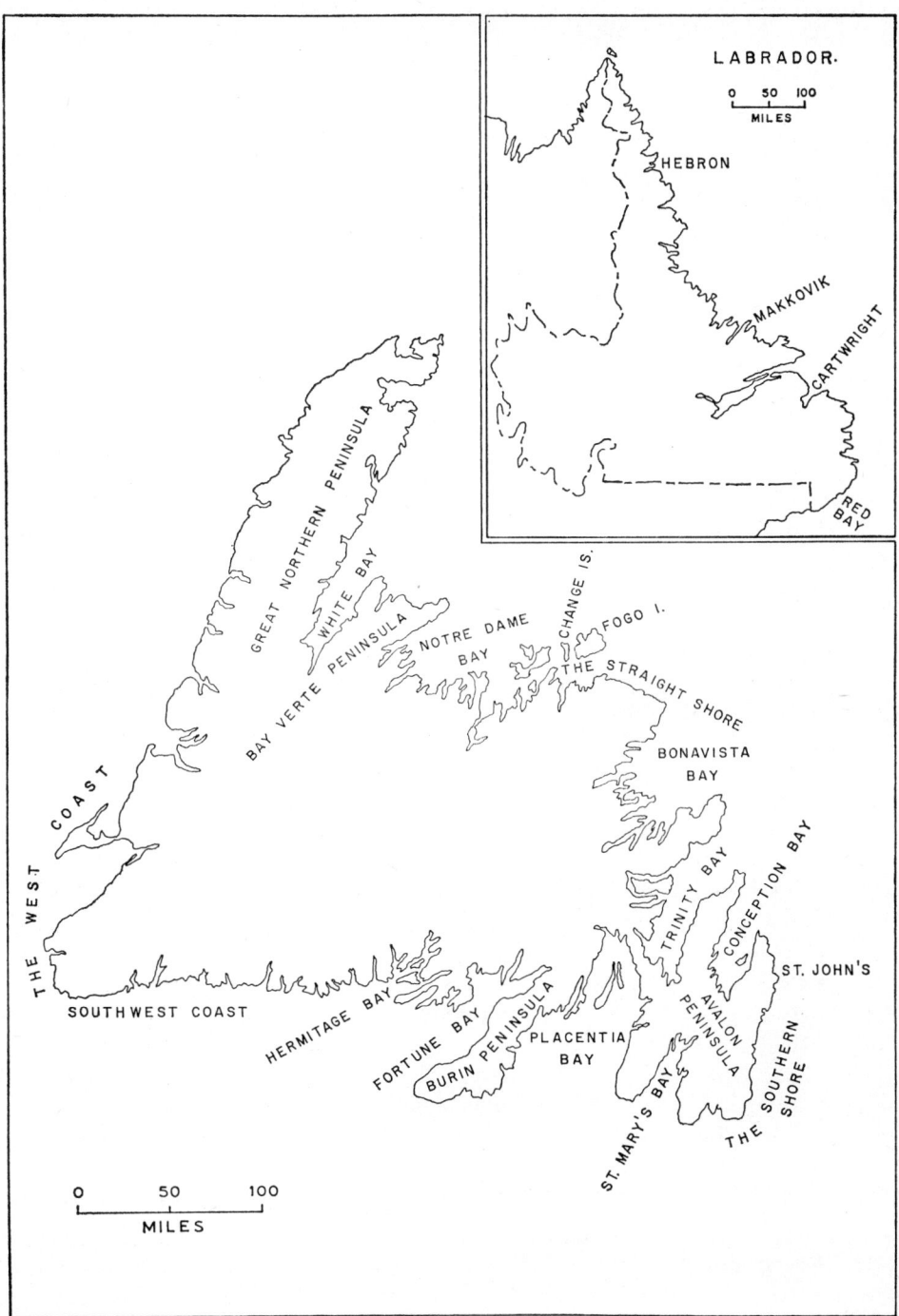

NEWFOUNDLAND

of deliberately retarded colonization, and its villages, such as they were, grew surreptitiously under the shadow of official British disapproval and even harassment as much by fellow-Englishmen as by foreign foe.

So Newfoundland remained outside the normal pattern of British colonial development and apart from the institutions and influences which created organized colonial communities elsewhere. Politically, the Island pursued an erratic course until the middle of the twentieth century; its settlements, shaped by the traditional fishing economy, remained (apart from the few towns) remote and undisturbed until the fourth decade of the twentieth century. In cultural terms, it was (like Iceland and Jamaica) an island-arrested society, and a rich repository of European customs and folkways on the very threshold of the New World.

Persistent family and local tradition in Newfoundland, despite the lack of documentary evidence, traces the earliest English settlements as far back as the late sixteenth century; and it is not unlikely that 'winter crews' were occasionally left on the Island to maintain the 'fishing rooms' used by the visiting summer fishermen in curing their season's catch. But the official English settlements were founded by the chartered companies which were such a pronounced feature of European colonial enterprise in the seventeenth century. All were established on the Avalon Peninsula, the most easterly portion of the Island: John Guy's colony at Cupids and Harbour Grace in Conception Bay (1610), Sir William Vaughan's at Trepassey (1617), and the colony of Sir George Calvert (later Lord Baltimore) at Ferryland (1621), these last two on the southern shore of the Peninsula. Groups of colonists were brought out, permanent houses erected, and 'planting' begun under the direction of the several governors of the colonies. Considerable information is available concerning the fortunes of the colonies, especially Guy's Colony.[4] These early colonies were remarkable, if for nothing else, for the literature they begat: Vaughan's *Golden Fleece* (1630), a fantastically mannered prose work, and Robert Hayman's *Quodlibets* (1628), verses composed at Harbour Grace, and one of the earliest books of poems written in English in the New World.

Ultimately none of these colonies was successful. They collapsed for a number of reasons. For one thing, their organizers failed to realize that the conventional "plantation" with an agricultural base, successful

---

4 / See the entry for "Willoughby" by Gilian T. Cell, *The Dictionary of Canadian Biography* (1966), I, 670–71. Sir Richard Whitbourne's *Discourse and Discovery of Newfoundland* (1620) is the best early account of the Island.

in Ireland, Virginia, or even New England, was not feasible in a northern country with a primarily fishing economy. For another, the interests of the colonists clashed, or seemed to clash, with those of the West Country fishing interests whose fishermen came and went each season. So the plantations were abandoned by their sponsors, and many of the settlers returned to Great Britain or removed to other more viable colonies in the New World; only a few remained as fishermen in Newfoundland to take their chances in competition with the transient fishermen from home.

In that struggle, successive British governments, with greater or lesser zeal, supported the visiting fishermen, and continued to do so until the nineteenth century. The basis of official British policy during this long period was succinctly reported before the House of Commons in 1793 by an Under-Secretary of State: "The island of Newfoundland has been considered . . . as a great ship moored near the Banks during the fishing season, for the convenience of English fishermen."[5] It was an attitude which had been given its first legal expression in the Western Charter issued by the Privy Council in 1634. This Charter, which confirmed long-existing custom, gave jurisdiction over the fishermen in Newfoundland to the mayors of the principal West Country ports and to the 'fishing admirals,' that is, the first, second and third fishing captains to arrive in a given harbour each spring. Since West Country mayors were uncommon visitors to Newfoundland harbours, the Charter gave effective jurisdiction over most of the east coast (from Cape Race to Cape Bonavista) to the rough, customary justice of the fishing smack and the rum-keg court.

The position of the settlers was briefly retrieved in 1637 by the arrival of Sir David Kirke. Backed financially by London merchants who saw the profits to be made in a fishery conducted by residents from the Island, and by a Court favourite, the Marquis of Hamilton, Kirke arrived with a royal charter granting him exclusive rights to the Island except that part of the east coast traditionally frequented by the West Countrymen. Kirke is a neglected figure in Newfoundland history. A resident Governor of the whole Island (not until 1817 was Newfoundland to have another), he ensured that "settlers for the first time were able to act as though they possessed the same rights in their own country as did residents of England."[6] But the Kirke interlude was short-lived. In 1651 he was arrested at his house in Ferryland and

5 / Quoted by D. W. Prowse, *History of Newfoundland* (1895), p. xix.

6 / G. O. Rothney, *Newfoundland: From International Fishery to Canadian Province* (1959), p. 8, a stimulating essay.

taken to England as a prisoner of Cromwell's republican Commonwealth.

His removal paved the way for the unrestricted operation in Newfoundland of the mercantilist policies which inspired successive British governments.[7] Briefly, the object of Cromwell's government was to help English merchants make money out of overseas possessions: West Country merchants formed a powerful lobby; the West Country–Newfoundland fishery was one of the mainstays of an important English regional economy; the settlers were comparatively few in number. A return, therefore, to the earlier anti-settler attitude towards the Island was both consistent and practical, and it was reinforced by the desire to preserve the Newfoundland fishery as a training ground for British seamen against times of war.

This policy remained fundamentally unchanged after the Stuart Restoration. A second Western Charter (1661) confirmed the provisions of the first. In 1671 an Order in Council forbade settlers to live within six miles of the coveted shoreline upon which their livelihood depended. A third Charter was contemplated, the effect of which would have been to deport all settlers from the Island; and although not passed, its primary aim was partly achieved by the act of the West Country fishermen who twice (in 1676 and 1678) burned down the houses and premises owned by the settlers between Cape Race and Cape Bonavista. Further official measures were not, however, taken against the residents. Possibly it was not considered worthwhile to apply techniques already devised by the state for Ireland, and later to be applied to the Scottish Highlands, for the uprooting of a troublesome people; perhaps the elusive nature of many of the communities defied such extreme methods.

For although the Island in the later seventeenth century contained a few substantial planters with considerable property,[8] it was not a settled colony, and the communities were not ordinary villages. Here, settlers became hunters. "Man'll go for a swile [i.e. a seal] where gold won't drag 'un," was a characteristic remark of a Conception Bay man to J. G. Millais in 1907.[9] Those who did not make this fundamental adaptation to their environment failed, as did the Norsemen in Greenland who tried to subsist on a farming economy instead of adapting their ways more thoroughly (like the Eskimo) to the richer harvest of the northern sea. Newfoundlanders became fish-killers, marine-trap-

7 / This, like the preceding paragraph, is indebted to Rothney, *Newfoundland*.
8 / See Prowse, *History*, pp. 205–8.
9 / *Newfoundland and its Untrodden Ways* (1907), p. 40.

pers, and dwellers of the seacoast – especially the remote coves and distant headlands and islands where fish were plentiful and officials scarce. Along the rocky sides of small inlets, or deep in the 'bottom' of the great bays, they perched their tiny log 'tilts' and their frail, easily replaced fishing-stages and flakes. Organized communities of the kind found elsewhere in British North America scarcely existed and therefore could not be permanently destroyed. Newfoundland baffled, and continued to baffle, orderly administrative minds. The best that they could do was to hope that the resident fishermen and their families would somehow go away, and meanwhile to pretend that they did not exist.

The recent publication of the journal of James Yonge, a Plymouth surgeon who made voyages to Newfoundland on three occasions during the 1660s,[10] provides valuable insight into the nature of the English fishery, and the condition of the east coast English communities, during the little-known period between the collapse of the official plantations and the emergence of the *de facto* colony in the eighteenth century. Around a nucleus of some two or three thousand permanent residents, scattered in nearly forty fishing villages from three to fifty families in size, there was a fluctuating body of perhaps fifteen hundred 'bye-boatkeepers' and their servants. These bye-boatkeepers were fishermen who were financed by merchants to come to Newfoundland as passengers on trading vessels; once here they hired small vessels and cheap labour to catch fish for the export trade. Some of them, and their servants, returned home the same year; others went to New England, with which Newfoundland carried on a flourishing trade; many remained as settlers on the Island where, in the eighteenth and nineteenth centuries, they came to be called 'planters,' that is, middlemen between the merchants and fishermen. Finally, there were the West Country fishermen, perhaps ten or twelve thousand in number at this time, who were summer inhabitants only, though many violated the terms of their employment and (like all settlers before the nineteenth century) the law, by deserting and settling.[11]

The detailed history of the settlements during this period cannot be written because the kind of institutions which would have left such written sources as parish records, letters, journals, and so on, did not, by and large, exist. Accounts of life in Newfoundland, especially

10 / *The Journal of James Yonge, Plymouth Surgeon: 1647–1721*, ed. F. N. L. Poynter (1963).

11 / The population figures, notoriously difficult to rely upon in this period, are from contemporary estimates quoted by Prowse, *History*, p. 698.

during the winter months when the fishing admirals and the British naval convoy vessels had gone, are rare before the later eighteenth century. Such evidence as does exist, the dry reports of naval officers, accounts of the depredations of the French, and occasional petitions of the settlers, have to be interpreted cautiously. The chief problem in using a Newfoundland historical source from this period is to discover the point of view of the commentator: to determine whether he is a naval officer upholding the official anti-colonial policy of his government, a clergyman seeking missionary funds from home by lurid tales of the ungodly, or a traveller of taste who would have drawn the same irrelevant contrasts with life in London after a journey through rural Ireland, Northumberland, or the Scottish islands. So one should assess the oft-quoted phrases about Newfoundland as a place where "the far greatest part of the inhabitants live as mere savages,"[12] where crimes are committed with impunity, for the offenders, "knowing there is no person to call them to account, rather look on it as merit than injury,"[13] and where intermarriage, disease, and famine produced "the gradual degeneration of a splendid stock."[14] No doubt conditions were harsh. But the settlers continued to come, and by 1715 they numbered a little over four thousand, a number which was to double itself, very roughly, every twenty years, until the tempo of immigration increased rapidly in the last decades of the century, tapering off again to a trickle by 1850.

Why did the settlers come? Desertion by seamen, whether from naval or fishing ships, is explicable given the conditions of shipboard life in the seventeenth and eighteenth centuries; and the economic and political disasters at home which led to the Irish immigrations have been amply documented. The question is usually asked of the West Country immigrants, often by visitors with fresh memories of Devonshire cottages in a rich and ordered English landscape; and the answer is that for West Countrymen too conditions at home were such as to make Newfoundland appealing. The detailed investigation of the social and economic history of the West Country–Newfoundland fishery has only recently been undertaken[15] and can be expected to throw light on the causes and pattern of the early immigration to the Island from Devon, Cornwall, Dorset, and Somerset. What some of these causes

12 / Report (1764) of Governor Palliser, cited by A. H. McLintock, *The Establishment of Constitutional Government in Newfoundland* (1941), p. 15.
13 / C.O. 194/21, 92.
14 / McLintock, *Constitutional Government*, p. 14.
15 / By Mr. Keith Matthews of Jesus College, Oxford.

were can, perhaps, be inferred from a recent study in rural sociology, E. W. Martin's *The Shearers and the Shorn* (1965).[16] The book is primarily concerned with a single region of Devonshire in the period after 1800, but much of the data, for example on endemic pauperism, workhouses, the marginal existence of the rural workers, and the oppressive power of the property elite, is valid for an earlier period. "The toiler in the fields became . . . not a slave or serf in the legal sense, but a creature without a modicum of mental freedom or social power."[17] A remote harbour of Newfoundland, of course, provided bonds of its own; and there were parts of the Island in which, until modern times, the economic relationship of fisherman and merchant could be described, by sober Royal Commissioners in 1933, as "feudal."[18] But in spite of this, the Newfoundland fisherman, unlike the farm labourer of the "Old Country," had much of the independence of the self-employed *entrepreneur*, and only limited contact with the merchant who took his fish and advanced him his supplies. An inshore fisherman, explaining recently to his interviewer his preference for fishing alone in a distant cove, was perhaps speaking as well for his West Country forbears when he remarked: "Dere's no one to bawl at you, you see."

Meanwhile, in the early eighteenth century, rule during the summer by fishing admirals (with some supervision by the commodore of the naval convoy protecting the fishing fleet from foreign attack and from pirates) became intolerable when the seasonal fishermen from England came to be outnumbered by the settlers. It was also impracticable as the English fishery gradually ceased to be a shore-based operation prosecuted seasonally from Island bases; by degrees, the English vessels turned their main attention to the offshore banks, and the catch, instead of being cured on shore, was salted down aboard ship and taken back to England as 'green' fish. In due course this development was to remove the visiting fishermen from direct and continuous conflict with the settlers. But before that happened, the untidiness of the administration of justice on the Island was sufficiently apparent to persuade the British authorities to appoint the first of a long line of naval governors (1729). Perhaps the persistent threats and incursions by the French (in 1696, 1705 and 1708), rather than concern for the

16 / The book is also, incidentally, rich in its documentation of widespread illiteracy and superstition (including belief in 'white witches') in the Devon community down to recent times.
17 / *Ibid.*, p. 71.
18 / *Newfoundland Royal Commission Report* (1933), sections 270–80.

settlers, was a deciding factor in the decision to create some kind of overriding authority; but created it was: some fortifications were built at strategic centres, and Newfoundland communities received their first official emblems of civility – stocks. The Governor was, of course, present only during the summer, and the law (that is, whatever the Governor from his quarterdeck thought was good and proper) was executed by his delegates, the commanders of naval vessels – 'floating surrogates,' as they were called – on patrol around the coast. For the regulation of the communities during the winter, justices of the peace were appointed from among the more substantial planters whose authority, however, was repeatedly ignored by those fishing admirals who happened to be around in the late season when no naval vessel was in sight, and who ordered floggings more or less at will.

Thus, at a time when the other British colonies in North America had entered on a generation of formal government and peaceful expansion, the settlers of Newfoundland had to draw what comfort they could from a Government whose policy was defined by Lord Grenville in 1789 as follows: "Newfoundland is in no respect a British colony and is never so considered in our laws. On the contrary, the uniform tenor of our laws respecting the fishery there, and of the King's Instructions founded upon them, goes . . . to restrain the subjects of Great Britain from colonising that island"; or as a Prime Minister, Lord North, described it: "whenever [the settlers] wished to have roasted the Governor was to give them raw, and whenever they wished to have the raw he was to give it them roasted."[19]

The turning-point in Newfoundland's development towards colonial status occurred during the second half of the eighteenth century, though formal recognition of the fact had to wait until after the end of the century. There were various signs of change. In 1750 authorization was given for the Governor to preside over a criminal court. The Anglican Society for the Propagation of the Gospel had for some time been conducting missionary work among the settlers; in 1765 the first Methodist mission in the New World was established at Harbour Grace; and in 1770 an undisguised Roman Catholic priest was permitted to minister to the Irish population in restricted areas. With the missionaries came a few schools to teach the rudiments of learning to a population which (like the majority of the British and Irish peasantry) was either illiterate on arrival or in danger of becoming so within a generation. And a Collector of Customs, responsible to a superior in

19 / Hist. MSS. Com., Dropmore Papers, 13 Report, vol. I, 548, quoted by Prowse, *History*, p. xix.

Boston, Massachusetts, was appointed in 1764 to ensure the return to the British Exchequer of its share of the proceeds from the thriving trade between the Island and New England. Modest advances, perhaps, but signs of change, and soon (not for the last time in Newfoundland's history) to be speeded up by war.

The French and English wars of the second half of the eighteenth century brought on one hand foreign troops and the torch to many Newfoundland communities, but on the other an opportunity to expand the Island's fishing economy and export trade. The war at sea disrupted the English Bank fishery, and the east coast ports of Newfoundland now became increasingly important as bases of fishing operations. A crucial development was the gradual rise of resident merchants in whose self-interest it was to finance planters and fishermen in a fishing venture, and whose import and export trade transformed some communities into substantial commercial centres. With this more varied and sophisticated local mercantile operation were to come, in due course, other signs of established society which made official recognition of a *de facto* colonial status increasingly inevitable. Fish prices were high; and the communities flourished.

It seems likely that the increased fishing effort with a limited technology led to some overcrowding of the older inshore grounds, and that this was an important factor which encouraged the spread of population beyond the east coast. The movement of population was able to take place because the French had, for the duration of hostilities, been driven from those parts of the Island's coast (principally the west and northeast coasts) where they had traditional rights to cure the fish caught in their deep-sea fishery. The focal points of English settlement were the Avalon Peninsula, Trinity Bay, Bonavista Bay, and Placentia Bay. But along the south coast, in Fortune Bay and Hermitage Bay, West Country and Jersey merchant houses had for some time conducted operations; and the larger islands of Notre Dame Bay provided bases for similar operations along the northeast coast. To these newer centres now came, in increasing numbers, settlers from the older east coast communities and fresh immigrants from the Old Country.

The settlement by the English of the northeast coast, past 'Cat Harbour' (a pseudonym) to Cape Freels and around the coast into Notre Dame Bay, began during the Seven Years' War (1756–63), and continued after its conclusion. But it was not a rapid process and the communities remained very small for some time. In Notre Dame Bay, the settlements and fishing operations were for a long time confined to the islands: Twillingate, Fogo, Change Islands, and others, for inside the island chain the cod fishery was not notably productive: operations on the coast itself were chiefly concerned with salmon and furs until the rise of logging operations in the area in the nineteenth century. The spread of population along the southwest coast, towards 'Deep Harbour' (a pseudonym) and Burgeo, took place about the same time; but it was not until after the Napoleonic Wars that numbers reached significant proportions.

Small as they often were, many of these communities were so firmly established that when, at the end of the different wars (1763, 1783, and 1815), French fishermen returned with treaty rights (granted by the British with a generosity characteristic whenever the affairs of the English settlers were concerned), the settlements remained. French rights to use these great stretches of coast, from Cape Ray to Cape St. John, for curing fish and maintaining premises, were held and exercised until 1904. These rights inhibited the growth of the English settlements and led to repeated disputes with the French over jurisdiction. And to this must be attributed some of Newfoundland's prolonged aloofness from its continental neighbour. When Confederation with Canada was first proposed in 1869, it was roundly rejected by voters in an Island whose principal communities were still facing eastward, more than 500 sea miles away from North America. This geographic fact received conscious recognition in an anti-Confederation song of the era which proclaimed:

> Her face points to Britain, her back to the Gulf
> Come near at your peril, Canadian wolf!

Nevertheless, the chain of English settlements gradually encircled the Island. When Archdeacon Wix visited the west coast in 1835, he found a number of English groups more or less peacefully mingled with Acadian French and Micmac Indians.[20] These communities were soon to be reinforced by Scottish settlers, primarily from Nova Scotia, creating the villages described under the pseudonym 'Ross' by Szwed (chapter VI). During a still later period, the communities on the western coast of the Great Northern Peninsula, including some of those described by Firestone (chapter IV), were also established. Further north, along the Labrador coast, European members of the Moravian Brethren had founded three missions between 1771 and 1782; simultaneously, English trading and fishing establishments were also set up

---

20 / *Six Months of a Newfoundland Missionary's Journal* (1836).

along the coast, some directed from Great Britain, others from the emerging Newfoundland commercial centres.

This movement of population was confined almost entirely to the six thousand miles of the Island's coastline. The interior, with its thick forests, its unknown mineral wealth, and its vast stretches of barren land, was unsettled, penetrated only seasonally and for short distances by fishermen-hunters stocking their winter larders with game or trapping for furs. It was the preserve of the Micmac Indians from Nova Scotia, of small groups of Nascopie Indians crossing occasionally from Labrador; and of the steadily decreasing Beothic or Red Indians, hunting the caribou herds on their seasonal migrations across the Island, and themselves hunted down and shot by the settlers whenever they ventured near the coast. Not until 1822, when W. E. Cormack crossed the Island from east to west,[21] did a white man systematically explore the interior. It was almost a century later before a substantial community which was not a coastal settlement was to be established in Newfoundland; the opening up of the interior of Labrador had to wait until the 1950s.

All the Newfoundland communities, old and new, were primarily dependent on the inshore fishery; and in Newfoundland, 'fish' means cod. Beginning in May, with a peak in late June and July, the cod swarm into inshore waters in incredible numbers after the 'bait-fish' – caplin; and they swarm in again later in the season, fewer in number but fattened by summer feeding, during the squid and herring 'scull.' 'Work in summer, play in winter,' is a Newfoundland proverb which reflects an intense, almost continuous fishing activity from spring to late fall.

The nature of the communities and the organization of the fishery varied considerably around different parts of the coast and at different times. Along the south coast, the bait fishery was itself an important activity, the settlers disposing of their catch to deep-sea fishing vessels from New England, Nova Scotia, and France and from Newfoundland ports. The larger, older east coast communities, with substantial merchant establishments, were centres of a quite specialized fishing operation, with 'professional' sharemen to catch, and a 'professional' shore-crew to process, the fish.[22] In smaller communities, the *entrepreneur* might be either a planter, organizing his operations with

21 / *Narrative of a Journey across the Island of Newfoundland in 1822* (1836).
22 / Sir Richard Burton, *Ultima Thule; or A Summer in Iceland* (1875), I, 197, speaks of the high degree of efficiency and organization in the Newfoundland processing operation in comparison with other North Atlantic island communities.

several 'crews,' or a small merchant financed by one of the big merchant houses in St. John's or one of the other larger centres. Fishing-crews were often family affairs: fathers and sons fished the nearby grounds each day with hook-and-line or cod-net from small craft, while wives and daughters split and cured the dried and salted fish which, throughout the Island, was the primary export product. The catch was ultimately disposed of to the merchant, not for cash but in return for provisions, clothing, and 'fit-outs' of fishing-gear. This "truck system" persisted in Newfoundland down to the end of the 1930s, a century after it had been banned by Parliament in Great Britain because it enforced economic servitude of producer to merchant.

From his summer and late fall fishery, the fisherman had to provide for the long winter season. Arable land and good fishing-grounds are uncommon neighbours in Newfoundland, and, apart from the cultivation of small 'gardens,' the economic activity of the inhabitants (outside a few agricultural areas) revolved around the sea; and the sea was frozen in winter around much of the coast, or else was too stormy even for the sturdy boats designed and built by the fishermen themselves. The conclusion of the 'fall voyage,' therefore, marked the end of the Island's principal economic activity except on the south and southwest coasts where a 'winter fishery' was prosecuted. Outside the few towns, winter was the time for securing further "non-cash" income: wood for fuel, for the repair of fishing premises in the spring, for boats; and game for the larder. In many parts of the Island and along the Labrador coast, the fishermen moved back from the exposed headlands and islands from which the fishery had been conducted, and settled down for the winter in their 'winter houses,' deep towards the 'bottom' of the bays where they were sheltered from the elements and close to wood and game.[23] And for all Newfoundlanders, in town and village alike, it was time for the long Christmas break.[24]

Along the ice-bound parts of the coast, this winter inactivity remained relatively unbroken until the start of the annual seal hunt. This 'fishery,' as it is still frequently called, was pursued principally by the inhabitants of the east, northeast, and Labrador coasts, and was

23 / Even within living memory, the inshore fishermen of St. John's went to their summer fishing-stations at the Battery, in Freshwater Bay and elsewhere, returning to the city each fall.

There are two especially good contemporary accounts of the Newfoundland fishery and the life of the communities in the earlier part of the nineteenth century: L. Anspach's *History of Newfoundland* (1819), chap. 15, and W. Wilson's *Newfoundland and its Missionaries* (1866), chaps. 6 and 10.

24 / See J. B. Jukes, *Excursions in Newfoundland* (1842).

prosecuted both by 'landsmen,' using guns and nets, and by vessels which sailed from the larger ports and pursued the seals amid the ice-floes far out at sea. The seal fishery ran from March to April (with considerable local variation) and, in the nineteenth century, became the great Newfoundland adventure, the source of heroic figures and legends, and of the only cash income a fisherman might earn. Men vied with one another to 'sign on' with celebrated sealing captains or 'jowlers': "Ye know, sir, that when we gets to be young men in this country they don't think much of a chap unless he's bin to de ice. It's a sort o' test o' hardiness, and the girls think a heap of the young fellers that's bin once or twice to the swoile fishin' and come back free with their money. It's jest dog's work while it lasts, but somehow there's an excitement in it that sets young fellers kind o' restless in the spring."[25] As late as the 1930s, the seal fishery generated an excitement throughout the Island difficult to exaggerate; as a source of cash income, it had no rival until the rise of the logging and mining industries.

The increasing size of the boats used in the seal fishery led, in the early nineteenth century, to the rise of a deep-sea fishery prosecuted from the Island on the Banks and off the Labrador coast. The sealing-vessels, having discharged their cargoes and crews, would 'fit out' for a summer voyage after cod. The Labrador fishery had developed rapidly after the Napoleonic Wars: each spring, hundreds of vessels sailed north from the east and northeast coasts to fish the Labrador waters. These were the 'floaters,' the schooner-fishermen. Most of them were owned and commanded by the planters, fitted out by merchants, and manned by crews drawn, in a pattern still to be studied, from settlements at the bottom of the bays where the inshore fishery was less productive than it was on the exposed headlands and islands.[26] From the same communities the Labrador 'stationers' also 'went down north.' They went as passengers, with wives and children, household belongings, dogs and goats, and conducted what was essentially an inshore fishery – repeating in Labrador from a Newfoundland home-base the pattern established by the original fishermen who came seasonally from the West Country to the Island itself. The Newfoundland Bank fishery was prosecuted on the Grand Banks and George's Bank principally by schooners operating out of south coast ports –

25 / Millais, *Newfoundland and its Untrodden Ways*, p. 40. Perhaps the best account of the seal fishery is G. A. England's *Vikings of the Ice* (1925).
26 / See W. A. Black, "The Labrador Floater Cod Fishery," *Annals of the Association of American Geographers*, I, no. 3 (1960), 267–93; and, for a planter's account, N. Smith, *Fifty-Two Years at the Labrador Fishery* (1936).

Fortune, Grand Bank, Burin, Burgeo, and the other principal harbours. Most of these 'bankers' were merchant-owned, and some of them would also make a late fall voyage to Labrador. There was also a considerable fishery on the near offshore banks prosecuted in smaller vessels called 'western boats' which were planter-owned.

Joint participation in the Labrador seal and bank fisheries (and later in logging operations) gives the lie to the conventional picture of the Newfoundland communities as populated by people entirely isolated and cut off from one another. Despite the almost complete absence of roads until the twentieth century, the population had a quite remarkable degree of mobility. Men travelled by sea.[27] Nor was this mobility exercised only within Newfoundland waters. South coast Newfoundlanders both commanded and manned a substantial part of the Nova Scotian and New England deep-sea fishing fleets. And the great fleet of locally built 'foreign-going' schooners which, from the early nineteenth century to the second decade of the twentieth, carried Newfoundland salt-fish to the West Indies, the 'Brazils,' and the countries of the Mediterranean, brought together Newfoundlanders from all parts of the Island, and made them familiar with the ports of three continents. Most significant of all, the building, equipping, and maintenance of these great fleets, both to catch and to carry fish, became an industry which, for the first time, provided some diversification of the Island's economy.

Some of the Newfoundland communities were developing into considerable towns – a new phenomenon in a land of small villages. The specialization of "urban" society occurred. In the 1790s, St. John's, the capital, had been transformed from a fishing village into a town in little more than a generation. It was the administrative centre, the hub of a growing trade, and the financial pivot of the Island's fishery and export trade. An unpublished census for 1794–95 provides the material for the following (incomplete) occupational analysis: 447 fishermen, 114 'shoremen,' 55 carpenters, 31 merchants, 24 publicans, 17 coopers, 10 boatkeepers, 10 taylors, 8 smiths, 7 shoemakers, 4 sailmakers, 4 butchers, 4 agents, 4 planters, 3 bakers, 3 clergymen, 3 watch-makers, 3 farmers, 2 justices of the peace, and the following with one member each: armourer, commissary, nurse, clerk, mason, accountant, gardener, midwife, barber, laundress, surgeon, doctor, schoolmaster, schoolmistress, Chief Justice, constable, collector, scrive-

27 / As late as 1941, the authoritative *Hand Book, Gazetteer and Almanac* by J. R. Smallwood (1941) gave distances between points not by land, but by sea miles.

ner, and (eloquent conjunction), one fiddler and one gentleman.[28] Together with the soldiery of the St. John's Garrison and the sailors of the Royal Navy's Newfoundland Station (not to mention the still numerous West Country fishermen), the census reveals a nautical community with an urban character. By 1839, Harbour Grace, one of the principal communities of Conception Bay, had a population of 3,000; its neighbour, Carbonear, had almost as many. On the south coast, Grand Bank had grown into a substantial community; Twillingate, in Notre Dame Bay on the northeast coast, was an important fishing and commercial centre; and the ancient settlements of Bonavista and Trinity were assuming even greater importance than hitherto in the affairs of the great bays whose names they bore.

After 1800 missionaries of all denominations arrived in increasing numbers, and with them appeared more schools as well as churches.[29] The first newspaper was established in St. John's in 1805; others soon followed not only in the capital but also in Harbour Grace, Carbonear, and Bay Roberts. There was a reading-room in St. John's; in the 1820s, a lending-library was formed in Carbonear.[30] The Island population went from 20,000 in 1804 to 56,000 in 1825, and six years later totalled just under 76,000. All this had taken place without the guidance of civil government and the institutions which, in other colonies, ensured the orderly development of society.

In law, Newfoundland was still "a great ship moored near the Banks," and on her quarterdeck stood naval governors committed, by government policy, "to restrain the subjects of Great Britain from colonising that island." But despite two centuries of neglect and even repression, the settlers had not gone away; and although a reactionary Governor (Sir Hugh Palliser) tried as late as 1784 to restore the West Country monopoly, recognition that a *de facto* colony had come into existence could not be ignored much longer. In 1817 a Governor was instructed to remain in the Island during the winter. In 1819 a Chief

28 / Manuscript census in the Gosling Memorial Library (St. John's), courtesy of Mr. N. C. Crewe.

29 / For a detailed account of the association of missionary activity and education, see F. W. Rowe, *The Development of Education in Newfoundland* (1964).

30 / Edmund Gosse, *Life of Philip Henry Gosse* (1890), p. 43. Gosse noted with evident surprise that "most of Scott, Bulwer's, Cooper's, Galt's [novels] and the O'Hara series were to be found within a year of their publication in England. Biography, poetry, travels, and even sciences were fairly represented, and the basis of a sound knowledge of contemporary literature could be, and was, formed in this remote harbour of Newfoundland."

Justice ruled that it was legal for Newfoundlanders to own their own homes and even the land they had built on. In 1824 came acknowledgement, at last, of Newfoundland as a British colony, the replacement of the 'surrogates' by circuit courts and civilian judges, and the repeal of the old Western Charters. In 1825 a Council was appointed to advise the naval Governor in the discharge of his office. Thereafter, the pressure in the colony for some form of representative government grew rapidly.

The movement for constitutional government in Newfoundland was led principally by some resident merchants and the small professional class, such as the Irishman, Patrick Morris (1789-1849), and the Scottish doctor, William Carson (1770-1843).[31] From a vigorous pamphlet campaign it grew into a movement with considerable popular support. Much of that support came from the Irish population of Newfoundland.

Ever since the seventeenth century, the Irish had formed an important part of the populace, brought over as 'youngsters' or fishing servants by bye-boatkeepers and West Country vessels calling at Waterford and Cork. They formed the population of such "Irish" parts of the Island as the southern shore of the Avalon Peninsula, Placentia Bay, and parts of Conception Bay. In the second half of the eighteenth century, economic conditions in Ireland, together with the political unrest endemic among the Irish, led to emigration. Many of those who came to Newfoundland were inadvertent settlers: stranded on the Island without passage-money to take them further, they hired out as fishing servants and soon became part of the large class of people more or less permanently indebted to merchant and planter. In the earlier period of their arrival they had, of course, been without even such limited educational services and religious ministrations as the English settlers enjoyed. But with the passage in Britain of the Catholic Emancipation Act (1829), they turned to win a place for themselves in a Newfoundland society dominated by an Anglican merchant 'Fishocracy'[32] and administrative establishment. The granting of Representative government in 1832 owes as much to the Roman Catholic population as to any other single group; and it was supported by a politically active Catholic clergy.

31 / The most detailed study is by A. H. McLintock, *Constitutional Government*. The account is continued by Gertrude E. Gunn, *The Political History of Newfoundland* (1966).

32 / The term appears to have been first used in print by Philip Toque, *Newfoundland in 1877* (1878), p. 86. It means the principal fish merchants.

No sooner had representative government been achieved than religious rivalry, hitherto covert, rapidly became the most serious political and social problem of the century. Between 1811 and 1830, over twenty-four thousand Irish immigrants landed: that is, a single ethnic and religious group almost doubled the total population of the Island in two decades. As early as 1828, Philip Henry Gosse, the distinguished naturalist, noted a growing fear of the Irish among the Protestant population of Conception Bay – a fear which is, perhaps, to be attributed as much to cultural differences and economic competition as to doctrinal differences. Five years later, Gosse left the Island with relief, so bitter had the rivalry become.[33] One instance will illustrate the explosive nature of the situation.

In 1832, Henry Winton, editor of the St. John's *Public Ledger* (an "establishment" newspaper), became involved in the first of a series of issues in which he and his newspaper were critical of the legislative representatives of the Catholic population. At Christmas, 1833, an enraged mob assailed his house in the capital, and it was saved from destruction only by the intervention of troops from the St. John's Garrison.[34] This Christmastide attack was followed, in May 1835, by a brutal assault on Winton at Saddle Hill (between Carbonear and Harbour Grace) when "a gang of ruffians hideously disguised, with painted faces," emerged from the woods by the roadside, struck Winton to the ground and cut off his ears.[35]

Throughout the nineteenth century, religious animosities were strong, and, especially during periods of political excitement, they frequently erupted into violence. Riots were common, especially during the almost continuous series of politico-religious clashes which culminated in the Conception Bay and St. John's disturbances in 1860 and 1861 (see chapter IX). In an attempt to control the rivalry, Newfoundland's educational system was remoulded (1856) along the denominational lines it still preserves; and the tradition of political representation in proportion to a denomination's share of the population as a whole, begun as a reaction against the virtual exclusion of Roman Catholics from public office, was carefully preserved,[36] and,

33 / Gosse, *Life*.

34 / Rev. C. Pedley, *History of Newfoundland* (1863), p. 391.

35 / A detailed narrative by Winton himself was printed in the *Public Ledger*, June 9, 1835, and it is from this that the quotation is taken. A ballad on the subject is still known among the Roman Catholics of Harbour Grace.

36 / See G. O. Rothney, "The Denominational Basis of Representation in the Newfoundland Assembly," *Canadian Journal of Economic and Political Science*, XXVIII (1962), 557–70.

indeed, extended into a tripartite or "troika" arrangement to represent the nonconformist Protestant sects.

Perhaps the turbulence of Newfoundland society in the nineteenth century has been exaggerated. Certainly it was not peculiar to the Island. For example, the English geologist Jukes who visited Newfoundland and travelled widely during a particularly excited period in its political history, thought that "scenes quite as bad have taken place at elections at home . . . but they naturally produce more excitement in a scattered and usually tranquil population."[37] But one does not have to go to nineteenth-century Britain (or the United States and Canada) for parallels; they are to be found, and for the same reasons, in contemporary (1966) Ulster. So far as I am aware, marked violence of an organized and public kind, despite the popular legend of the "fighting Newfoundlander," was confined to the large centres with divided religious denominations and, equally important, where a middle class existed side by side with a substantial 'servant' class. Eras of economic depression were particularly marked by social turbulence. In such periods, the urban Irish population was peculiarly vulnerable.

The Irish arrived, as we have seen, in large numbers during the prosperous war years. The collapse of prices in the post-war period (1815) ended several decades of prosperity in Newfoundland, but not the immigration. Many of them collected in the larger towns of the Avalon Peninsula. There they joined those from other parts of the British Isles who, chiefly employed as fisheries servants and seasonal labourers, lacked even the precarious independence of the outport fishermen, who were at least sustained by their "feudal" relationship with the local merchant. Especially during the winter months, these English and Irish servants were often unable to support themselves. The solution of the British authorities – the wholesale export of shiploads of the indigent back to Ireland or to such favoured parts of the New World as Nova Scotia – was both unpopular and not always feasible, and there were frequent local outbursts. One of the worst of these occurred in 1817, 'The Winter of the Rals,' as it is known in local annals: bands of these masterless men, driven to desperation by privation, hunger, and cold, resorted to violence, and the word 'ral' (an Irishism) entered the Newfoundland vocabulary to distinguish a volatile element of the populace which, for several generations to come, was to play its part in history.[38] When associated with Christmas mum-

37 / Jukes, *Excursions in Newfoundland*, I, 239.
38 / In St. John's, which by this time had a population of ten thousand, bands of armed citizens formed nightly patrols to protect the wharves and other property. See C.O. 194/59, 20, Enclos. Magistrates/Gov. Pickmore, April 1, 1817.

ming, this tradition of violence led to the phenomenon of mummers in conjunction with rals, the subject of a later essay in this volume (chapter IX).

All the communities of Newfoundland were alike in their dependence, direct or indirect, on the fisheries: fisherman and merchant were equally involved in a single, dominant industry. But it would be misleading to suggest that the larger communities of the Avalon Peninsula, which experienced such rapid changes during the period with which we have been dealing, were typical of the Newfoundland communities elsewhere on the Island and along the Labrador coast, or of the smaller settlements on the Avalon Peninsula itself. For one thing, the smaller communities, indeed, whole stretches of the coast, were frequently homogeneous in both religion and racial origin – a fact frequently observed by nineteenth-century writers on the Island.[39] The small settlements therefore avoided the worst excesses of denominational rivalry so common in the towns. They were, moreover, close knit in a peasant economy with a considerable non-cash income, and the curve of their economic fortunes was less steep than that of the urban proletariat. And as culturally distinct groups, they were largely unaffected by the thin overlay of town culture.

In the towns there was not only a greater diversity of occupation and trade, there was also a greater degree of cultural diversification. The popular culture of the towns was in part a modified 'outport' culture, a reflection of the continuous movement of rural people into the urban centres, but it was also in part derived independently from the British Isles, especially from Ireland. Gosse, who lived in Carbonear for some years in the 1820s, noted the contrast between outport Newfoundlander and urban Irish as follows:

> The North Shore men were tall, well-made handsome fellows, singularly simple and guileless, with a marked aversion and dread of the Irish population of the harbours, to whom their peculiarities of idiom and manners afforded objects of current ribaldry. ... Their dialect was peculiar. It sounded particularly strange in the ears of the English peasantry. One of its traits was an inability to pronounce the *th*, which became *t* or *d*. Most of them were Wesleyans, and it was amusing to hear them fervently singing in their odd language: –
>
> "De ting my God dut hate
> Dat I no more may do."[40]

39 / Cf. Toque, *Newfoundland in 1877*, p. 366.
40 / Gosse, *Life*, pp. 49–50. Gosse was evidently not familiar with all the dialects of the English peasantry; a visit to west Somerset would have given him a clue to the origin of the softened *th* sound he noted on the lips of the north shore men.

The rural communities were themselves, of course, of great variety. Archdeacon Wix noted this in 1836, when he observed that "The inhabitants of Conception Bay, although a neck of land of only a few miles extent separates them from Trinity Bay, differ from the inhabitants of the latter, as much as if they were of a distant nation; the same may be said of the differences between those who live in Placentia and those who live in Fortune Bay."[41] Yet rural Newfoundland communities – especially those of non-Irish affiliation – were alike in their separateness from the towns. In St. John's the Irish colouring of popular culture was particularly strong.

By the middle of the nineteenth century the towns also had a dominant middle class culture. It was nurtured not only by the presence of English merchants, clergy, and professional men, but by English teachers in the grammar schools which were founded for the education of sons of the professional and merchant class (including, of course, the children of the outport merchants). The more substantial merchants sent their sons to the minor public schools in England, a practice which remained common until the outbreak of the Second World War. There was no higher education on the Island. Indeed, until the institution of the Rhodes Scholarships in 1904, not many Newfoundlanders went abroad to attend university except for training in medicine and law. With few exceptions there was no liberally educated class to develop an interest in regional culture. Its very existence being dependent on foreign trade, the Newfoundland merchant class was notably outward-looking and even cosmopolitan. Although controlling the economic affairs of the Island, the dominant merchant families sought formal political power and office less often than might have been expected. Nevertheless, Newfoundland political parties tended to be led by merchants and professional people (from St. John's), and the appearance as a political force, early in the twentieth century, of Sir William Coaker's Fishermen's Protective Union was a rare popular phenomenon.[42] Non-intellectual and essentially English bourgeois, the merchant class was sturdy, self-confident, and very distant from the folk-culture of the outports.

The primary purpose of this essay has been to provide a background for the communities treated elsewhere in this volume. Stress on these communities as they had developed down to the middle of the nine-

41 / *Six Months of a Newfoundland Missionary's Journal*, p. 168.
42 / See J. Feltham, "The Development of the Fishermen's Protective Union in Newfoundland, 1908–1923," Memorial University History thesis, 1959.

teenth century must not be taken to imply that thereafter Newfoundland community history ceases to be of importance. On the contrary, the rest of the century witnessed a continuous process of change. The population increased steadily, though after the middle of the century, migration outward slowed the growth. Responsible government was granted by the Crown in 1855. A railway was built across the Island between 1881 and 1893. A large logging industry followed together with paper manufacture (at Grand Falls in 1907, and at Corner Brook in 1923), and mining (Bell Island in 1895, Buchans in 1927). These developments provided not only economic diversification; they introduced the beginnings of a cash economy and they also opened the interior of the Island for settlement. For the first time in the Island's history, employment unconnected with the sea was possible for considerable numbers of people.

Even so, these changes did not alter fundamentally the nature of Newfoundland society, especially of the communities in rural Newfoundland where the bulk of the population still lived in fishing villages. Indeed, for many decades afterwards, the logging operations, which in numerical terms provided the greatest employment outside fishing, were conducted by fishermen in the off-season; and even at Bell Island, the iron mines in the early years were worked by winter and summer shifts of fishermen from Conception Bay, and not by professional miners. The great events of the earlier part of the twentieth century had but a limited effect on the nature of the rural communities. Prosperity and high prices for fish during the first World War had comparatively little impact on those communities in which the "truck system" kept to a minimum the spread of profits to the primary producers. In good times or bad, these outports tended to remain the same.

Not until the Second World War, with its unprecedented demand for natural products and the population shift generated by the construction and maintenance of American military and naval bases, did industrialism and urbanization and cash incomes arrive in Newfoundland and begin the thorough transformation of the old economy and the old society. In this sense, Confederation with Canada in 1949 was but the culmination of a process which had already begun a decade earlier.

That process disguised a change which was already occurring in the fishing industry and markets, a change which has increasingly threatened the economy and the existence of the traditional Newfoundland communities. Those communities had originally been founded, and had survived, because the fishery in inshore Newfoundland waters with small boats was more efficient than the old English and European ship-fishery. As late as 1933, three-quarters of the Newfoundland catch was taken from inshore waters. The collapse of foreign markets for the traditional salt-fish product in the 1920s and during the Great Depression led to a gradual shift to fresh-fish products, principally for New England markets. But Newfoundland was not able to match the deep-sea efforts of foreign fishing fleets using modern technologies and factoryships, and buttressed by the subsidies of nationalist economic policies. The continuous, year-round operation of modern fish-processing plants, a necessity which follows from their high capital costs, could not be sustained without either a great deep-sea fleet or a year-round inshore fishery; the one was excluded by the limited financial resources of both the Island's government and its merchants and the other by the winter ice-blockade which made the inshore fishery a limited seasonal operation. Only within the past few decades has the demand for fish products on the world markets brought to Newfoundland the enormous capital investment necessary to sustain a competitive deep-sea fishery. By 1966, 40 per cent of the fish-landings in Newfoundland were made by deep-sea trawlers.[43]

The investment which made this shift possible, although in part local, is coming increasingly from outside – from New England, from Great Britain, and from Canada. The Island, "a great ship moored near the Banks," seems likely, once again, to become the centre of an international ship fishery. When fully under way, it will operate from centralized east and south coast ports with a sophisticated modern technology. In this fishery, the traditional small-boat operation, prosecuted seasonally in inshore waters with a now primitive technology, seems unlikely to remain viable; not viable, that is, without a massive infusion of new techniques, more versatile fishing-gear and boats, and, perhaps more basic, producer-oriented marketing institutions and policies which are themselves not altogether compatible with the capitalism upon which the present general direction of expansion apparently depends. In many areas, the continued survival of the small-boat fishery and its dependent communities must therefore remain in question because the size of these villages, their location, their economy, and their values are in conflict with the current direction of change not merely in the fishing industry but in the Newfoundland economy and society.

43 / On the Northwest Atlantic fishery, see Harold A. Innis, *The Cod Fisheries* (1940). Recent trends in the fishery are sketched by E. Pazdior, "The Fishing Industry," in *Newfoundland and Labrador: The First Fifteen Years of Confederation*, ed. R. I. McAllister (1966), pp. 117–32.

This essay will not – perhaps no essay could – attempt to describe that change. The pace is so rapid, the implications so unpredictable, that – apart from quantification in terms of miles of new roads linking communities for the first time to one another and to the outside world of the towns, and kilowatts of developed hydro-electric power bringing industry to hitherto remote rural areas; in terms of tons of proven ore reserves on the Island and in the interior of Labrador leading to the creation of new mining-towns; and of numbers of settlements abandoned for the centralized educational and medical services of the towns – apart, that is, from the crude statistical facts, meaningful generalization is all but impossible. Certainly, in taking the final step of political union with a North American industrial nation, a choice was made whose full implications are only gradually becoming apparent.

Most apparent is the end of the age of the fisherman, hunter, planter, and merchant: the replacement, in a decade and a half, of an economy dependent on the sea to one dependent on the land; and the change from a traditional, pre-industrial society to an increasingly urbanized, industrial, and consumer society. For rural Newfoundland – as for similar societies throughout the world – the present era is one of emergency. Once again, these settlements are "odd men out"; at odds with outside economic forces which, this time, seem likely to prove more decisive influences than West Country merchants because they are part of a more general process of social and cultural change brought by modern communications to the very doors of the most remote villages.

Throughout most of their history these villages existed without many of the institutions which, in other parts of the overseas English-speaking world, shaped the development of organized societies. Their "laws," were those of a different pattern of custom, unenforced by magistrate, constable, or town council and with their own rationale for the maintenance of harmony within the community. Their people, though today they would be classed as "unskilled" on the modern industrial market, achieved a virtuosity in technical accomplishments which enabled them to construct their own houses, build their own boats, and conduct a fishing operation requiring judgement, skill, and daring. Often without the easy opportunity for much formal education, they yet produced a people with a culture rich in oral literature and music and particularly creative in song. They were, above all, communities on a human scale and societies with a consciousness, or an illusion, of mastery over their environment.

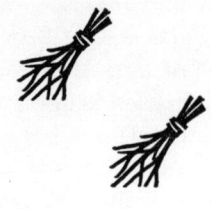

A Typology of Mumming

BY HERBERT HALPERT

1 The Typology

The anthropologists represented in this volume have each proposed theoretical frameworks within which their separate studies of Christmas mumming in Newfoundland communities, especially the "house-visit," may be viewed.[1] The historical documents and plays present other data on mumming, but describe a more varied range of Christmas activities. All this is Newfoundland data.

But the full range of mumming activities in the English-speaking tradition, whether British, Irish, or North American, as well as related European traditions, is very much wider. It includes such contemporary phenomena as the Philadelphia Mummers' Parade, the New Orleans Mardi Gras, the North of England Sword Dance, the St. Stephen's Day Wren-boys, the Shetland "skaklers," the "belsnickles" from German tradition in Nova Scotia, Pennsylvania, Virginia, and West Virginia, mediaeval and renaissance pageants, the court masque of England, the *perchtenlauf* of Austria, and the folk plays of Thrace. Clearly we have here an enormous body of customs.

So far as we can determine from the literature in English, no one has proposed a simple descriptive framework or typology for the whole mumming complex. The diversity of the material makes such an attempt difficult; at the same time because this has not been done, the popular view, and even some specialist treatments, of the subject are misleading. We have in mind here such assumptions as that the Newfoundland house-visit represents the mummers' visit but with the play lost, that the Philadelphia Mummers' Parade derives from the mummers' play,

[1] / I wish to thank G. M. Story, my co-editor, without whose patient firmness this essay would not have been completed.

and that the play itself is invariably and in all its forms derived from mediaeval drama.

Study of this material in the English-speaking world has been largely historical, and its interpretation has been heavily influenced by the eclecticism of Sir James Frazer with his emphasis on magic and ritual. There has been rich historical documentation and description and extensive collecting, particularly by British folklorists and folksong and dance specialists, some of it involving comparison with related European materials.

Though the material assembled in Newfoundland (both from fieldwork and from library sources) is by no means complete, yet it seems sufficiently exhaustive and varied to permit speculative generalization. The typology proposed here, which is intended primarily to view the subject of this book in a wider framework, may be regarded as one attempt to organize a complex body of material.

The typology proposed is a classification of mumming into two grouped pairs. These are as follows:

A

1 *The Informal Visit*
   a) The house-visit (e.g., Newfoundland janneys)
   b) The visitation by inquisitors (e.g., Eskimo 'naluyuks,' St. Nicholas and Black Peter)
   c) The collectors' performance (e.g., wren-boys, carolers, mayers, soulers)

2 *The Visit with the Formal Performance*
   a) Renaissance dumb-show, masque
   b) The dance (e.g., Sword Dance, Morris Dance)
   c) The folk play (e.g., Sword Dance Play, Plough or Wooing Play, Hero-combat Play)

B

3 *The Informal Outdoor Behaviour*
   a) Undirected wandering (e.g., general carnival behaviour)
   b) Going from point to point (see A, 1, above)

4 *The Formal Outdoor Movement*
   a) Groups moving to give performances at fixed points (e.g., dancers, players, etc.)
   b) The dance procession or "running" (e.g., the Helston Flora Dance or Furry Dance)
   c) The formal procession (e.g., parades, pageants)

In Newfoundland, for a variety of historical and ecological reasons, most of the calendar customs celebrated in the Island were restricted to the Christmas season. Indeed, there were few holidays in rural communities outside the twelve days of Christmas. It might be worth testing the typology against the variety of roughly similar disguising practices spread over the calendar year in the milder climate of Great Britain and Ireland. In this study, however, concentration is primarily on this unique period of holiday activity and some of its associated customs in Newfoundland and Labrador. The discussion does not necessarily follow the order of the typology; nor does it give each subsection equal weight, particularly where Newfoundland data are lacking.

2 The Informal Visit

Christmas mumming in Newfoundland, as currently or recently practised, centres largely on the informal house-visit. This is clear from chapters IV-VIII of this book, and supported by field recording and responses to questionnaires in the Newfoundland Folklore and Language Archive. The salient features of the house-visit are as follows:

a) The visitors are an informal group of varying composition (see especially Chiaramonte's discussion in chapter v on some of the possible variations).

b) Members of the group attempt complete disguise. This involves (1) disguise of face and body with varying degrees of elaboration, and with sex-reversal (the man-woman figures) as a frequent pattern; (2) disguise of gestures and body movement; (3) disguise of voice, especially, though not invariably, the use of ingressive speech.

c) The behaviour of the disguised visitors tends to be uninhibited and the reverse of normal. On request, however, they may entertain by singing, playing musical instruments, and dancing.

d) The hosts attempt to penetrate the disguises by a form of guessing-game, sometimes accompanied by roughness; unmasking by the visitors usually, though not invariably, follows successful identification.

e) The unmasked figures return to their normal social roles and are usually offered, and accept, food and drink. Unlike the pattern of

38 A Typology of Mumming

many of the English "collectors,"[2] however, no part of this offering is taken away.

The mummers' house-visit, with its accompanying guessing-game, is the core of this book. It has received little attention so far as we know, and its significance for the student of folk culture has not therefore been recognized.

It might, theoretically, be posited that the house-visit is a peculiarly Newfoundland development, originating perhaps in special local conditions and spreading internally through the movement of population or through contact in the seal hunt, the Labrador fishery, or logging. But against such an assumption is the fact that many parts of the Island, and Labrador, were settled at different times and by different groups who often came directly from Great Britain and Ireland. Moreover, the spread of the custom only internally seems unlikely since contact between people of different regions was substantially confined to the men. And while oral narrative, song, and other verbal lore unquestionably spread from one region to another by direct contact of men engaged in common pursuits, it is unlikely that a custom such as the house-visit, limited to a particular season when the men are nearly always at home, and with its special ramifications of behaviour, would have spread so widely in such a fashion. An origin in the British Isles is therefore to be assumed despite the lack of detailed reports from England itself.

In Great Britain and Ireland there are numerous references to disguised house-visits at Christmas and other seasons, connected with a variety of customs. There are, for example, soulers, pace-eggers, wren-boys, and the like, most of whom are "collectors."

I have not as yet been able to document from the printed sources at my disposal that in England the guessing-game is associated with the holiday disguise of the house-visitors. Mr. E. C. Cawte, however, in an informal communication to me in 1966, mentioned in Northern England "people going about disguised . . . in old clothes, jackets

---

2 / "Collectors" is the term conventionally used by English folklorists to refer to the figures (usually performers) who on various calendar occasions collect food or money in return for their visit and occasional performances. Not all "collectors" wear disguises.

The Folk-Lore Society's books on British Calendar Customs for England, Scotland, etc. are full of details, as are the journals and county volumes of the Society. Excellent descriptions are also given in many books on British folk customs; in the great miscellanies of Brand, Chambers, and Hone; and, of course, in *Notes and Queries*. See the bibliographical note in E. O. James, *Seasonal Feasts and Festivals* (1961), pp. 329–30.

inside out, clothes of opposite sex, black faces or masks at Christmas, or New Year's Eve. . . . They often had a rhyme to say or sing, visited houses, had food and drink, and in some cases the people visited had to try to guess the identity of the Guisers."[3]

As the evening set in, numerous bands of grown-up persons, male and female, sallied forth with their "false faces," and their extraordinary guises on, to sing and "act" at the houses of friends and acquaintances. In many instances money was given to them, but the most of the guisers did it for the fun of the thing. There were usually refreshments offered and accepted, consisting of bread and cheese, currant loaf, hogmanays (or three-cornered biscuits), and in some houses whisky to whose who were grown up.[4]

When we turn, however, to the printed literature outside of England, we find a number of widely distributed parallels to the Newfoundland house-visit pattern. There are, for example, the Scottish Hogmanay "guisers" who go out on December 31; the "skaklers" from Shetland who appear on Hallowe'en; the "belsnickles" reported from German tradition in North America; a South American report from Quito, Ecuador; and a famous literary description from Tolstoy's *War and Peace*.

The Scottish Hogmanay "guisers" and their behaviour are described in the two following reports. The first suggests that the "guisers" were occasionally "collectors," while the second is much closer to the Newfoundland emphasis on the guessing-game and roughness.

Kennoway. – Men and women, boys and girls, dressed themselves in strange costumes, and blackened their faces, or otherwise disguised them, and went off to village and farmhouses, sang songs, and danced to the banter and amusement of the onlookers. It was rare fun not to be known. ... Then the ability and cleverness of those who detected the "guisers" were something to boast about. Sometimes a strong youth would seize a damsel, and keep her in his clutches until he was sure of her identity, but he might get into trouble by the walking-sticks of the males under whose protection she was placed.[5]

3 / I draw attention to the incomplete description of the festival of St. Andrew in Thomas Sternberg, *The Dialect and Folk-Lore of Northamptonshire* (1851), pp. 183–84: "Towards evening the sober villagers appear to have become suddenly smitten with a violent taste for masquerading. Women may be seen walking about in male attire, while men and boys have donned the female dress, and visit each other's cottages, drinking hot 'eldern wine,' the staple beverage of the season."

4 / Alexander Stewart, *Reminiscences of Dunfermline and Neighbourhood* (1889), pp. 152–53.

5 / John Hutton Browne, *The Golden Days of Youth, or a Fife Village in the Past* (1893), p. 121, reprinted in *Examples of Printed Folk-Lore Concerning Fife*, ed. J. E. Simpkins (1914), p. 144.

40   A Typology of Mumming

Although the Shetland "skaklers" at Hallowe'en are "collectors," some of the details of their costume and behaviour parallel the Newfoundland data. Groups of boys go from house to house, in separate bands, disguised with straw caps drawn over the face, or alternately "a piece of thin fabric veiled it." The costume itself apparently changed over the years and the old straw garments were replaced by long white shirts, the straw caps by a white one covered with ribbons. "They disguised their voices by speaking while drawing their breath."[6]

A form of mumming – belsnickling – reported from North American communities of German stock, involved, with variations of detail and fullness, disguise and the guessing-game. Creighton's note from Lunenburg, Nova Scotia, is brief: "We *belsnickled* by mouth organ and musical instruments, but had no singing. We wore masks and people had to guess who we were."[7] The Virginia description is fuller:

During the period between Christmas and New Year, bands of young people, about fifteen to twenty years of age, went about in disguise visiting neighbors. ...

Belsnickles, travelling about in the evening, on approaching a house they wished to visit usually called out in falsetto voices until they attracted the attention of the inmates. There was no set pattern of behavior, but usually some of the mummers represented a family group of husband, wife (made very buxom by means of padding), and child. Some time was spent in trying to discover who the persons disguised were, the attempt resulting in a struggle to remove the false face of the mummer. After the visitors had removed their masks, they would ordinarily be served cider and cake.[8]

A private communication from Mrs. Dorothy Howard (1966) has a description from Pendleton County, West Virginia:

It was the custom of young people (from fourteen or fifteen years old to twenty-two or three) to organize Bell Schnickling parties in October and November each year. (Mr. Dunkle said there were no "Halloween" practices in Pendleton County.) The plans were kept secret; the members of the party – both boys and girls – wore costumes; disguised themselves completely; changed their voices. They planned to visit three or four homes in one evening

---

6 / L. G. Johnson, "Laurence Williamson," *Scottish Studies*, VI (1962), 56–57. Cf. the Halloween visitors described in R. Menzies Fergusson, *Rambles in the Far North* (1884), pp. 158–61.

7 / Helen Creighton, *Folklore of Lunenburg County, Nova Scotia* (1950), p. 59.

8 / Ruth H. Cline, "Belsnickles and Shanghais," *Journal of American Folklore*, LXXI (1958), 164.

– homes where they had friends of their own age – especially homes where bell schnicklers had ambitious amorous interests.

The bell schnicklers rode horseback and tied their horses at some distance "down the road" from each house visited because the horses could offer clues about their owners.

Once inside a home, the bell schnicklers each performed – singing a song; reciting a poem. They never unmasked nor acknowledged their identity even when they were correctly named. After their performances, they were served refreshments – cookies and hard cider usually; occasionally methelglin (a fermented honey drink of the area). Sometimes eating and drinking underneath the mask became an impossible problem. No food was taken from the home.[9]

Finally, there are descriptions of belsnickling from nineteenth-century Pennsylvania, some of which parallel the above accounts.[10]

A recent communication from Miss Yvonne Lange describes a Trinidad masking-and-house-visit custom which I have not seen reported elsewhere. It occurs from early January to Shrove Tuesday, involves body, face, and voice disguise with frequent reversal of sex-roles, the guessing-game and unmasking, the offering of refreshments, and much boisterous behaviour.[11]

A single South American report records what the author, of Cornish origin, calls 'guise-dancing,' from Quito, Ecuador. After describing the carnival atmosphere of children and adults, who run about and dance in disguise through the streets between Christmas and New Year, she adds: "The more respectable members of Quiteño society often make up parties and visit their friends' houses, dressed in fancy costumes, and wearing masks. They have great fun making their friends guess their identity, and usually the party ends with dancing and refreshments."[12]

Finally, from nineteenth-century Russia we have what is no doubt one of the most celebrated European references to the disguise and guessing aspect of the house-visit – Tolstoy's famous and delightful account of the Rostovs' winter amusements in the country.[13]

9 / Mrs. Howard collected the description from Mr. John L. Dunkle (b. 1884).

10 / Alfred L. Shoemaker, *Christmas in Pennsylvania* (1959), pp. 73–85. I owe this reference to Professor Don Yoder.

11 / Miss Lange's full description, it is hoped, will soon be available in print.

12 / S. Freda Paynter, "Guise-dancing at Quito," *Old Cornwall*, II, no. 9 (Summer 1935), 19.

13 / Leo Tolstoy, *War and Peace*, trans. Louise and Aylmer Maude (1938), I, part 7, sect. 10.

The mummers (some of the house-serfs) dressed up as bears, Turks, innkeepers and ladies – frightening and funny – bringing in with them the cold from outside and a feeling of gaiety, crowded, at first timidly, into the anteroom, then hiding behind one another they pushed into the ballroom where, shyly at first and then more and more merrily and heartily, they started singing, dancing, and playing Christmas games. The countess, when she had identified them and laughed at their costumes, went into the drawing-room. ...

Half an hour later there appeared among the other mummers in the ballroom an old lady in a hooped skirt – this was Nicholas. A Turkish girl was Petya. A clown was Dimmler. An hussar was Natasha, and a Circassian was Sonya with burnt-cork moustache and eyebrows.

After the condescending surprise, non-recognition, and praise, from those who were not themselves dressed up, the young people decided that their costumes were so good that they ought to be shown elsewhere. ...

Surrounded by the screaming children the mummers, covering their faces and disguising their voices, bowed to their hostess and arranged themselves about the room. ...

Pelageya Danilovna, having given orders to clear the room for the visitors, and arranged about refreshments for the gentry and the serfs, went about among the mummers without removing her spectacles, peering into their faces with a suppressed smile and failing to recognize any of them. It was not merely Dimmler and the Rostovs she failed to recognize, she did not even recognize her own daughters, or her late husband's dressing-gowns and uniforms, which they had put on. ...

Sometimes, as she looked at the strange but amusing capers cut by the dancers, who – having decided once for all that being disguised, no one would recognize them – were not at all shy, Pelageya Danilovna hid her face in her handkerchief, and her whole stout body shook with irrepressible, kindly, elderly laughter. ...

Pelageya Danilovna began to recognize the mummers, admired their cleverly contrived costumes, and particularly how they suited the young ladies, and she thanked them all for having entertained her so well. The visitors were invited to supper in the drawing-room, and the serfs had something served to them in the ballroom.

We have yet to mention the specialized form of the informal visit, the visitation by inquisitors, described in chapter VII. Here there are distinct differences from both the house-visit and the informal collectors' visit. First, the group is a limited one known to the adults of the houses they are visiting, though not to the children. Second, they come in the role of inquisitors or judges of the children's behaviour, and are there both to frighten and punish and to reward and bring gifts. The masked figures appear in specific roles, but though actors, they invert the normal relation with the audience: it is the children whose houses they visit who must sing for the masked visitors, or at least answer questions on their behaviour.

Examples of this visitation of inquisitors are found in North American German tradition from Nova Scotia, Virginia, and particlarly nineteenth-century Pennsylvania, again called belsnickling,[14] in Holland, Germany, Austria, and elsewhere, in the visit of either a single figure, or a pair of 'black and white' inquisitors (e.g., Black Peter and St. Nicholas, etc.);[15] and, curiously, among the Pueblo Indians of the American southwest, in the visitation of masked figures.[16]

The informal Christmas visit in disguise is, of course, a widely known custom, especially in connection with collecting or begging for food or money. Certain features, for example the kinds of facial disguise and the disguising of the voice, are presumably also widespread, though the examples we have found are not many and have therefore been presented in some detail. It is, however, the existence of the house-visit with its concomitant guessing-game that we wish to stress. Despite the limited number of clear parallels we have been able to find outside Newfoundland (Scotland, North America, Trinidad, Ecuador, and Russia) it is evident that we apparently have here a custom of wide distribution and presumably of respectable age. Its significance has hitherto been, if observed, ignored in favour of the colourful aspects of mumming, namely, the play, the dance, calendar songs, or the spectacular behaviour of the hobby horse, the Christmas bull, the Old Tup, and so on.

It is apparent that the whole subject of mumming as it is related to the informal visit, especially the house-visit, needs to be reopened.[17]

14 / Creighton, *Lunenburg County*, pp. 58 and 59; Cline, "Belsnickles and Shanghais," pp. 164–65; Shoemaker, *Christmas*. It should be noted that the term belsnickling covers more than one kind of informal visit.

15 / Paul Mok, "Folklore of the Netherlands," *New York Folklore Quarterly*, VI (1950), 227–28; Louise Van Nederynen Atteridg, "Dutch Lore in Holland and at Castleton, N.Y.," *ibid.*, X (1954), 251–52. For a variety of European examples, see Clement A. Miles, *Christmas in Ritual and Tradition* (1913), pp. 201–2, 206–7, 218–20, 222–23, 230–32, 243, etc.

16 / Elsie Clews Parsons, "The Zuñi A' doshlĕ and Suukĕ," *American Anthropologist*, n.s., XVIII (1916), 339–47; Ruth L. Bunzel, "Zuñi Katcinas," *47th Annual Report of the Bureau of American Ethnology* (1932), pp. 931–41; Leo W. Simmons, ed. *Sun Chief* (1942), pp. 45–47, 70–71, 84–85.

17 / The private communications I have received (from Mr. Cawte, Mrs. Howard and Miss Lange) suggest that the attention of students, once drawn to the custom, may well reveal its existence in other areas not known to us. The editors would be grateful for additional data either published or unpublished.

As a start, we need more information on points which the older collectors ignored either because they did not know of their existence, or because they seemed too obvious to record. One suspects that the social class and preconceptions of folklorists may have limited both their view of what seemed significant and even what they were able to observe. In a highly stratified society such as nineteenth-century England, the informal house-visit tended to be confined to visits among one's equals. Consequently it may be that the English educated classes had little opportunity to observe intimately such behaviour. It is possible that the practice had been common among the upper classes, as it continued to be in Ecuador and Russia, but had died out. At any rate the falsetto voice, the extrovert behaviour of the disguised figures, and the guessing-game are nowhere treated with the richness of detail and seriousness that the studies in this book show they clearly merit.

3 The Informal Outdoor Behaviour

The central interest of most of the anthropologists' papers in this book is the behaviour of the mummers within the house on their informal visits. Only incidentally do most of them discuss the behaviour of the disguised figures outdoors. Chiaramonte and Ben-Dor, however (chapters v and vii), each dealing with widely separated and ethnically distinct communities, describe this outdoor behaviour in some detail. Moreover, both the historical (chapter x) and our archival data from questionnaires and field recordings indicate that this is a topic worth separate examination.

The mummers in 'Deep Harbour' are sociable, musical, peaceful, and very friendly; there is no suggestion that these wandering groups come into conflict with other such groups or with bystanders. And this friendliness and lack of antagonism form a pattern of behaviour that is commonly found over many areas of the Island, though I confess I have very few other reports to match Chiaramonte's description of the mummers singing as they make their rounds.

But such peaceful outdoor behaviour of mummers does not apply to all mummers' groups in Newfoundland. There are many communities in which mummers behave in a way which is close to that of the ethnically distinct Labrador 'naluyuks' described by Ben-Dor. In these other areas groups, often carrying 'splits,' or sometimes large sticks, fight when they meet other groups of mummers; attack with sticks and even whip with rope unmasked bystanders or toss them roughly off the path or road. In such communities mummers are generally regarded by adults as well as by children as frightening figures to be shunned when met outdoors. We have reports of people taking to their heels on the approach of the mummers, and of being pursued even into houses.[18]

Some of these violent mummers, especially those who go around with the hobby horse, take especial delight in frightening women and children, whether indoors or outdoors. Indeed, it is for this very reason that many households refuse to admit mummers or even bar the door for fear they will force an entrance. The historical reports in chapter x are full of accounts of the 'fools' who either individually chase a bystander or as groups attack spectators. Some of these reports are from communities divided in religious denomination, economic status, and ethnic origin (e.g., Protestant English *versus* Catholic Irish). But other reports from communities without such marked divisions contain evidence of hostile behaviour scarcely less 'rough.' The extent to which the fools or other mummers use the occasion to pay back old grudges (as suggested by Prowse),[19] or whether, as with the 'naluyuks,' the hostility is directed at socially disapproved people, has yet to be determined.

The proceedings of the more friendly and peaceful mummers, by the very absence of noticeable behaviour, go relatively unnoticed in the printed literature of British and Irish calendar customs. The behaviour outdoors of the more violent types of mummer is, however, well documented.

Hunt, describing guise-dancing in St. Ives, Cornwall, remarks that disguises "for the most part consist of old clothes, arranged in the oddest manner, even frightfully ugly. It is dangerous for children, and aged or infirm persons, to venture out after dark, as the roughs generally are armed with a sweeping-rush or a shillalagh. The uproar at times is so tremendous as to be only equalled in a 'rale Irish row.' "[20]

Courtney has another Cornish parallel: "From Christmas to Twelfthtide parties of mummers known as 'Goose or Geese-dancers' parade the streets in all sorts of disguises, with masks on. They often behaved in

---

18 / From Boston, Massachusetts, Shropshire, and Ulster there are reports that mummers who went around with the Christmas Play would burst into houses, whether or not they were welcomed. There are no such reports from Newfoundland. In a personal communication Mr. Alex Helm also calls to our attention that there are many English reports of groups of players frightening people.

19 / D. W. Prowse, *History of Newfoundland* (1895), p. 402. See chap. x.

20 / Robert Hunt, *Popular Romances of the West of England* (1865), II, 187.

such an unruly manner that women and children were afraid to venture out. If the doors of the houses were not locked they would enter uninvited and stay, playing all kinds of antics, until money was given them to go away."[21]

The Cornish behaviour outdoors at Christmas seems remarkably close to the behaviour of carnival crowds in Italy, France, the West Indies, Louisiana, and elsewhere. This is too well known to require documentation here. Although carnival behaviour, ranging from good-natured boisterousness to considerable roughness, undoubtedly qualifies for inclusion under this sub-section, from the point of view of the Newfoundland data it can be largely ignored.

Violence associated with the Christmas bull and hobby horse is common. From Dorset, for example, we have a late nineteenth-century account of the bull.

The Bull, shaggy head with horns complete, shaggy coat, and eyes of glass, was wont to appear, uninvited, at any Christmas festivity. None knew when he might or might not appear. He was given the freedom of every house and allowed to penetrate into any room, escorted by his keeper. The whole company would flee before his formidable horns, the more so as towards the end of the evening, neither the Bull nor his keeper could be certified as strictly sober.[22]

At the feast of St. Michael at Minehead in nearby Somerset, "a hideous figure called a hobby horse used to frighten girls and children, holding great pincers and 'acting the devil.' . . . Though called a hobby horse he was simply a man with a mask and made up as a devil."[23]

The white horse at Cowbridge, in Glamorganshire, Wales, who appeared at the end of November, was more of a true horse-figure.

The essential part of the thing was a framework in the shape of a horse's head, over which was fastened down a white drapery, which fell like a sheet over a boy's body. The white horses, I remember, had gay knots of coloured ribbon stuck on the head. The horse was led by a young man or youth, and

---

21 / Miss M. A. Courtney, "Cornish Feasts and 'Feasten' Customs," *Folk-Lore Journal*, IV (1886), 118; also reprinted in her *Cornish Feasts and Folk-Lore* (1890), p. 10.

22 / Marianne R. Dacombe, ed., *Dorset Up Along and Down Along* (1936), p. 103. Cf. the Wiltshire account of the Christmas bull by E. E. Balch, "In a Wiltshire Village: Some Old Songs and Customs," *The Antiquary*, n.s., IV (1908), 381, also cited in A. R. Wright and T. E. Lones, *British Calendar Customs: England* (1940), III, 222–23.

23 / Frederick Thomas Elworthy, *Horns of Honour* (1900), p. 140.

the great purpose of it all seemed to be to run after, threaten to bite, and frighten the maids and children. Some of the horses had jaws, which the boy beneath could open and shut. I was told, in December last, that the white horse was put down by the police at Whitland, in Carmarthenshire, only about ten years ago, because there had been some servant girls frightened into fits; and another man in the neighborhood told me that some very rough play was carried on sometimes in connection with it.[24]

These selected parallels, which could, of course, be amplified, show again the wide distribution of boisterous or violent behaviour of the informal outdoor rambling of the mummers, a behaviour which is often carried into the house. This violence is a subject that is taken up again later in this essay in connection with the formal outdoor procession of the mummers, and, to a more limited extent, in connection with the play.

4 The Formal Outdoor Movement

The formal outdoor movement of mummers takes several forms. It ranges from formalized dance processions to parades and pageants. The nineteenth-century Newfoundland descriptions of the formal outdoor movements and behaviour of the Christmas mummers are unusually rich in detail. From St. John's in particular we have fine descriptions of processions which can properly be called parades, as well as of the behaviour of other mummers on their way to perform their play. We lack, however, reports of such formalized dance processions as the Padstow May performance, and the procession of the Abbots Bromley horn dancers.

It is suggested that the formal outdoor movement of mummers and other costumed figures may be grouped, though not rigidly, in the following ways:

(a) Groups of performers who go in costume to a particular place, offer their performance, often, if not invariably, ask for and take up a collection, and then move on to another point. The progress of the performers is not usually important, though occasionally it may, in varying degrees, be stylized (i.e., marching); it is the performance at fixed points that is most significant.[25]

24 / Frances Hoggan, "Notes on Welsh Folk-Lore," *Folk-Lore*, IV (1893), 122.
25 / As will be seen from the Patrick Kennedy example below, it is possible to combine the parade with the progress to a performance.

(b) The dance procession or "running" in which the performers may continue to do their formalized step as they progress from farm to farm, or weave through a village, possibly entering various houses or shops, or perhaps merely pausing briefly to greet or sing to the inhabitants, or to perform a stationary dance; but then immediately continuing with their dancing progress. Although it is important that they do stop at houses – the so-called "luck visit" – the distinctive aspect of their behaviour is the dynamic, almost continuous outdoor flow and movement.[26]

(c) The pageant and the formal parade which often incorporate such pageant elements as the float. One is expected to admire the movement itself and its music, the elaborate costumes and paraphernalia borne in procession. Here within the steady flow of the main marchers, there may be performances at various intervals by individuals or by groups. The nineteenth-century Mummers' Parade in St. John's, for example, called on important people both to honour them and to take up a collection. In a modern parade, the important people may be on reviewing stands, but the parade continues on to the end of its course – a course which is usually fixed and predetermined.

Though we have stressed the formal nature of these three types of movement, this does not preclude the association with the main body of individuals or groups who interact dynamically with the crowd.

It is clear that the parade is a distinct part of mumming activities that should not be confused historically, as it has so often been, particularly in the United States, with the mummers' play with which it has no necessary relation.

Historically, the parade and/or pageant is one of the oldest documented forms of mumming. It appears in an already elaborate form apparently derived, Miss Welsford suggests,[27] from folk and ritual ori-

---

26 / For three examples of the kinds of movement described above, see chap. 5, "Dance Processions," in Douglas Kennedy, *English Folk Dancing, Today and Yesterday* (1964), pp. 68–80.

We should probably also include here the Morris dancers who accompanied the rushcarts in Lancashire and Cheshire. According to a recent study "for a long time the North-West Morris has been a processional dance, performed while moving along the street. The dancers might occasionally stop and perform part of their dance on the spot, but this was the exception rather than the rule." Daniel Howison and Bernard Bentley, "The North-West Morris: A General Survey," *Journal of the English Folk Dance and Song Society*, IX, no. 1 (1960), 43. For a delightful description from Didsbury in Lancashire, see Fletcher Moss, *Didisburye in the '45* (1891), pp. 23–25.

27 / Enid Welsford, *The Court Masque* (1927).

gins, in Italy in the fifteenth century, and is soon afterwards found as a regular part of entertainments in royal and aristocratic households throughout the Renaissance period. The masked figures seem to have been of two kinds: the silent mummers, and the ribald maskers. These seem to be connected with both the formal and informal visit, but Miss Welsford's discussion emphasizes the magnificence of the formal processions themselves. On this aristocratic level, the documentation is copious; on the non-aristocratic level, however, although we have made no attempt to examine in detail the history of the subject, one or two examples may be helpful.

These descriptions not only provide parallels with the Newfoundland parade but also illustrate very usefully that the formal procession may have boisterous and aggressive elements in association with it. The Newfoundland eyewitnesses draw particular attention, for example, to both the fools who belaboured the bystanders with whips and inflated bladders, and the 'oonchooks,' who were even "more persistent and punishing in their thrashing of people."[28]

There is a particularly interesting fifteenth-century account from Norfolk in eastern England:

John Hadman, a wealthy citizen, made disport with his neighbours and friends, and was crowned King of Christmas. He rode in state through the city, dressed forth in silks and tinsel, and preceded by twelve persons habited as the twelve months of the year. After King Christmas followed Lent, clothed in white garments trimmed with herring skins, on horseback, the horse being decorated with trappings of oyster-shells, being indicative that sadness and a holy time should follow Christmas revelling. In this way they rode through the city, accompanied by numbers in various grotesque dresses, making disport and merriment; some clothed in armour; others, dressed as devils, chased the people, and sorely affrighted the women and children; others wearing skin dresses, and counterfeiting bears, wolves, lions, and other animals, and endeavouring to imitate the animals they represented, in roaring and raving, alarming the cowardly and appalling the stoutest hearts.[29]

One of the best nineteenth-century parallels we have found to a combination of the formal parade with elaborate costumes and the putting on of a dance performance is Patrick Kennedy's delightful account of the procession of Irish May-boys in County Wexford in

28 / William Whittle, *Evening Telegram* (St. John's), December 24, 1885. See chap. x.
29 / C. H. Stephenson, "King Christmas," *Notes and Queries*, 4th ser., VIII (December 23, 1871), 525.

50   A Typology of Mumming

1812.[30] Though from another season, and involving a much smaller group, it has some of the major elements of the Newfoundland Christmas parade of the mummers.

After a reasonable pause, we had the delight of seeing twelve young men come forth, accompanied by the same number of young women, the boys dressed much more showily than the girls. They were in their shirt-sleeves, waistcoats, knee-breeches, white stockings, and turned pumps; sashes of bright colours round their waists, and ribbons of every hue encircling hats, shirt sleeves, knees, and bodies, the shoulders getting even more than their due. The girls, their hair decked with ribbons, were in their Sunday garb; but, for once, the admiration of the crowd was given to the rougher sex, or rather their bedeckings. To heighten the beauty of the spectacle, out sprung the fool and his wife, the first with some headdress of skin, a frightful mask, and a goat's beard descending from it. Though we knew that the big, bluff, good-natured countenance of Paudh himself was behind the vizard, we could scarcely refrain from taking flight, most country children not being able to look on an ugly mask without extreme terror. His wife (little Tom Blanche, the tailor, there being a bigger Tom) was in an orange-tawny gown, flaming handkerchief, and mob-cap, and had a tanned, ugly, female mask, fitting pretty close to her face. Paudh's first salute to his friends was an Indian yell, a charge in various directions, and a general thrashing of the crowd with his pea-furnished bladder suspended from a long stick. Mrs. Clown had a broom, and used it to some purpose when she found her friends disposed to crowd her.

After a few charges and retreats, we got into marching order, the performers in front, the fool and his wife around and behind them to prevent annoyance, and the delighted assembly bringing up the rear. In this state we reached the big fields of Tinnock, and proceeded by the long, straight fence dividing them till we crossed the road, entered the grove, and defiled on the castle lawn. Considerable amusement was excited as we passed along the big field by a sportive youth devoting some soft compliments and caresses to the fool's wife while his (the husband's) attention was momentarily occupied by other matters. But that was nothing to the fun of seeing the jealous husband, when he found his domestic repose invaded, rushing at the libertine, chasing him through the crowd, and bestowing noisy chastisement on innocent and guilty alike, till the culprit sued for mercy. The farce of reconciliation succeeded the tragedy. It was sweetly affecting to see the

---

30 / Patrick Kennedy, "Hibernian Country Pastimes and Festivals Fifty Years Since," *Dublin University Magazine*, LXVII (1863), 582–83; also reprinted in his *The Banks of the Boro: A Chronicle of the County of Wexford* (1867), pp. 222–25.

false siren with apron to eyes, and sobs in voice, sidle up to Goat'sbeard, and wheedle him into good-humour again. Sealing the re-union with a hearty embrace, they showed their joy by a new foray on the assembly, and scattering them to all points of the compass, amidst shouts of laughter and ludicrous fright.

The turbulent behaviour of the disguised figures is evident in the above accounts as it is in the informal outdoor behaviour treated earlier. Mediaeval and Renaissance bans against masking are noted by Chambers and Withington.[31] In a later period, roughness by "goose-dancers" became "such a term to the respectable inhabitants of Penzance [Cornwall] that the Corporation put them down" around 1876.[32]

In the long history of mumming in Great Britain and America, and probably elsewhere, a common pattern is evident: the rowdiness and dangerous (sometimes criminal) behaviour of the disguised mummers have been met by repeated civic bans on the practice. These bans have a curious habit of repeating themselves in time, suggesting the deep-seated nature of the custom of mumming, which has been suppressed only to rise again in the old or a new form. It is worth examining this pattern, especially, though not exclusively, in connection with the parade.

In Newfoundland, it was this boisterous and aggressive behaviour of the fools and 'oonchooks' that led directly to the first banning of the mummers in St. John's. Subsequent mummers' violence elsewhere on the Island (though not, apparently, connected with a formal parade) led to the statutory ban in 1861 on the custom of disguising throughout the colony, a ban, it may be observed, technically still in effect (see chapter x).

The immediate effect of the prohibition of disguising was to bring to a halt the elaborate parade of the Christmas mummers. Nonetheless, both disguising and parading persisted – though now dissociated. The disguising, despite the ban, continued particularly in the custom of the house-visit, amply documented in this book.

Most Newfoundland accounts of the behaviour of mummers on their way to perform the play (as distinct from the house-visit) suggest that there was rather formalized marching under the direction of the Captain of the Play, or a similar figure, and the players made formal

31 / E. K. Chambers, *The Mediaeval Stage* (Oxford, 1903), I, chap. 17, "Masks and Misrule"; supplemented by Robert Withington, *English Pageantry, An Historical Outline* (Cambridge [Mass.], 1918), I, 103–4.
32 / See Courtney, *Cornish Feasts*, p. 119; p. 11.

request for permission to enter. Thus far we have found no parallels in Newfoundland to the occasional but widespread reports that the players themselves might be rowdy. In North Antrim, Ireland, Foster tells us "doors used to be bolted at dusk during the week or so before Christmas when the Christmas Rhymers were abroad, and women would not venture out alone."[33] Burne and Jackson describe the eye-witnesses' report from Shropshire that when the performers of the play were going about "at the first alarm of their approach, all the household hurried to bar the door, and if they were not in time to do so, in rushed the rabble rout of masquers without leave asked or given."[34] Finally, Boston, Massachusetts, provides an eighteenth-century report of interest:

I forget on what holiday it was that the Anticks, another exploded remnant of colonial manners, used to perambulate the town. They have ceased to do it now, but I remember them as late as 1782. They were a set of the lowest blackguards, who, disguised in filthy clothes and ofttimes with masked faces, went from house to house in large companies; and, *bon gre, mal gre*, obtruding themselves everywhere, particularly into the rooms that were occupied by parties of ladies and gentlemen, would demean themselves with great insolence. I have seen them at my father's, when his assembled friends were at cards, take possession of a table, seat themselves on rich furniture, and proceed to handle the cards, to the great annoyance of the company. The only way to get rid of them was to give them money, and listen patiently to a foolish dialogue between two or more of them. One of them would cry out, "Ladies and gentlemen sitting by the fire, put your hands in your pockets and give us our desire." When this was done, and they had received some money, a kind of acting took place. One fellow was knocked down and lay sprawling on the carpet, while another bellowed out,

> "See, there he lies,
> But ere he dies
> A doctor must be had."

He calls for a doctor, who soon appears, and enacts the part so well that the wounded man revives. In this way they would continue for half an hour, and it happened not unfrequently that the house would be filled by another gang when these had departed. There was no refusing admittance. Custom had licensed these vagabonds to enter even by force any place they chose.

---

33 / Jeanne Cooper Foster, *Ulster Folklore* (1951), p. 35.

34 / Charlotte Sophia Burne and Georgina F. Jackson, *Shropshire Folk-Lore* (1883), p. 410.

What should we say to such intruders now? Our manners would not brook such usage a moment.[35]

The fate of the mummers' parade is curious. Though the parade itself ceased, and has never been reinstated in its old form, Story makes the suggestion (chapter x) that the deep-rooted tradition of formal parades during the Christmas season led to a partial transference in Newfoundland. The Orangemen in many fishing communities, instead of holding their official parades on July 12, held them on December 26 (St. Stephen's Day). Similarly, fishermen's fraternal societies, which began to spring into existence shortly after the ban, held their parades in full regalia on January 1. Here, clearly, is a phenomenon which needs more study. Some of the implications are discussed later in this essay.

The transfer suggestion, calling attention as it does to the deep roots of the parading custom, is of particular interest in view of the history of three of the most celebrated mummers' parades elsewhere in the New World: the Trinidad Carnival Parade, the New Orleans Mardi Gras Parade, and the Philadelphia Mummers' Parade. In all three areas, the boisterous behaviour of mummers on the several holidays originally led, as in Newfoundland, to the banning of all mumming.

In Trinidad there was a series of bans:

In 1846, on account of the general unrest in the city and the numerous cases of arson, the practice of appearing masked in the streets for Carnival was expressly forbidden by the Governor, the writer of the *Port-of-Spain Gazette* commenting "we trust this will prove a final . . . stop to the orgies which are indulged in by the dissolute of the town at this season of the year, under pretence of Masking," and then, three days later, presumably in response to representations, the paper points out that the prohibition does not prevent bands of maskers dressing up and going from house to house, putting on the masks as they get to the houses.[36]

In Philadelphia:

Towards the end of the eighteenth century, this custom of shooting and mummery apparently grew to serious proportions, in the opinion of the

---

35 / *Recollections of Samuel Breck with Passages from his Note-Books* (1771–1862), ed. H. E. Scudder (1877), pp. 35–36, quoted in a note by G. L. Kittredge, *Journal of American Folklore*, XXII (1909), 394.

36 / Andrew Pearse, "Carnival in Nineteenth Century Trinidad," *Caribbean Quarterly*, IV (1956), 185. Pearse lists other bans and controls by the police, pp. 187 and 190.

elders of Philadelphia, for in the year 1808 an "Anti-Masquerade" act was passed. This act decreed that masked balls and masquerades were "common nuisances," and all persons who allowed masked balls in their homes, or co-operated in any way to organize them would be subject to a fine of between $50.00 and $1,000.00, and would be liable to imprisonment for up to three months. In addition, the recalcitrant masquerador was required to give a surety to be on good behavior in the future.[37]

Welch also[38] calls attention to the banning of the mummers associated with Mardi Gras in New Orleans in 1806:

An interesting parallel to this action may be found in the Mardi Gras which was outlawed in 1806. To Pennsylvanians there is still a stronger connection with the Mardi Gras, as may be seen from the following quotation concerning the first major parade after the Mardi Gras was reinstated in 1827: A young man named Michael Krafft, who had been born in Pennsylvania and who had nothing that was Latin in him, had organized the Cowbellion de Rankin Society in Mobile in 1831. It was this organization which first paraded with torch and float, although in Mobile the pageants appeared on New Year's Eve. (Not until 1866 did Mobile have parades on Mardi Gras.) The entire conception of the parades of the Cowbellions and of those later to become popular in New Orleans seems to have originated in the minds of Krafft and a few of his friends.[39]

The earliest known club to be formed among the Mummers was the "Chain Gang," which, according to legend, was formed sometime around 1846. Nothing is known of this club, except that it did exist, and did parade throughout the South Philadelphia area. There are still some men living whose fathers remembered this organization. Other groups soon were organized; this changed public opinion and forced the repeal of the "Anti-Masquerade Act" in 1859.

The point to be noted is that when mumming (i.e., disguising) was legalized once again in Philadelphia and New Orleans, it reappeared in the guise of formal parades – this time under the sponsorship of particular societies which could be held accountable for the behaviour of the mummers. Indeed, it was pressure from these societies and organizations which led to the repeal of the prohibitions. By the end of the nineteenth century, Welch points out, the separate Philadelphia groups banded together in a single parade.

37 / Charles E. Welch, Jr., "Some Early Phases of the Philadelphia Mummers' Parade," *Pennsylvania Folklife*, IX (Winter 1957–58), 25.
38 / *Ibid.*, 25–26.
39 / Robert Tallant, *Mardi Gras* (New York, 1948), p. 100.

What this examination shows clearly in each case is that the violence and disrespect for authority concomitant to the reversal of roles common to masking by "the lower orders," whether at Carnival or Christmas seasons, disturbed the dominant, well-to-do middle class, who succeeded in having masking officially banned; that the deep-seated custom in certain areas of expression through disguises and parades was so strong that it found vent in a compromise through which organized societies accepted responsibility for the behaviour of their members. Today we have the phenomenon whereby an originally spontaneous folk tradition is present in Trinidad, Philadelphia, and New Orleans on civic sufferance, and subject to civic censorship. A recent example of such civic censorship is that the universal phenomenon of mummers blackening their faces was banned in Philadelphia in 1963 for fear of the sensitive colour issue.[40]

In a curious way, this transfer of responsibility is a distant parallel to the later mediaeval practice of the guilds taking responsibility for and indeed sponsoring pageants and parades.

5 The Visit with the Formal Performance

Since we are suggesting here a typology for mumming activities, we might properly refer to other kinds of formally rehearsed and performed activities, put on at specific places and not necessarily in the house. Here one might mention the elaborate performance of the dance, such as the Morris and Sword dances, and probably could examine historically such mediaeval and Renaissance phenomena as the dumb-show, masque, and other kinds of popular plays. The former group, the dances, have been ably studied by a host of distinguished workers (Cecil Sharp, John Graham, and others, particularly those associated with what is now the English Folk Song and Dance Society);[41] the latter, the dumb-show, masque, and popular plays have been treated by Chambers and Welsford. None of these activities,

40 / Charles E. Welch, Jr., "'Oh, Dem Golden Slippers': The Philadelphia Mummers Parade," *Journal of American Folklore*, LXXIX (1966), 533–35.

41 / For a useful list of references, see the bibliography in the interesting analysis of ceremonial dances by E. C. Cawte, Alex Helm, *et al.*, "A Geographical Index of the Ceremonial Dance in Great Britain," part 1, *Journal of the English Folk Dance and Song Society*, IX, no. 1 (1960), 1–41. E. O. James, *Seasonal Feasts and Festivals* (1961), p. 329, calls attention to a number of general studies. To these add: Violet Alford, *Sword Dance and Drama* (1962), and Douglas Kennedy, *English Folk Dancing, Today and Yesterday* (1964).

apparently, was transferred or practised in Newfoundland, except the folk play. Our discussion, therefore, is confined to the folk play.

In chapters x and xi we have published all the printed texts, fragments and references to the mummers' play that have so far come to light in Newfoundland. The three printed texts in chapter xi, and several other references, show that all of these plays were performed only at Christmas. What is the relationship of these plays to the British folk plays performed in England, as well as in parts of Ireland and Scotland, not merely at Christmas but at other seasons of the year?

The play and its performers have a limited number of names in Newfoundland – "The Tragedy of St. George," "Soldiers acting at Christmas."[42] When we turn to the British and Irish reports, however, we are overwhelmed by such names for the performers as, not only mummers but, Christmas Guisers, Christmas Rhymers, Sword Dancers, White Boys, Soulers, Tipteerers, Jolly Jacks, Plough Jacks, and so on. The plays themselves may have a variety of names; some are connected with the season at which they are performed: the Plough Monday Play (the first Monday after January 6), the Pace Egg Play (usually at Easter), the Souling Play (All Soul's Day, November 2), and the various Christmas plays; others are performed at particular seasons with which their names are not necessarily connected. Some of these latter may be described by their localities, for example, the Earsdon Sword Dance.

All of these plays, the English scholars Cawte, Helm, *et al.* suggest, fall into one of three classifications: Sword Dance, Wooing, or Hero-combat plays. The Newfoundland plays seem to have no connection with dancing. A 1936 study[43] shows that in the West Country of England mummers' plays are not associated with dancing; and the same is largely true of the Irish mummers' plays. The bulk of Newfoundlanders are presumed to be descendants of West Country immigrants (especially from Devon, Somerset, and Dorset) and settlers from Ireland – though the precise county origins are apparently mixed. This fits in very well with the presumed provenance of our texts. For this reason I shall not attempt to discuss the Sword Dance type.[44]

42 / "The Christmas Masque" at Herring Neck is Ross Mercer's description (see chap. x).

43 / Joseph Needham, "The Geographical Distribution of English Ceremonial Dance Traditions," *Journal of the English Folk Dance and Song Society*, III, no. 1 (1936), 20–21.

44 / For recent discussions of the subject see Alford, *Sword Dance*, especially part II, "The Sword Dance in Great Britain"; and D. Kennedy, *English Folk Dancing*, chap. 4, "The Sword Dance and the Play."

The Wooing Play, usually or frequently connected with the Plough Monday, or Spring, Play, is also – so far as present records go – absent from Newfoundland. Since the Plough plays, so far as we know, are not found either in the West Country or Ireland, this is not, perhaps, surprising. The Wooing Play is of particular interest, however, since it seems to represent a very old tradition. It has close parallels to the plays collected in Thessaly, Northern Greece, and the Southern Balkans, including Albania, Yugoslavia, and Bulgaria,[45] in some of which the act of ploughing or of making a plough is connected with mimicry of the sexual act, and the surprisingly sudden birth of a child; and often with a death and rejuvenation. Scholars and folklorists have suggested that in these plays we have a magical ritual involving sympathetic or imitative magic connected with agriculture. In other words in their eyes the Plough Play may well represent the oldest stratum of the folk play.

The third classification, that of the Hero-combat Play, is the one to which our Newfoundland texts belong. This is the play which in the older literature was often misleadingly referred to as the play of St. George and the Dragon. While it is true that our three chief texts refer to St. George, or, thanks to the Hanover dynasty, to King George, it should be observed that though George appears frequently in Hero-combat plays, other characters may replace him. Other characters, too, shift and combine in bewildering ways; historical characters, figures from popular tradition or chap-books, and contemporary notables are often introduced. Basically, the Hero-combat play, as its name suggests, presents a combat between two or more antagonists. It might be useful to adapt here E. K. Chambers' analysis of the normal play.[46] In reduced form, it can be divided into four parts: (1) The Presentation, (2) The Combat, (3) The Cure, (4) The Collection.

In the Presentation, some character comes in and demands room to

45 / See: J. C. Lawson, "A Beast-Dance in Scyros," *The Annual of the British School at Athens*, VI (1899–1900), 125–27; R. M. Dawkins, "A Visit to Skyros," *ibid.*, XI (1904–5), 72–4; A. J. B. Wace, "North Greek Festivals and the Worship of Dionysos," *ibid.*, XVI (1909–10), 232–53; A. J. B. Wace, "Mumming Plays in the Southern Balkans," *ibid.*, XIX (1912–13), 248–65; R. M. Dawkins, "The Modern Carnival in Thrace and the Cult of Dionysus," *Journal of Hellenic Studies*, XXVI (1906), 191–206. For some related descriptions see also: G. F. Abbott, *Macedonian Folklore* (1903), pp. 30–31, 41, 80–83, 88; John Cuthbert Lawson, *Modern Greek Folklore and Ancient Greek Religion* (1910; reprinted 1964), pp. 221–31. For a useful recent summary see George A. Megas, *Greek Calendar Customs* (1963), pp. 60–67.

46 / E. K. Chambers, *The English Folk-Play* (1933), p. 13.

perform the play. Then the Presenter, who may or may not be the same as the one calling for room, either introduces each character as he appears, or introduces only the first character who in turn calls in the second, the second calls in the third, and so on. (A third possibility is for each character merely to appear and announce himself.) Each character when he comes in makes his *gab* or vaunt in which he usually gives something of his background and, if he is one of the warriors, announces his warlike prowess.

The combat then follows, frequently after an exchange of insults between the antagonists. The first two antagonists draw their swords and come to blows. One wounds or kills the other. Upon this there often follows what Chambers has called the Lamentation. Either the victor or the Presenter (or sometimes even the wounded warrior) cries out at the terrible deed that has been done and calls for a Doctor.

When the Doctor appears, after some nonsensical discussion about his fee, he usually parodies the brags of his warlike predecessors. He may discuss his own education and travels and then tell about the remarkable cures he has made. In many versions we have here a great deal of nonsense talk, "backward talk," and other examples of foolery.

Sometimes the Doctor makes mock attempts to raise the combatant from the dead, often with some rather earthy horseplay. At other times he comes directly to the point and says that he has a bottle of magical stuff, giving it a nonsense name and a list of its improbable ingredients, and claims that it will work wonders. He applies this magical nostrum and raises the dead or wounded man. It is this regeneration scene, found in practically all versions of the play, which has made many folklorists feel that the mummers' play has ritual connections with agriculture, spring, or the general notion of death and rebirth.[47]

There may be more than one combat, each with its separate, or mass, rejuvenation. Usually, after the final cure, other miscellaneous characters may be introduced. The roll of characters is one of the most variable parts of the play – for obvious reasons. These characters are introduced in the same spirit in which distinguished guests are commonly presented at such contemporary functions as testimonial dinners, a political rally, speech day, or commencement exercises, not to mention university convocations where a Public Orator introduces candidates for honorary degrees. Some of these characters may be described by the Presenter, but others imitate the bragging of the main combatants and describe or praise themselves. One of the characters almost invariably present, though often without a speaking part, is a man in

---

47 / Margaret Dean-Smith, "The Life-Cycle Play or Folk Play," *Folklore*, LXIX (1958), 237–53.

woman's disguise. Scholars interested in ritual have placed much emphasis on this transvestite figure, reading many complicated ideas into her, his, or its presence in the play.

After the more formal characters have been presented, one or more grotesque figures are introduced or introduce themselves, and announce that they are there to take up a collection from the audience. Presumably while the collection is being taken, the performance ends either with the playing of an instrumental number, or by the assembled cast singing a farewell song – frequently one with little relation to the play in tone or content.

An attempt to write the detailed history of the folk play must await the results of current investigations by British and Irish scholars.

It is clear that some forms of the folk play, particularly the Wooing or Plough Play, have very old origins as was suggested above. The same cannot be said of texts of the usual forms of the Hero-combat Play as found in the British, Irish, and Newfoundland traditions. The qualitative assumption many people make of a direct mediaeval origin is not supported by documentary evidence. The earliest reference to what seems clearly to be a Hero-combat Play is in a 1685 manuscript from Cork, Ireland, in which such characters as St. George, St. Dennis, St. Patrick, the Turk, Oliver Cromwell, Beelzebub, a little Devil, a Doctor, and an old woman appear. Such mumming may well have been an "ancient pastime" even in 1685, since it apparently came full fledged from England, but how much older is an unanswered question.[48] Many versions of the Hero-combat Play show distinct influences from chapbook versions. The earliest fragment of a text that can be safely identified as a Hero-combat one is in a scarce Devonshire work (written by Andrew Brice in 1737 or 1738 – though not published till 1770 – *The Mobiad: or Battle of the Voice*, n. p. 90).[49] It may not be merely a coincidence that the Newfoundland texts are of Irish and West Country provenance. The first full text collected from oral tradition is from Oxfordshire, appearing, oddly enough, in a 1794 Welsh collection.[50]

The three mummers' texts printed in chapter XI and the fragments in

48 / See William Smith Clark, *The Early Irish Stage: The Beginnings to 1720* (1955), pp. 4–5; also given in Alford, *Sword Dance*, p. 52.

49 / Reprinted by Cuthbert Bede [Rev. Henry Bradley], "Christmas at Exeter in 1737," *Notes and Queries*, 2nd ser., X (December 15, 1860), 464, and by Cecily Radford, "Three Centuries of Play-going in Exeter," *Report and Transactions of the Devonshire Association*, LXXXII (1950), 249–50.

50 / Edward Jones, *Musical and Poetical Relicks of the Welsh Bards*, 2nd ed. (1794), p. 108, n. 9. Reprinted in J. B. S. "Waits and Mummers," *Notes and Queries*, 6th ser., XII (December 19, 1885), 489, and in John Ashton, *A righte Merrie Christmasse* (n.d.), pp. 128–29.

chapter x are far from giving a complete picture of our knowledge of the folk play in Newfoundland. In fieldwork over several summers subsequent to the point at which data presented in this book were collected, informants have given us many full or fragmentary versions as well as rich details and descriptions on many aspects of costume and performance. In some cases these came from old men who had taken part in these plays in their youth, or from eyewitnesses who recalled vividly such performances and could recite large sections of the plays.

It is worth observing that these performances are invariably recalled with pleasure. Hardy comments, in *The Return of the Native*, that "They [the audience] took the piece as phlegmatically as did the actors themselves. It was a phase of cheerfulness which was, as a matter of course, to be passed through every Christmas, and there was no more to be said."[51] Though Hardy's observations may apply to the region he was describing, and to the social conditions of that period, they do not reflect the attitudes, feelings, and tone of Newfoundland performers and eyewitnesses as they recall the past.

Most people unfamiliar with the folk drama find it hard to view these plays as plays. They are obviously limited in scope and dramatic action. Just as obviously they are not attempting to be plays in the convention of realistic drama. Indeed, because the term "play" immediately suggests, to most people, the realistic convention, Alex Helm has proposed that the term should be avoided and replaced by some phrase such as "Mummers' Ritual."[52] According to his view, in the folk plays we are interested in the ritual significance of the death and revival of a character; all else is added decoration. But this, though it stresses the non-realistic nature of these performances, is to take too narrow a view of drama. For stylized drama is an old and thoroughly accepted tradition; and one must learn to accept the conventions of a particular kind of drama. Certainly from the information we have from people who can recall performing in or witnessing such a play in Newfoundland, the possible ritual significance had little meaning for them and they watched it as a performance which had its own special kind of pleasure.

In no area have we yet found an explanation of why the traditional performances of the play died out, apparently shortly before the First

51 / Thomas Hardy, *The Return of the Native* (1878), book 2, chap. 6.
52 / Alex Helm, "In Comes I, St. George," *Folklore*, LXXVI (1965), 126. For an excellent survey of the folk play in England and its historical affiliations, see E. C. Cawte, Alex Helm and N. Peacock, *English Ritual Drama* (London, 1967) which appeared after this chapter was completed.

World War. When we contrast this with the continuing vitality, in most areas, of Newfoundland's most popular form of mumming, the house-visit, we can only assume that, as the essays in this volume show, the mumming of this latter kind has continued to live because it serves various useful functions. For some reason the mummers' play, perhaps because of its formal nature, did not take on a new functional significance, and was allowed to die out.

The typology presented in this essay, it must again be stressed, is intended as a descriptive framework within which the diverse material of the whole mumming complex may be viewed. What has not, perhaps, been sufficiently emphasized is that the diversity of this material is such that any categorization is extremely hazardous, for frequently what a typology seeks to delimit is, in practice, found in overlapping areas.

It must also be emphasized again that the typology does not profess to encompass the full range of British, Irish, and general European tradition, but stresses the Newfoundland and Labrador practice; together with a sampling of other traditions brought in to enlarge that limited perspective.

Nevertheless, the proposed typology, it is hoped, will prove of general interest to folklorists engaged in the study of other aspects of the mumming complex. It will be their task to correct, qualify, or verify the suggestions proposed here. Meanwhile, it may be claimed that the typology has, for Newfoundland students, the particular merit of focusing attention on the various aspects of the Newfoundland custom, yet seeing them in some relation both to one another and to the broader body of data from some other parts of the world.

Mummers and Strangers in Northern Newfoundland

BY MELVIN M. FIRESTONE

Along the Straits of Belle Isle during the twelve days of Christmas, mummers, or 'janneys,' go from house to house adding to the merriment that characterizes this holiday.[1] Although the spirit of these masked performers is overtly festive, there are covert implications to their behaviour. By donning disguises they make themselves unknown and so escape their customary social roles. It removes some of the inhibitions normal to individuals in their daily lives, and as 'janneys' their behaviour becomes somewhat unpredictable and capricious. The donning of a disguise removes them from the normal interactional sphere, in which behaviour is predictable, and makes them temporarily akin to those who have no identity in local society – strangers.

The Northern Peninsula of Newfoundland, some forty miles wide, juts up 140 miles from the western side of the main body of the Island. This area was sometimes referred to by Newfoundlanders as the 'French Shore'[2] since the French, to whom it was known as the Petit Nord, had fishing rights there until 1904. The janneys that I wish to discuss are those to be found along the western coast of the peninsula, the Newfoundland side of the Straits of Belle Isle, that narrow band of water which separates northern Newfoundland from Labrador.

The settlement in which most of these data were gathered, Savage

1 / This paper is based on fieldwork done in 1964 under a Fellowship from the Institute of Social and Economic Research of Memorial University of Newfoundland. I wish to thank Baxter Coles, Lewis Langness, Alisdair Smith, Melford E. Spiro, and James Watson, along with contributors to this volume, for helpful comments and criticisms.

2 / E. R. Seary, *Toponymy of the Island of Newfoundland . . . The Northern Peninsula* (1959), p. 55.

Cove, lies close to the southwest entrance to the strait and near its narrowest point some thirty miles from Cape Norman, the northern tip of the peninsula. Savage Cove, population about two hundred and fifty, is one of a number of small settlements dotting the coast, the most important of which, politically and economically, is Flowers Cove, three miles away. All the settlements in the area are on the coast, and are located in small coves, after which most are named. So one finds: Bear Cove, Sandy Cove, Nameless Cove, and so on.

The economy of the area is mixed: the people fish, work in the woods, plant gardens, and hunt. Inshore fishing, the most important activity, not only provides the greatest amount of income, but also influences local social organization (to be discussed later) and underlies the dominant orientation toward the world – a nautical one. This is reflected in the use of nautical terms to cover various "land" situations: a group of people is 'a crew,' an individual is a 'hand,' and everyone is 'all hands,' a person of higher status is addressed as 'skipper,' visiting from house to house or community to community is 'cruising,' one gets 'on board' a car, potatoes are 'capsized' into bins, and the front porch is called 'the bridge.' There are also practices which reflect this orientation, such as the storing of clothes in chests rather than in closets and the use of 'lockers' like those on boats, which run the length of the kitchen wall and also serve as benches.

For many years the cutting of pulp wood was also important in the economy; but more recently the local company logging camps have closed down and relatively few men cut wood commercially. An increase in the price of fish, plus, perhaps, social welfare funds, have offset this loss. Gardening has also declined in importance. Previously almost all vegetables were grown locally since not much produce was brought in and there was little cash. With the increase in the price of fish many prefer to put more time into fishing and buy their vegetables.

In the spring the men don their 'rackets' (snowshoes) and walk out onto the ice in the straits to hunt seals. Sealing has been more intensive in the last two years because of a sudden rise in the price of skins. They are worth so much now that few are 'barked'[3] for sealskin boots even though these are desired items. At one time fur trapping was of some importance, and people reported fabulous amounts paid for certain foxes; but now only a few beaver, otter, and muskrat are taken. Most of the meat consumed is game. Many 'rabbits' (varying hares) are caught in snares, and quite a number of birds are shot – mostly murres.

3 / A form of dressing in which the sealskins are soaked in water containing spruce and vur (fir).

More fish is eaten than meat. Cod is the staple, but salmon and halibut are also taken, and people avidly wait for 'a feed of mushels' (mussels) or 'whitefish' (smelt) in the spring. Squashberries, bakeapples, and other berries are gathered, and occasionally wild greens.

Fishing is related to social structure in the straits in that the ideal unit of production is a group of brothers who hold property in common and fish together, dividing the return into equal shares. When their boys grow up there will usually be a split and each man will fish with his sons, although in the past there were frequent instances of brothers and their adult sons all fishing together. When the father dies the boys normally stick together until their children in turn grow up. In conjunction with this we find that after marriage the couple lives with or near the groom's father and, with the exception of household goods, inheritance is only through males. This co-operating group is 'a crew,' and its head, the father or oldest brother, is the 'skipper.'

Mummers

In the Christmas season along the Straits of Belle Isle, the behaviour of mummers, or 'janneys' as they are usually called, is probably similar to that of mummers in other parts of Newfoundland. Since, however, a given cultural form may have different functions in different social settings, its social significance may not be the same as that elsewhere.

When one dons the mummer's disguise in the straits, one is said to 'janney-up.' There are 'big janneys,' adults, and 'little janneys,' children. There are fewer big janneys than little ones today. The children do not take the pains to disguise themselves completely that the adults do; their actions, however, follow closely those of the big janneys except that their behaviour is more inhibited.

Janneys wear all sorts of garments – anything outlandish that they feel will not be identified. Such disguises are difficult to assemble in so small a community. Some cover their boots with 'brin' (burlap) bags tied around their legs, and hands are usually covered since their peculiarities are known. People wrap themselves in quilts, drape themselves in tablecloths, and put on odd garments. Sometimes only a sheet is hung around the body. Shapes are often changed by tying pillows over stomachs to represent fatness or by making humps on the back with stuffings of various kinds. Mummers may walk with a stoop or change their gaits as habitual mannerisms and postures are easily identified in so close a community.

The face is quite often covered by a veil which hangs in front of the face and down over the sides of the head hiding the neck. Outdoors the veil may be raised for better navigation, only to be lowered just before entering a house. Grotesque rubber masks are a recent introduction, but homemade ones of various types are still constructed.

There was until recently a 'hobby horse' or 'horsey-hops'[4] in Sandy Cove, the next settlement northeast of Savage Cove. This is a frightening mask in the shape of a horse's head with a movable jaw controlled by a string. The jaws contain teeth of nails. "You could tell that it was a horsey-hops outside by his jaws snocking [knocking] together: snock, snock." Hobby horses are largely of the past: few in Savage Cove remember them.

Some other infrequently seen types of costume consist of the skin of a moose head worn over the face. Once a man went around from house to house with cowbells and chains fastened to him. At one time little janneys would come in under a single large piece of canvas. The people in the house might then grab hold of protruding limbs and attempt to drag individuals out, or throw a rope around the lot and tie them into one bundle.

There are other ways of disguising the face than those already mentioned. Nylon stockings may be pulled over the face, and in conjunction with this it may be rouged or partially blackened. Dentures are sometimes removed as a means of disguise; it can be surprisingly effective as most adults and many late adolescents have upper plates and are usually not seen without them. Some quite successful janneys have not covered their faces, and a prank of one of these will be presented later as an example of the parallel between the janney and the stranger. Here let me mention one middle-aged woman who took out her teeth, pulled back her hair, put on a long white gown, and knocked upon her son's door. He did not recognize her and would not let her in. A factor undoubtedly involved in this refusal is that only strangers knock in this area, and so the son's perception of the situation was altered before he reached the door: his mother would never have knocked but would have walked right in.

Insofar as they speak at all the speech of mummers is disguised. Some are able to 'talk like a janney' – ingressive utterances at a high pitch. ("Yes" and sometimes "no" are indeed normally uttered ingressively in this area as in other parts of Newfoundland.) When a group of janneys enters a house, only one or two of them speak. These "spokesmen" are not the leaders of the group but merely those who are

---

4 / I have heard the term 'horsey-hops' used only by one person.

not afraid of being recognized by their speech. They may, however, tap the others with the sticks they carry and admonish them if they do anything that might give themselves or their fellows away. Mummers who can hold long conversations without being recognized are rare. The ideal janney is one who can do this even with his face uncovered. Those who can accomplish this may be disguised only by the removal of teeth, face blackening, and strange clothing.

When janneys come to the door they knock loudly and impressively. People are not obliged to let them in, and many do not. Their knocking clearly sets them apart as strangers. When visitors come they normally walk right into the kitchen and sit down; they do not usually venture into the other rooms. The kitchens of the area are in a sense communal. The mummers march in imperiously after being admitted and station themselves around the room. Someone initiates a conversation with them, often asking where they have come from. Typical replies are "the North Pole," "France," or "Germany"; thus emphasizing strangeness by distance or foreignness.

Sometimes janneys 'step-dance.' The mummers are often asked if they can dance, and they may then do so. Occasionally they will perform without being prompted and may even bring their own musicians. Hosts may give big janneys beer, or small ones candy.

Those in the house attempt to ascertain the mummers' identities by asking them questions in the hope that they will inadvertently give themselves away. If a janney will not speak, he may answer with nods. They are often ridiculed by the hosts who attempt to embarrass them by making fun of their appearance, clothes, or attitudes. The janneys, on the other hand, intimidate by their frightfulness and strangeness.

Someone may declare that a janney is a particular individual, but unless the janney is positive that he has been identified he assumes that the person is merely guessing. Many will try to notice if the janney's behaviour changes when they call the name of a person who they feel he might be. When the mummer is certain that his identity has been discovered, he ceases his uninhibited behaviour and usually unmasks. People say that "It spoils your fun when people know who you are."

The twelve days of Christmas are a period of licence during which drunkenness on the part of men is expected. Violence sometimes accompanies mummery. If someone attempts to lift a janney's veil, the latter may give him a 'snock' with his stick, or at least make a warning swing. Janneys are sometimes tripped, which may lead to roughhousing. Sandy Cove has a reputation for being rough with janneys;

on occasion they have been thrown into snowbanks and otherwise tormented.

People look forward to the coming of Christmas and the coming of the janneys. Their visits are a source of amusement both to those visited and to those in disguise. Children, however, are afraid of janneys and will often cry and whimper when they enter a house. Adults are not usually overtly fearful but may run from janneys if they encounter them outdoors.

Strangers

The role of the stranger, a person who has no place in local society, is emphasized in the straits by two factors: the pervasive intimacy in social relations (everyone knows everyone else well), and the isolation of the area (you rarely see anyone you don't know).

Settlement is only along the coast, and people maintain that they know almost everyone from Eddies Cove East (thirteen miles to the northeast) to Anchor Point (eleven miles to the southwest) or even to Ferolle (twenty-eight miles to the southwest). Individuals are actually known, or known about, much farther than these points. The inhabitants of Big Brook (twenty-six miles northeast), the next settlement northeast of Eddies Cove East, are known as are many people in Cooks Harbour (forty miles northeast), where many of the men on the southwest side of Savage Cove go as sharemen. Individuals and relatives are known as far around the tip of the peninsula as Main Brook.

To the southeast the number of people known beyond the "social area" gradually fades until one reaches Bonne Bay where the Northern Peninsula begins. Friends and relatives of those in the straits live in Deer Lake and Corner Brook; occasionally they are to be found in other parts of Newfoundland, mainland Canada, and even the United States.

Much of the intimacy that exists throughout the straits area is due to the small population and the fact that there has been little population movement. Almost all of the inhabitants are descended from a handful of early settlers. Patrilocal residence, coupled with the lack of mobility, has made for only a few surnames in each settlement. Many children are produced in each generation, and people keep track of a large number of their relatives. First-cousin marriage is common, as is the marriage of a cluster of siblings to another group of siblings.

Intimacy within the area is reflected in terms of address. Males call each other 'my dear,' 'boy,' 'my son,' and females are generally addressed as 'maid' or, less frequently, 'my maid.' Older people are called 'uncle' and 'aunt.'

Hospitality also fosters familiarity. People walk into houses without warning and are given 'a lunch.' The charter for such activity is "Around here [in contrast to the city] you goes where you likes and does what you wants." Prior to thirteen years ago land transportation was by foot in summer and by dog- or horse-sled in the winter. When travelling you would go on until night overtook you and then put up at whatever home was at hand. In this way hospitality reinforced intimacy while serving a practical end which would be reciprocated. I have heard it said that in earlier days your own relatives might come through and you wouldn't see them because they would have put up with someone else. With the opening of the roads this custom is starting to die out.

The road that now links the area with the rest of Newfoundland to the south has been open only since November 1962. Prior to this, since the coast was icebound from Christmas to the beginning of summer, it was the rare man who could make the trip by dog-team to Corner Brook. It has only been about five years since the road across the tip of the peninsula to St. Anthony has been open. Although strangers are not as rare as they once were before cars and snowmobiles appeared, they are still scarce and stared at. The values which existed in the previous period of extreme isolation are still strong.

'The Runaway' is the archetype of stranger. He is the fantasy figure of whom children and some adults, particularly women out berry-picking, are afraid. He is the man who has no home, is on the run from something or somebody, and he is dangerous. Runaways are thought to carry guns. If big janneys wish to remain undisturbed by groups of children who gain their courage from the crowd, they may take a rifle along and remain undisturbed.

Occasionally adults are more specific about what the Runaway is supposed to be running away from. Some of the early settlers were deserters from ships.[5] Life aboard ship was hard: there was little food and punishments were severe. I am told that the Goulds of Bear Cove were descended from Alexander Duncan, a naval lieutenant on one of H.M. war ships, who deserted to marry a local girl and then took as his surname his mother's maiden name.[6] Desertions continued until

---

5 / For another instance of fantasy figures being derived from fugitives, see Felix J. Oinas, "Spirits, Devils, and Fugitive Soldiers," *Journal of American Folklore*, LXXVI (1963), 225–30.

6 / Also mentioned by J. T. Richards, "The First Settlers on the French Shore," *Newfoundland Quarterly*, LII, no. 3 (1953), 19.

fairly recent times. There are at least two old men living on the peninsula today who ran away from a French ship. After jumping ship boys and young men were taken in, and sometimes adopted, by local people, whose names they took.

Now let me present some similarities between janneys and strangers.

The first is that both janneys and strangers knock. When a knock comes at the door in the straits, a person in the house may say, "There's a stranger at the door." When janneys knock, they are known by their loud thumps and attendant noises. Before I left St. John's for the straits I was informed by a Newfoundlander who had worked in the area that people enter houses without knocking; if you knock, he said, they probably will not let you in. This turned out to be an exaggeration, but disclosed an essential truth. In a society characterized by familiarity and intimacy with all those living over a wide area, the knocker demonstrates by his action the absence of these qualities.

People are apprehensive and tense when a knock comes at the door. Little children are sometimes teased by an adult knocking secretly and saying in an apprehensive tone that someone is at the door.

Insofar as janneys knock they announce their presence and set the stage for their performance before they enter. Their knocking also provides an opportunity for turning them away, as they sometimes are, perhaps with the reason given that a child in the house is afraid of janneys. If they are to be admitted it provides the host with a chance to admonish them not to be too loud or to dance if there is someone sick in the house. In knocking they also set themselves apart from their normal roles as community members who would normally enter freely and without formality. Someone must go to the door to see to them as one would see to a stranger. Their knocking is a ritual by which they announce their strangeness.

A second similarity is that people attempt to discern the identities of both mummers and strangers. Trying to find out who a janney is is the object of those who entertain him. Similarly people are quite curious about strangers and attempt to find out who they are, what they are doing, and what they are like. They are approached and drawn out.

Another parallel is that people are apprehensive of both mummers and strangers. We have already mentioned that children show overt fear of janneys whereas the feelings of the adults are not as open. Adults are sometimes a bit apprehensive at the entrance of big janneys, may run from them outdoors at night, and some tell stories of their encounters with janneys in which they claim they were not frightened at all!

Fear of strangers is also somewhat covert. People are conscious of the changes brought about by the opening of the roads and some are fearful of the long-term effect. There is very little crime in the area and there was even less in the past. The nearest policemen are the Mounties in St. Anthony who cruise the road, but are not often encountered. People say that the reason that there was so little crime in the past was that there was almost no one around who was not a native, and you couldn't hope to get away with anything because it would soon be obvious who had done the deed. Now, they say, people can come in from anywhere on the road and you have no idea who they are, where they are from, or what they might be up to. They could come in, commit a crime, and then drive off.[7]

That strangers are feared does not imply that anyone is in any way unkind to them. On the contrary the people of the straits are genuinely hospitable, friendly, and eager to establish relationships. The outsider is urged to visit, stay late, and partake of meals. One man said to me, "People around here are good to strangers, aren't they?" He was right. However, covert fear and overt friendliness are complementary. The more you find out about an outsider, what he is up to, and what he is like, the less of a threat he is.

In keeping with the notion of 'The Runaway' it is strangers passing through that are most feared. Once someone settles in the area and becomes known he is readily accepted. This is not only true today but also held in the days of the real runaways: they were quickly and easily incorporated into local society.

One also finds that children are threatened with strangers and with janneys. When I was new in the community parents would frequently tell misbehaving children that I would take them away, and one said, "Don't do that or Mr. Firestone will put it in his book." Children are also threatened with people from other settlements who are strangers to them, but not to their parents. Similarly, a child upstairs might be told to quiet down and get to sleep because janneys are coming. Children may be afraid to go outside because of the mummers, and I have already mentioned their fright when janneys come into the house. A few parents also tell their children during the year that one or two of the older women of the settlement who are socially distant from them are janneys and will take them. These children show fear of such women, even though the latter are not 'janneyed-up.'

I have been told by children that when I first arrived they were

---

7 / This general attitude is not limited to the straits. I have heard several people in St. John's remark that since Confederation with Canada, 1949, or some say since the arrival of U.S. servicemen during the Second World War, one must be more careful with people one does not know as they might be outsiders.

afraid when passing my house. Somewhat later, when I complained to two men of the danger to children involved in chasing my car, I was told to threaten them and that this should be particularly effective as I was a stranger. But some time after this, when I was better known, a little boy showed that he was not intimidated by his uncle's threat that I would take him, by saying, "Oh, I knows he!"

Other figures with whom children are threatened are the Mounties, the Nurse (at the Grenfell nursing station), The Boo Man, and Santa Claus. Youngsters flee at the sight of the car the RCMP constables drive. The Nurse, it is said, will give the child (painful) needles and keep him in the nursing station. The Boo Man (or The Boo, a euphemism for the Devil) takes children 'down to his fire' if they misbehave or lie. One type of toadstool is called a 'Boo Man's Hat.' I have heard parents tell their offspring no more than that they would not receive anything from Santa Claus if they did not obey; however, the fear children display of him suggests that more is involved. One woman says that her mother used to tell them that Santa Claus "put the hammer into" a certain man's head, and he might do the same to naughty children. Children show an intense fear of the costumed[8] Santa Claus at the yearly Christmas parties held at the school. Many will not go up for their presents, and many cry. Those who do neither are thought to display a remarkable bravery in approaching him.[9]

The final similarity has already been touched upon, that the behaviour of janneys is uninhibited. They are not constrained until their identity is established. The behaviour of strangers is similarly unpredictable. You do not know how they will behave until you have got to know about them. Even though it is known that janneys are, in fact, not strangers but members of one's own or adjacent communities, they are feared because they have temporarily shed their identities, and so one might just as well be interacting with strangers. Once in Flowers Cove men outdoors backed away from a janney who they knew was a friend of theirs. Such fear is the result of an accumulation of experiences based upon childhood training.

The most successful piece of janneying that was ever carried out in Savage Cove illustrates the similarity between mummers and strangers. This was brought off by a man who armed himself with an old breech-

8 / It may be that the children's fear of approaching the party Santa Claus is that, like a janney, he is in disguise.

9 / Note that the Stranger, the Nurse, and The Boo Man will all take, or keep, the child away. It may be that fear of the Mountie is related to his potential of removing individuals from the community.

loading musket, put on old clothes, blackened and rouged his face, but did not otherwise hide it. He went up to one house and told the inhabitants that he was the man who had been dragging the boom-log. There was a story going around that a man had been seen pulling a forty-foot boom-log through the country, and it was thought that this was the Devil or a spirit. He then asked them to direct him to a certain man's house, and they fearfully told him the way and slammed the door. He then went from house to house and at each place asked for a certain item, a pound of tea at one place, a pound of butter at another, a pair of sealskin boots at a third, and so on. The people were so frightened of him that they gave him these articles to get rid of him. As he received the extortion from a house he would stuff it into his knapsack and go on to the next place. At each house he asked for things that he knew would be there and that would be no mean loss. People thought that he was a runaway and were completely intimidated.

Here was a man who came along painted up during Christmas, when everyone expects janneys, and was so successful in his mummery that people who had known him all his life thought him a real stranger, or rather the archetype of the stranger – unpredictable, threatening, and malevolent.

I do not mean to imply that the people of the straits consciously feel that mummers symbolize strangers or feel that the two categories necessarily have anything in common. However, they are functional equivalents. They both provide individuals with socially approved means of displacing hostility.[10] They do so in two ways.

First of all they enable parents to turn away from themselves the hostility that their children feel when disciplined. Donald T. Campbell states the general notion as follows:

... our theories of learning and cognition predict trouble for the modern emancipated American family. According to learning experiments, conditioned fear and conditioned hostility are the unrational product of temporal contiguity between stimulus and pain, or between stimulus and frustration. And if we go to cognitive psychology we find that the perception of causality, and with this the phenomenon of blaming, are likewise functions of temporal and spatial contiguity.... From these theories it follows that in a

---

10 / The fears, hostilities, and functions that I have discussed should not distort what is manifest in the straits regarding mummers and strangers. Janneys are the focus of much fun and merriment, and I doubt if the kindness shown to strangers can be exceeded.

society such as intellectual suburbia, where the parents stand alone in representing the restraints which society passes on to children, the parents will become the stimuli for conditioned hostility on the part of children, the children will perceive the parents as causing, as to blame for, their frustrations. Thus, the conditioning and/or causal perception processes predict a chronic divisive force within the modern family.... one can expect that in stable societies preventive customs will have grown up around this inevitable parental-resentment problem... such as the role of shamans and kachina dancers as devices serving to deflect the discipline-induced hostility of the child away from the parent, and thus as preserving intrafamilial solidarity... one [has]... sympathy for those unsophisticated parents in our own culture who attempt a similar deflection of childish hostility away from themselves through invoking the sanctions of the policeman, the boogeyman, Santa Claus, or a reified God. (On the other hand, perhaps it is well that in our culture the socialization-induced hostilities are associated with parents, for our occupational structure requires new entrants to the labor force who are willing and eager to leave home permanently. Just such a labor force is lacking in some of the underdeveloped countries, perhaps in part because of the greater "wisdom" of their intrafamilial relationships....)[11]

Life in the straits usually calls for continued residence with or near one's father and brothers, and also continued economic co-operation with them if one is a male. About half of all women marry within the settlement and are never far from their parents. Families work together well and in the summer and early fall in particular spend many long hours working 'at the fish,' when all except infants and very old people help. I have heard it said that to work together you have to have a boss, and this boss is the father if alive, or the eldest brother if he is not. All of these factors make a displacement device, such as is suggested above, integrative in the straits. The mummer and the stranger who will take the child away if he is bad, plus the other frightening figures mentioned, help preserve home and community.

Secondly, fear of janneys and strangers is a means by which adults

11 / Donald T. Campbell, "The Mutual Methodological Relevance of Anthropology and Psychology," in *Psychological Anthropology*, ed. F. L. K. Hsu (1961), pp. 335–36. Campbell offers the notion quoted as one of a number of "several condensed and oversimplified examples" of ways in which cross-cultural research can "... put to more rigorous test psychology's tentative theories" (334–35). One must not, therefore, take the quotation as a demonstrated relationship which Campbell is asserting. Note that he says "... one *can expect* [italics mine] that in stable societies preventive customs will have grown up...."

can displace generally acquired hostility. Kluckhohn[12] has analysed Navaho witchcraft as a means by which hostility engendered by relatives and various other frustrating agencies are displaced, and Spiro has shown how the fear of ghosts on a Micronesean atoll functions to displace in-group aggression.

It requires little insight to infer that hostility, as well as fear, motivates the performance of rituals to defeat ghosts. Indeed, the Ifaluk are quite consciously hostile toward the ghosts. But though consciously hostile to ghosts the Ifaluk, like all people, have occasion to be hostile to their fellows, particularly to their close kinsmen. By displacing hostility from fellows to ghosts, their hostility is acceptable, and their subsequent aggressive motive can be gratified in a socially sanctioned manner in the performance of these rituals.[13]

In the straits the fears regarding malevolent figures that are engendered in childhood remain and function similarly in adulthood.

The parallel between janneys and strangers is disturbed in that a member of local society cannot become a stranger, but anyone can janney-up. One can actually become a mummer and, whatever one's conscious motives, intimidate and frighten others with one's strangeness and potential aggression.

Conscious motives of fun and amusement aside, covert hostility is undoubtedly a factor in janneying. However, the desire for esteem is also involved and many who are otherwise quite shy can show off. When groups of men get together and drink, either going from house to house during Christmas and Easter week, or at weddings and other occasions, individuals are encouraged by the group to sing or dance. The introverted are embarrassed by these promptings and the extroverted readily accept. Some may be motivated to escape their normal roles in society and utilize janneying to this end. Perhaps temporary anonymity in so intimate a society is in itself rewarding.

In becoming mummers people temporarily make themselves strangers in their own society.

12 / Clyde Kluckhohn, *Navaho Witchcraft* (1944).
13 / Melford E. Spiro, "Social Systems, Personality, and Functional Analysis," in *Studying Personality Cross-Culturally*, ed. Bert Kaplan (1961), p. 112.

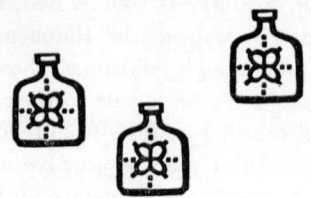

Mumming
in 'Deep Harbour':
Aspects of Social Organization
in Mumming and
Drinking

BY LOUIS J. CHIARAMONTE

1 Introduction

'Deep Harbour'[1] is one of the relatively isolated communities located on the south coast of Newfoundland. Travel between these communities is by sea. It is extremely difficult to connect most south coast communities by road because of the sheer cliffs which rise from 500 to 1,000 feet above sea level, and the fiord-like harbours extending as much as fifteen miles inland.

The entrance to Deep Harbour is about 500 yards wide. Inside the entrance the harbour narrows quickly to a width of about 300 yards, and then widens again to about 400 yards as the harbour makes a slow 'S' curve over its mile-and-a-half length. Water from ten to forty fathoms deep and towering cliffs make it an excellent shelter for ships of all sizes.

The sixty-five houses of the settlement are built along steep hills at the head of the inlet. At the time of this study, there were 338 residents, of whom 171 were adults, 120 school children, and 47 infants.

Most of the houses are built very close to one another, sometimes separated by no more than a couple of yards. Close as their houses are, men seldom visit other houses during the work week – from Monday through Saturday. Usually men do not fish on Sundays, unless they have not been able to haul their gear earlier because of foul weather,

---

1 / 'Deep Harbour' is a fictitious name. This paper is based on fieldwork carried out under a Research Fellowship of the Institute of Social and Economic Research of Memorial University of Newfoundland from October 1962 to October 1963, with a return visit of three weeks during the Christmas of 1963. I wish to thank the residents of Deep Harbour for their help and co-operation. I am indebted to Dr. Herbert Halpert for his many suggestions during the several rewritings of this paper.

and so most men spend the day relaxing at home, or if it is a pleasant day they may join other men on the government wharf where they will sit, talk, and smoke for an hour or so. For children and many women, however, Sunday is the big visiting day and they may call briefly at several houses.

For most of the year the tempo and tone of life in Deep Harbour is characterized by separateness. Although households are linked by a complex of relationships and obligations as well as by proximity, each household maintains its self-containment. Indeed, a household as a separate unit of social organization may be defined in terms of its opposition to other households.

This separateness and self-containment are illustrated by the fact that in a household talk about other members of the community, or about problems that concern the household, ceases when someone from outside comes in; the subject is changed when the outsider enters and resumed when he leaves. This is done automatically with no reference to the interruption or comments about the outsider who has just left.

Each member of the household has equal access to all household information. A letter or telegram from father, son, or some other relative is read by all; even the four-year-old who has not learned to read handles it. Although there are the usual disagreements between siblings, they keep each other's secrets and defend one another against other households. Relationships between husband and wife are especially close.

Each member in a household has his role to perform. The children have chores which are graded according to their ages. Associated with a person's role is the expression of individuality: each person has his own cup, his place at the table; the mother has her chair, the father his, and all have the right to 'have their say.'

Normally women are more mobile within the community than men. Women will often borrow small quantities of sugar, molasses, eggs, and the like, from their neighbours. When borrowing an item they frequently visit for a while, passing the time of day and exchanging gossip. Women will also go to another's house for the sole purpose of visiting, talking over a cup of tea for an hour or so. They tend to visit with their sisters, aunts, and mothers far more than men visit their equivalent relatives. Husbands seldom visit another household by themselves unless it is for an express purpose, for example, to borrow a necessary tool or to ask a favour. When the husband is home, the mobility of the woman is, however, restricted: she feels she should be home to attend to her husband's needs.

The household, as an important unit of Deep Harbour social organization, complements another, that of the dyadic relationship. An understanding of both the household and dyadic relationships is vital to a discussion of Christmas in Deep Harbour.

A dyadic relationship refers to the social interaction between two persons. Each man in the community defines his relationship with a particular man on the basis of experiences he has had with him. The fact that every man makes a separate definition for each of his relationships to all other men makes each man the nucleus of his own universe. The structure of the social network in Deep Harbour can be drawn, then, as a number of individual universes which overlap in various ways.

During the course of his life, a man tries out relationships with others in the community. His evaluation of another depends more on his own private assessment of specific involvements than on the other's role in the community at large, that is, a judgment is made at each point a man touches on experience with another. For example, a fisherman will decide how he will act toward a shopkeeper on the basis of prior personal experiences which he and others have had with the shopkeeper, not on the basis of the role that the shopkeeper plays as shopkeeper.

Ties are made, broken, and re-made, in the ongoing life of the community. As these ties alter, the universe of each man changes and with it the interlacing of the structures of all the men's universes. Along with the constant altering of ties, tensions between members of the community may increase or decrease. The increase of tension is made most evident in the constant evaluation taking place between men who have established ties and between men who are about to establish ties. Even a long-standing relationship may be broken because of a conflict.

Ties that two men in the same social grouping have with others in their group will be of unequal strength. Each may have with the others long-standing relationships which will vary in intensity with the number and quality of experiences shared. Thus the 'closeness' one man may feel towards another, or the degree of 'trust' that one may express towards another, varies. The above complication yields a picture of each man's social network as a structure composed of ties of varying intensity.

In the process of forming his network a man will become obligated to others and will, in turn, obligate them through exchanges of labour, borrowing, work done, and work received for payment, and through reciprocal drinking. Later, it will be shown how dyadic relationships affect mummering and drinking during the twelve days of Christmas.

Most Deep Harbour men earn their livelihood from the sea. The exceptions are the postmaster, the few school teachers, the shopkeepers and their helpers, and the lumberjacks (the latter part-time fishermen). Deep Harbour fishermen are away from home for varying lengths of time, depending on the type of fishing engaged in. Some fish from the home community all year, leaving early in the morning and returning late in the afternoon. Others fish from other ports for varying periods of time. Since men may combine various types of fishing in any one year, their absences from home may range from two months on long-liners or halibut boats to eleven months on draggers.

2 The Coming of Christmas

All members of the community try to come home for the Christmas season. The young unmarried men and women working in nearby fish plants, and the men who have been fishing from other ports, make every effort to arrive in Deep Harbour on or before December 24, for Christmas in Deep Harbour is a unique event in the adult world of the fisherman. It is the only extended period of the year when a man, relieved of his daily toil, relaxes. When Deep Harbour men are at home they are always busy. Even on a 'looard [leeward] day' (that is a stormy one) when men cannot fish, there is always the net to repair, a trawl-buoy to be 'chopped out,' wood to be cut, repairs to be made on the houses, a wharf that needs shoring, an engine to be tinkered with, or the gasoline washing-machine that a man may have to fix for the fourteenth time.

The varied yet plodding beat of daily living is stepped up as the community experiences the rhythmic variations of Christmas. The earlier part of the day is taken up with the ordinary chores and preparations for social events in the evening. For everyone involved the ordinary is put to one side as the tedium of routine daily tasks is interrupted by twelve days of play. The fisherman may sleep late in the morning, and drink, dance, and sing at night. Women and their daughters are kept busy making soups and cakes and cookies for family and visitors. Christmas 'sweet-bread' is eaten every day; Sunday clothes are worn daily; and gifts are exchanged. For twelve days time is suspended, while the community releases the restrained energy stored through a year of workaday living. The celebrations of Christmas in Deep Harbour represent, therefore, a sharp break in a routine which is otherwise characterized by predictable daily behaviour.

A few weeks prior to Christmas an outside observer has little sense of anticipation of the coming celebrations. People carry on their normal work until the last moment except for the women, who begin their preparations making fruit-cakes and sweet-bread a few days before. And then, suddenly, 'Christmas is in.' Sons and fathers chop down the Christmas tree, presents are wrapped, and beer is bottled.

Other festive events interrupt the ordinary pattern of life, but Christmas is more significant because of its duration. There is, of course, a 'good bit of fun to be had' at weddings. But although there 'are lots of drinks on the go,' dancing, singing, and the telling of tales, a wedding does not carry the sustained excitement out to an entire community, as does Christmas. Festivities which go on for twelve days gather a momentum, which builds to a point where the entire community is carried away with the all-pervading excitement.

Particularly during Christmas evenings the separateness of households, the usual withdrawal of each family to its own kitchen, is dramatically broken. Crowds of men tour from one household to another – singing, dancing, telling stories, and drinking. Groups of mummers of all ages and descriptions are also visiting from house to house. On some evenings entire households may leave home to attend the evening function of that day, for there is hardly a night during Christmas when some organization does not have an event in the Orange Lodge or the school. Tensions built up during the year are eased, as alienations between households and men are put aside. For this is the season of the year when the community reaffirms its sense of unity.

Throughout the twelve nights of Christmas each house has its kerosene lamps burning until well past midnight, whereas during the working year houses are usually darkened by ten o'clock. Not only are the lights burning later during Christmas, but there are more lamps in use. Throughout the year most of the daily living is carried on in the kitchen, where one, or at most two, lamps provide light for an entire family. Children sit at the kitchen table labouring at their homework, while the mother cuts down an old pair of pants for the youngest boy. With all the family assembled in the kitchen there is no need for lights in the rest of the house. During Christmas – with mummers and others constantly coming and going – the kitchen, living room, and sometimes even the upstairs bedrooms, where some of the younger children have retreated to play, all beam light through normally darkened windows.

In the Christmas season houses announce their hospitality with this blaze of lights. Visitors need not carry their usual flashlights: the kerosene lamps shining from houses illuminate the narrow footpaths. Elderly persons who are not able to go visiting sit at their windows watching, listening, and commenting on the 'goings on' to the rest of the household.

At night throngs of "social-drinking" men threading their way along the narrow footpaths sing between visits. A popular or ribald song becomes the theme song of a group for that night. The next night the same men might sing a different song.

Besides wandering in crowds of men and mummers, people attend the many 'soup suppers,' 'concerts,' and other 'times' given throughout the Christmas holiday. A 'time' is any function given in the school, or local Orangemen's Lodge: a card party, a dance, or a dance combined with a 'soup supper' (the soup, twenty-five cents a bowl, is usually a substantial moose or caribou stew) may be given by any organization that wants to raise money. A 'concert' resembles a variety show – with or without a theme – and might include one-act plays, skits of various kinds and individual acts, or a three-act play by itself.

Regardless of what kind of a 'time' is taking place at the Orange Lodge, the crowds of social-drinking men make their rounds as do the mummers. Each group, however, eventually finds its way to the Lodge at some point in the evening.

In a community where even the bi-weekly arrival of the coastal steamer is a major social event, it is difficult to picture the effect of a sesason when one or more functions take place every night.

Mummering is an important part of Christmas in Deep Harbour. The behaviour of mummers in different rural Newfoundland communities is similar in many respects. But what is especially interesting about mummering in Deep Harbour is that the custom reflects many features of the social organization of this particular community. This correspondence between the forms that mummering takes and the social organization of a community means that mummering can be used as one of many indices for comparative studies of the social organization of Newfoundland communities.

A Deep Harbour mummer might be described simply as a person who, having disguised himself in a costume, visits houses in the community. His object is to try to fool the people he visits; they in turn attempt to guess who the mummer is. But while ostensibly we might define mummering as an elaborate guessing-game, this definition would not be sufficient. For mummering involves people in social relationships which while differing from normal behaviour are nevertheless influenced by it. Indeed, normal relationships determine, not only the composition of any mummer group, but also the attitude of mummers to those whom they visit.

Both the 'little mummers' and 'big mummers' give the same cue before entering a house: they knock on the door, and give an ingressive shout (that is, they draw in their breath) while saying, "Mummers allowed in?" Mummers always knock and are usually asked to enter, though occasionally they are turned away. When a household refuses entrance to a mummer the occupants do not go to the door to make their excuses. They shout through the door, "Mummers aren't allowed in." Some people will offer an excuse, such as that they are feeding the baby or that the baby is afraid of mummers. (Often very young children are frightened by mummers, although mummers in Deep Harbour are not generally thought of as scary figures, nor are costumes designed with the intention of frightening people.) Sometimes occupants of the household will not say anything until the mummers knock a second time and repeat the question, "Mummers allowed in?" Then the door is opened and in come the mummers. The guessing-game begins as members of the household try to determine the mummers' identities.

The mummers approach the Lodge in a different manner from the social-drinking men: the latter announce their approach with the singing of their theme song. The mummers are silent in their approach to the Orange Lodge, but clump up the steps, bang on the door, and burst in singing and dancing. The unmasked men also enter the Lodge singing and dancing, but (if anything) they are more boisterous than the disguised men, perhaps because, as they would say, they are 'three parts under.'

Dancers of all ages may be in the middle of the floor in a square-dance when the men of either group weave into the Lodge. The accordionist continues to play the tune, but the dancers move off the floor to enjoy the men's antics.

The men 'get off,' one supporting the other, each doing 'his step.' Most men have a characteristic dance step, and others may imitate this, since people try to guess whose step it is. Disguised men may walk all around the Lodge, shaking hands with one person and wishing him a Merry Christmas, pulling another's hair, and having a little 'step' while joking with a third. By disguising himself as a mummer, an adult commits himself to making a public display.

The young mummers make their own fun at the 'time.' They swing to the music on the sidelines, chase each other around the hall, and pester their parents for money for homemade ice cream. Children keep their costumes on all evening, but may eventually remove their masks.

Adults who stay in the Lodge usually remove their disguises after fifteen to twenty minutes as the Lodge is hot and dusty. They may then settle down to a game of cards or have a few dances. Others keep their masks on, leave the hall, and continue their rounds from house to house.

3 Christmas Drinking Customs

Deep Harbour fishermen have traditionally celebrated Christmas by group visiting, whether as mummers or as "social drinkers." Though the older tradition of mummering continues with surprising strength, most would agree that there is more fun to be had simply in going from house to house singing, dancing, telling stories – and drinking.

During the year men do not generally drink, except at weddings and in the fall when those who have been away fishing return home. A few drinks relax the stiffness of posture characteristic of these fishermen, and a few more drinks allow some men to be as uninhibited as drinking norms permit.

Tradition dictates that Christmas drinking is almost always done in the company of several men. It would be considered strange if a man were to drink alone or even drink for an extended time with only one man. The greatest quantities of alcohol are consumed by members of a crowd, who having had a number of rounds in one house, move on to another. Such a group I term a "social-drinking" group.

It has been observed by several Deep Harbour men that when there is a scarcity of alcohol in the Harbour, "Christmas isn't the same." When there is less available to drink, fewer men visit, and those that do are more inhibited.

The mood of Christmas is set to a great extent by the groups of social drinkers who spread the spirit from house to house. On an evening when there are many groups of men 'on the go' the entire community is influenced by the air of excitement and anticipation created by their singing. Throughout the earlier part of the evening and into the early hours of morning, others join existing groups and new groups are formed.

In most cases the groups start out after supper; they leave their houses between 7:00 and 8:00 P.M. and continue with their celebrations until three or four the next morning. Carousing around for eight or more hours whets the appetite, and towards the end of their house visits, one of the men might suggest to those in his group that everyone come over to his house for a 'scoff.'[2] This late supper might include a meal of 'bottled moose meat,' warmed-over soup from the Church of England Women's Association 'time,' homemade sweet bread, 'pork-buns,' and 'a good cup of tea.'

There are several patterns of visiting followed by both mummers and social-drinking men. First, men stop in succession at the houses of each

2 / A 'scoff' is a big meal held at any time of the day, usually late at night.

man in the group. In this way everyone becomes a host in turn, reciprocating the hospitality he has received. If the 'crowd' has not had time to stop at each of the houses, the same men may start off together the next night.

Another pattern followed by both groups is that the men will stop at the houses of those who have earlier visited them. One man might say, "Let's go over to Bill's now, he told me to come over." Bill's invitation was not for a specific night; he was fulfilling his side of an obligation when he extended the invitation. The men may go to a house because they expect 'a good drink of rum,' or because the host is known for his particularly fine homebrewed beer. The sounds of singing men, accordion music, and step-dancing may also draw a group into a house.

There are, however, some houses at which no one will stop; these houses do not provide any drinks because the owners do not drink. One of these men has said, "The only reason men come to visit during Christmas is to get a drink. They don't come to see *you*." Such men limit their ties with the community by not participating in the drinking rounds.

Reciprocal drinking obligations are closely and self-consciously observed. Every man who drinks is expected to reciprocate by providing drinks for those from whom he has received one. One of the men who does not join a group making the rounds was offered a drink in a household where he and his wife were visiting. Although he takes an occasional drink in his own house, he refused the offer explaining that he couldn't accept because he didn't expect to provide drinks in turn.

The awareness of reciprocity is also observed in the manner in which drinking takes place. For example, six men enter a man's house; after they sit down a preliminary conversation begins as the man of the house inquires where they have been. The men will be rather quiet if it is early in the evening; later they come into the house arm-in-arm, bellowing a song. They may continue to sing, or one man carrying an accordion may play a jig to which the men dance. The head of the house may wait until the men have settled down before he goes into the other room or reaches into a cabinet for a bottle or a jug of homebrewed beer. He places these on the table with one or two glasses from which each man will drink in turn. Then the host says, "Now John, have a drink." John steps up to the table, pours himself a drink, drinks it, and returns to where he was sitting. Then another of the men is invited to have a drink; the second man steps up to the table, fills the same glass, drinks, and returns to his place. Each in turn takes a drink, and no man drinks until he is invited to do so. If George, when the host says, "Now George, it's your turn," pours a small amount into the glass, the host may say, "Now George, don't be shy, take a good one."

If a man continually takes more than his share, he will be silently censured by the group. The host and the rest would not say anything to him at the time, but everyone would 'take notice' of how much he drank. If he continued to take more than his share, men would speak critically about his greed and in all probability he would not be invited to go around with the same crowd the next night. He might also be penalized by not being offered a drink when drinks are scarce.

Although there is no formal relationship between the amount of entertainment furnished by the social-drinking men and the number of drinks offered, the host usually provides more drinks if the men and the host's family are enjoying themselves. No one would begrudge a drink to Uncle Ben who plays a good accordion, one of the few who still plays the fiddle, sings, and tells stories, or to William Henry who, it is said, can sing three hundred songs without repeating himself once. These men take pride in their ability to sing and play and do not feel obligated to reciprocate with drinks to the same extent as others. Most men can sing a song, make a toast, or do a 'step'; it is only the recognized specialist who is under less obligation.

Reciprocal drinking, then, is characterized by a host-guest relationship. The number present is irrelevant to the relationship between host and guest. This is essentially a dyadic relationship; the host offers, the guest accepts. Men do not take drinks out of turn or before they are invited. The playing out of this two-person relationship amidst a crowd further illustrates the importance of the dyadic relationship as one basic unit of Deep Harbour social organization.

Similarly, no adult male mummer would take a drink without first removing his mask, for, if a man were to take a drink without exposing his identity, he would not be able to fulfil the obligation he incurred by accepting the drink. The understood norm in Deep Harbour is that no man wants to feel obligated to another. Ideally each man likes to believe that he has fulfilled all of his obligations. When the mummer removes his mask before drinking, the host is free to visit the mummer's house with or without a disguise. For this reason, adult mummers seem anxious to unmask and reveal their identities. If the host is a man who would not generally come over to the mummer's house during the twelve days of Christmas, the mummer will make a point of inviting him to "Be sure an' come by for a drink now; I'll be savin' one for you."

Adults disguised as mummers often call at a house where a group of social-drinking men are dancing and singing. The following example illustrates how mummers may stop mummering for the evening and join the group of social drinkers.

Four mummering men banged on the door of a house in which there were a crowd of social drinkers. "Mummers allowed in?" they shouted in unison. "Come on in," the host's wife replied. In came the mummers with their declarations of "Merry Christmas" to the fourteen men crowded in the kitchen. About half of the latter were out in the middle of the kitchen floor stepping out a lively jig. The others were accompanying the dancers with the beating of their feet. The four mummers danced their way to the centre of the floor. One, carried away with the tune, began to do his special step.

Almost immediately, everyone recognized him by his characteristic step, and calling him by name, shouted encouragement as he danced. The men moved back to give him the centre of the kitchen floor and towards the end of 'his step' one of them joined him in the middle of the floor. The two men faced each other, each doing his favourite step. The mummer, a very good step-dancer, began to do a different step. The second man moved back slightly from the centre of the floor, 'stepping out' an accompaniment.

A type of dance-duel then began – something which takes place frequently whenever two or more good dancers get together. When the mummer had finished his special step, the second dancer took over the centre of the kitchen floor and began to tap out a new step. In turn, the mummer responded by beating a steady rhythm to the opponent's variations. The friendly duel came to an end when several of the other men and mummers joined them in a step. Every few minutes one man would 'take hold' of another and give him a swing. (Both men and couples always swing in the waltz position.)

While all the dancing and carrying-on of the men was taking place, the wife of the host and their children stood by enjoying the fun. Every now and then one of the men pulled her out onto the floor amidst her laughter and protest and gave her a swing.

After about thirty minutes of dancing the mummers sat down, joining the crowd of men already assembled. By this time all of the mummers had been identified and most of them had their masks off. There was a slight, expectant pause in the activity. The host's next move, as his guests had anticipated, was to offer each a drink in turn, both to those in the first group and to the now undisguised mummers.

The host is able to control the tempo of the gathering because a man will not usually take a drink until the host invites him. The host may invite each in turn to take a drink with little or no time lapse between the moment when a man finishes his drink and sits down, or he may wait several minutes before inviting the next man. After each has had a drink, the host may delay starting another round. If his guests have not been visiting very long, they will usually take this as a signal that it is their turn to entertain. If a well-known singer is in the crowd several men may tease him until he finally consents to sing. Once he has sung a few songs others will sing without coaxing. Another man might then tell a story, using lively gestures to dramatize his tale. A well-known story-teller will frequently be called on for one of his humorous specialties, for example, a skating story. The guests will sing, recite, dance, and 'carry on' until there is another break. The host will now usually offer them another round of drinks.

A host usually starts with a limited amount of liquor on the table. If he wants the men to stay, he brings out more liquor. But even if a host becomes involved in the spirit of the evening and wants the social drinkers to stay until the 'last drop' is gone, he continues to place only a limited amount of liquor on the table.

Each time the host leaves the room to get more drinks he is demonstrating his generosity. He does not make a display of going into the other room, but the very act of placing more liquor on the table several times in an evening is enough to evoke comment on the host's generosity.

Hosts may not be consciously trying to obligate the men and mummers; nevertheless the host of the evening described previously commented later, on one of those who had been present, "He shouldn't ought t'ave said that against me, he knew where ta come when he wanted a drink." This host felt that the man should have been loyal instead of 'backbiting,' not only because of this one night, but because the host had extended his hospitality to him on several occasions.

Another group visiting the same host had stayed only for two rounds of drinks when one of the men suggested that it was time to make a move. The rest of the men agreed with the suggestion, and the social drinkers soon left, even though the host was protesting that there was, "lotsa time to stay." In this instance the man suggesting they leave did not want to be obligated to the host. He reported later that if they stayed too long he would not be able to reciprocate and would, thereby, place himself under the host's obligation.

4 Costumes for Mummering

There are two disguises used frequently by mummers of all ages and sexes: "the fisherman" and "the woman." "The fisherman" disguise consists of a padded suit of rubber clothes, cotton work gloves or woollen mitts (both used for fishing), rubber boots, and a piece of cloth for a mask. Basic to "the woman" disguise is a loosely fitted dress or a nightgown, preferably one that reaches to the ankles and has long sleeves. Short sleeves will do, but then the mummer must wear a sweater or blouse to cover his arms. Outmoded women's hats and handbags complete the costume. As with the fisherman disguise a mask is worn.

Everyday clothes are usually worn under a mummer's disguise. Wearing these clothes makes mummering more comfortable on a frosty evening; and further, allows men to leave their costumes at a house where they have joined a 'crowd' of social drinkers. The next day, the mummer's children will be sent to retrieve the costume.

In recent years, rubber masks have become a familiar part of the mummer's costume. Made in either Japan or Hong Kong, these masks were designed for use on Hallowe'en. They are great favourites with little children, who beg their parents for money to buy a new monster mask.

Three chief types of cloth-masks are used: a flour sack, with or without holes, a flour sack with a painted face, and a piece of lace. The lace is preferred by some because the mummer can easily see through it; however, with it one must also use face make-up with lipstick and eyebrow pencil. All households save large flour sacks. They rip them up the seam for use as towels, for embroidery, and for many other things, including mummers' masks. When worn as a mask the rectangular piece of sacking is merely draped over the head, the mummer peering from beneath the folds. Faces painted on flour-sack masks are of simple design; the eyes, nose, and mouth are drawn with black paint from a child's water-colour box. A variation which is not used as frequently as the rubber or cloth masks is an old nylon stocking stretched tightly over the face to distort the features. Make-up is used either under or on the outside of the stocking.

The dressing up is as much a social activity as mummering itself. All members of the household help the mummers with their costumes.

As an illustration, suppose four girls, between sixteen and seventeen years of age, are planning to mummer. They will meet at one house, stopping off on the way at friends and relatives to pick up additional pieces of clothing for their disguises. One girl borrows an old suit of fisherman's rubber clothes. She adds to her costume by filling out the rubber pants with pillows. With a sou'wester on her head and her face covered with the remnants of a tattered lace tablecloth, her disguise is complete. Not quite complete, some one points out, for she would be recognized by her shoes. Result – one pair of rubber boots, and white mittens to conceal her hands.

As one girl helps the other into her costume, they poke and pull at each other making sure their costumes will stand up to the pinches and prods they are sure to receive. The entire household looks on, laughing at the girls' shenanigans, and helping where they can. 'Dressing up' the girls becomes a household project with everyone participating.

One of the girls asks, "How am I going to hide my hair?" Her father suggests an old felt hat. Mother's flannel nightgown covers her from neck to toe, and with appropriate padding, a rubber mask, and a pair of a neighbour's shoes, she is dressed. After a few more trips to the clothes closet, all four girls are decked out in well-padded, ill-fitting disguises. All dressed up, the quartet start out on their tour of Deep Harbour.

5 Who goes Mummering with Whom?

The Deep Harbour folk classification of who goes mummering with whom is relatively simple: mummers are either 'big mummers' or 'little mummers.' 'Big mummers' are generally married persons, and boys and girls who are no longer attending school. But the dividing line between 'big' and 'little' mummers is often relative to a specific household. A household with children between the ages of thirteen and sixteen in school might think of them as 'big mummers'; another household without children in this age range might think of them as 'little mummers.'

One reason for making the distinction is that on some occasions people will receive 'big mummers' when they will turn away 'little mummers.' 'Big mummers' are seldom refused entrance; nearly everyone is interested in playing the guessing-game with them. 'Little mummers' usually make several appearances at the same house during the twelve days of Christmas, unaffected by the obligations of reciprocity. If many groups of 'little mummers' have called at a house that day, some of the subsequent groups may be turned away.

This twofold classification into big and little mummers, however, is an oversimplification of the many combinations of who goes mummering with whom. From observations during two Christmases in Deep Harbour I distinguished ten types of mummering groups. These types correspond to social and age groupings within the community.

The types of mummers are as follows: (1) an individual male adult; (2) a group of male adults; (3) married couples; (4) two married women; (5) bachelor boys between sixteen and twenty; (6) single girls between fifteen and twenty; (7) boys between eleven and sixteen; (8) girls between ten and fifteen; (9) children under nine; (10) older brothers and sisters escorting their younger siblings.

Dyadic mummering, or mummering in pairs, is common to all except adult men (Types 1 and 2). Married men apparently never mummer in pairs because they no longer have the "buddy" relationship with other men common before marriage. When a man marries, his spouse replaces the "buddy" and the latter is relegated to a less important position in the network of dyadic relationships. Similarly, a girl will have a "best friend" who upon marriage will no longer be her *confidante*. However, because of the prevalence in Deep Harbour of dyadic relationships, there are many pairs of mummers among Types 4 through 9.

The groups of mummers that always accept a drink when offered are the male adults (Type 2), the bachelor boys (Type 5), and the male members of Type 3 (the married couples). The single male mummer is the exception; he does not always accept a drink at the houses he mummers in. This appears to be associated with the fact that the single male mummer does not usually unmask in the houses he visits. If he does unmask, he will accept a drink if offered.

The bachelor boys (Type 5) do not usually drink with the married men (Type 2). The exceptions are the few bachelors in the community who are over twenty-five; most of these will go mummering and drinking with the married men, and enter into reciprocal relations with the men they include in their social network.

The only types that are relatively unstable in composition are Types 1 and 2. The individual adult mummer may decide to join a group; and other men might join the adult male mummers, or several Type 2 groups may combine.

A man would not normally join a group unless he was on good terms with all of them. One would not, for example, mummer with an 'enemy,' for mummering involves a continuance and a strengthening of a man's social network which is a structured complex of dyadic relationships.

However, when a band of mummers joins a group of social drinkers, a man might well find himself in the company of one with whom he has had a 'falling out.' It is possible for him to join such a group because no commitment is made to the individuals in that group. Even if there have been longstanding animosities, the men who have been at odds tacitly agree on a truce and make their rounds with the group from house to house.

The stable groups (bachelor boys, single girls, boys between eleven and sixteen and girls between ten and fifteen, i.e., Types 5 to 8) represent units of social organization constantly together throughout the year. Normally, such groups may be seen on a Saturday night promenading up and down the footpaths; congregating first in one shop, then in another; or organizing a dance on one night, on another making plans to attend the movies. In summer such groups might pile into a couple of motor-dories and visit a nearby community for the day, or go for a picnic in one of the many coves.

Each of these four types may have several groups. Their composition varies as new alliances are formed and old ties broken. The boys' groups tend to be more constant than those of the girls. The girls break relationships, influenced by petty gossip or by squabbles over boys.

Mummers, like other visitors, make a commitment to the house they visit by their very presence. The amount of time a mummer is in a house as well as whether or not he enjoys himself seems to determine whether or not he unmasks. During the rest of the year, a visit will be appraised by the host by how long the visitor stays, as well as by what he says, for the amount of time a person remains in the host's house is one recognized measure of commitment. This may, of course, be true of many communities, but it is to be particularly noted here because so little visiting takes place in Deep Harbour during the course of the year.

Mummers always come into a house through the door normally used by the householders and, in accordance with general Newfoundland practice, leave by the same door they entered to avoid bad luck. In most houses the door commonly leads into the kitchen.

The only type of mummer not likely to unmask is, as observed earlier, the adult male mummer. Other types of mummers might not unmask in each house they visit, but they will usually unmask in some. Mummers almost always unmask in houses where they have enjoyed themselves. It's not as much fun, they say, if some people do not find out who you are.

Mummers are more inclined to remove their masks if they have been in a house for more than thirty minutes – mummers who leave after fifteen minutes do not usually remove their masks. Mummers who have unmasked always offer an excuse before leaving, for an unmasked mummer resumes his normal behaviour when his identity is revealed. And normal behaviour in this instance is that a person always makes his apologies to the host when leaving, regardless of how long he has been visiting or how late it is.

Masked mummers *never* tell where they are going next, and no excuse is made for their exit. Having retained their masks, their identities unknown, they are free of normal obligations. On the other hand, mummers who share the secret of their identity with the people of the house usually tell the hosts whom they plan to visit next. In this way the hosts share vicariously in the mummers' next visit as host and mummers laugh about the friends they are going to fool.

No mummers make the rounds in Deep Harbour on either Christmas Eve or Christmas Day. The first mummers to be seen on the footpaths are the younger children's groups; these groups (Types 7, 8 and 9) make their first appearance on December 26. The other groups do not begin to 'dress up' until the next night.

The ten types listed above are parallel to the normal units of social organization in the community.

Type 1, The Single Male Adult The single male adult mummer is today rare, for mummering in Deep Harbour is a social event. While a man may start out from his house alone, and perhaps even visit a couple of houses by himself, he will usually join a group of mummers either on the road or in one of the houses at which he has stopped.

Thirty years ago, when men competed in devising imaginative costumes, the single male mummer was a more frequent caller. Disguises in this older tradition might include covering the body with a black bearskin, or a man might spend considerable time in carving a wooden head. In recent years, however, most costumes are hastily improvised.

In my two Christmases in Deep Harbour only one single male mummer was 'on the go.' It is worth describing his actions in detail because his reception indicated that today this form of mummering is atypical.

Joseph was unquestionably one of the best-disguised mummers in Deep Harbour. Few people expected him to mummer, for he does not drink and has not mummered in recent years. Also, he is one of the few with a job outside the community; and since he also does not fish, his network of close social ties is limited. With his slim body he was able to wear one of his sister-in-law's tight-fitting dresses. He first made up his face with lipstick and eyebrow pencil; pulled a nylon stocking over his head, and wriggled into the red dress. He drew on a pair of long brown cotton stockings, borrowed a neighbour's high-heeled shoes, wore a matching hat with veil and carried one of his sister's old handbags.

While mummering Joseph rarely spoke. He knocked at the door, but failed to utter the mummer's usual ingressive "Mummers allowed in?" Only 'strangers,' outsiders unaccustomed to Deep Harbour practices, knock; normally, a person who visits a house simply walks in unannounced. In one household the people were uneasy at the knock followed by silence because they knew there were no 'strangers' in the harbour. Joseph continued to knock. The mother suggested that it was probably a crowd of boys 'carrying on.' He knocked again, slowly and deliberately, until she asked one of the children to see who it was. The fifteen-year-old son opened the door. Joseph came in and stood silently in the middle of the kitchen.

The first response of the family was relieved laughter. Then they proceeded to ask could the mummer dance? Joseph shook his head. "Can you sing? Do you want a drink?" Joseph stood there, his hands crossed holding his handbag, shaking his head negatively in response to each question. He stood silent and motionless until the mother offered him a chair. He sat down with his hands in his lap while everyone in the household tried to figure out who he, or she, was. Still a little unsettled from the knocking at the door, they refrained from poking and pulling his padding. After ten minutes of questions, Joseph rose with all the aplomb of a model and walked out saying only, "Good night" in the ingressed mummer's voice.

As soon as he left, everyone began to speculate as to who he was, each person substantiating his guess by identifying an article of his clothing, or commenting on his stature, his stance, and his movements. Not one member of this family guessed who he was. Nor, apparently, did most of his later hosts, for when, several months later, a colour-slide of Joseph dressed in his disguise was shown to the community, many people in the audience still did not know who the mummer was.

Type 2, A Group of Male Adults The second type of mummers may number from three to eight men, but four or five mummering together is more usual. Such a group will travel from house to house, revealing themselves at one or more houses. The pattern continues as they either link up with another group or, after taking off their disguises, make the rounds as social drinkers.

The decision to go mummering, like many plans, is made on the spur of the moment. A man may not know in the morning whether or not he is going to mummer that night. There are no community pressures on the adult male to go mummering. People expect that some men will mummer every Christmas, while others might, and some will not.

On nights when there are only a few social drinkers making the rounds from house to house, adult men are more likely to mummer. If there is some kind of function going on at the Lodge, men might mummer earlier in the evening, and afterwards come to the 'time.'

The strong individualism of Deep Harbour adult males shows up clearly in contrast with other types that will be described. Whereas women of all ages, teenage boys, and children respond to suggestions for group activity such as mummering, a man will only mummer if he is so inclined. He has, after all, the alternatives of joining a social-drinking group or simply wandering over to the 'time.'

The behaviour and attitudes of the adult males of Type 2 may be illustrated as follows. One group of four men started out from the east side of the harbour about 8:00 P.M. The men had stopped at several houses before reaching the place where I stayed. They approached stealthily and then pounded on the outside door, asking, "Mummers allowed in?" The woman of the house said to her oldest son, "John, go see if they are big mummers; we have had enough of the little ones for tonight."

John opened the door, and the men came in. The first mummer to enter came up to the man of the house, took his hand and said, in ingressed speech, "Merry Christmas, Uncle Charlie." He then shook hands with the woman of the house and me, repeating the greeting. The other mummers followed suit, mimicking the Christmas greeting of the first. Sarah, the wife, shrieked with laughter when the four mummers first came in. After their greeting she said, with a smile in her voice, "I wonder who they can be?" Guessing immediately who one of the men was, Sarah went over to him and poked him in the midriff, saying, "He can't be a woman; he's too hard."

The first mummer was dressed in "the woman" disguise. He was covered from head to toe with a faded nightgown, heavily padded in front, a belt holding everything together. Sarah tugged at the belt and asked, "Where didya get that belt? Isn't that Mary Rose's belt?" At Sarah's last comment, William Henry pulled away, for she had recognized his wife's belt.

Charlie stepped up to one of the other mummers and asked, as he took hold of the ample bodice, "Watcha got there, Uncle?" Both men laughed, and the mummer gave Uncle Charlie a rough hug. Next, he sat on my lap and gave me a big hug. I promptly asked the mummer for a kiss and made a move to lift his mask. "No, not tonight," he said, jumping up.

Charlie said, "I wonder, can the mummers dance? John, John, go get the accordion and give us a tune." John started playing a lively jig as we all entreated the mummers to "give us a step." A second mummer began to 'step,' his legs swinging high. The first mummer, still masked, joined in with a low shuffling step, barely lifting his feet from the floor. Toward the end of the jig, the second mummer reached over to Sarah saying, "Give us a swing, missus." "Go to it," said Charlie, and they whirled around the kitchen floor. John played away and we all stamped out the time to the tune. I jumped up, and imitating the second mummer said, "Give us a swing, missus." Everyone laughed as we swung. John played another jig, and we all got out on the floor together, each of us doing his own step.

At the end of the dance I asked if the mummers would like a drink. The second mummer replied, "Well, now, I wouldn't refuse one." As I brought the bottles in from the other room, I noticed he was standing slightly bent from the waist, head inclined forward in a stance that many men ordinarily take. His bent posture anticipated his next action, for he removed the old lace tablecloth from his head, and resumed his bent stance. Once his mask was removed he stopped his joking and acted as he would have when visiting this particular household under ordinary circumstances.

The others now also removed their masks and stood revealed as William Henry, Calvin, Harold, and Gerald. They sat down almost simultaneously. These four men have shared many experiences and have strong ties of work and mutual obligation.

Sarah said to William Henry, "I knew it was you; I could tell by your walk." William Henry gave his quick laugh, and sat down resting his arms on his legs. His back was bent forward and his head down in the position that he might take when visiting the house at another time of the year. Harold assumed a similar position, though not quite as bent over as William Henry. I invited each man in turn to take a drink, as is the custom.

William Henry asked Sarah to sing "Annie Dear," one of her favourite songs. She refused at first, but after a few minutes of persuasion she sang the ballad in her rich voice. We asked her to sing another; she did, and then said, "Now, William Henry, you sing one." He bowed his head a little lower, saying, "No, no, not yet, not ready yet." We implored him to sing and then I suggested, "Have another drink, and then sing us a song." He took the drink, relaxed a little, and sang several songs he had learned from his father.

When he finished, Harold spontaneously interjected, "I'll sing one now." He sang a song he had composed, describing the hardships a fisherman must endure.

After another round of drinks Harold said to me, "Why dontcha come around with us?" With everyone's help and a couple of trips upstairs to the clothes closet, I was finely adorned in "the woman" disguise. We travelled around the community stopping at a couple of houses as mummers, and then, at one of them, unmasked and joined a crowd of men who were swapping stories between rounds of drinks.

Type 3, Married Couples In most instances mummering by married couples in single or double pairs is merely incidental to the party or 'time' they plan to attend of an evening. Perhaps one reason a couple does not usually mummer together is that they would be too easily recognized.

If a couple is going to a card-game at a friend's house, they might decide to dress up at the last minute. Or, one couple calling in at another couple's house, both bound for the same party, might suggest that all four dress up. In this case, they would stop at several houses on the way, remaining in each for about fifteen minutes. Such couples usually unmask quickly in the house they visit, keeping their masks on long enough for the persons in the houses along the way to have some fun in guessing who they are. However, when they reach the party, they will 'carry on' until the hosts and other guests figure out who all of them are. Along the way the man or men, as the case may be, accept a drink if it is offered, thus obligating themselves or freeing the host of his prior obligation.

In many instances, most of the persons making up the dozen or so invited to such a card party will be neighbours. Giving and attending card parties is one way that neighbours affirm their identity as a neighbourhood.

Type 4, Two Married Women A married woman and her married neighbour are a frequent mummering pair. Their social ties have been continually reinforced throughout the year as they borrowed small items from each other, and perhaps helped each other with their spring-cleaning.

One of the best-disguised married female mummers was Aunt Susie, who went around from house to house with her neighbour, Mary Jane. The latter was conventionally outfitted in the pillow-padded fisherman disguise. Aunt Susie would come into the house with an exaggerated roll, mimicking the fisherman's walk. She wore a pair of men's shoes, and an oversized borrowed dress that covered her from neck to ankle. She had pulled a woollen stockingcap over her hair and around her head had draped a lace curtain, doubled to conceal her features. With her back humped with padding and a pillow in front, her shape was so distorted that it was impossible to determine her identity.

Aunt Susie's uniqueness was that her costume gave no clue to her sex. The men's shoes suggested she was a man and led the hosts to name all the small-framed men in the harbour in an attempt to guess who she was. To no avail, the hosts asked if the mummer could dance, could sing, where she had come from? Aunt Susie said nothing but nimbly avoided their prodding fingers. While the guessing was going on, the oldest unmarried boy of the house brought out his accordion and started to play a jig. Aunt Susie 'took hold' of Mary Jane and gave her a swing. Before long everyone in the kitchen was dancing and swinging. Aunt Susie was breathing hard and laughing at the same time. She seemed to be bursting to show everyone who she was. At last she tossed back her mask and amazed everyone: none had guessed who she was. Still breathing hard, Aunt Susie sat down and related delightedly how many people she had fooled that night.

Type 5, Bachelor Boys between Sixteen and Twenty; Type 6, Single Girls between Fifteen and Twenty Most of the mummering in Deep Harbour is performed by the unmarried young people: the greater number of mummers are boys under sixteen and girls under fifteen. Unmarried boys and girls between fifteen and twenty will mummer, if at all, once during Christmas with their peers, and possibly again as escorts to their younger brothers and sisters. Those younger than fifteen might mummer two or three times during the twelve days.

Boys seldom mummer with the opposite sex. Indeed the only male-female mummering is Type 3 – married couples. There are fewer mummers in Types 5 and 6 because many of the boys and girls are married before they are twenty, while others leave Deep Harbour for work in larger Newfoundland communities and on the mainland of Canada.

Bachelor boys follow a pattern similar to adult men. They start off mummering with two or three friends, planning to stop in later at the dance in the Lodge.

They assemble at the house of one of the boys, sending the young children out to fetch any extra clothing the house cannot provide. Their disguises are simple; usually they dress in "the woman" disguise, with a few wearing "the fisherman" disguise.

These boys are distinguished from their older counterparts by the greater degree to which they 'carry on' in the houses they visit. Often, one of the boys will carry an accordion; he is then quickly identified by his style of playing.

Singing and step-dancing as they enter the house, the boys seem to be more concerned with having a good time than with fooling the hosts. The accordionist, called 'a fiddler,' plays a 'tune' while each of the mummers has 'a step.'

After five to ten minutes of playing the guessing-game of "I wonder, is that young Sam?" the boys are invited to take a drink. Most of them will accept if they belong to the older group, that is, nearing twenty. Like the men, the boys take off their masks before accepting a drink. While drinking, they may relate some of their Christmas exploits. If offered a round of drinks, they will remain about thirty minutes; but if none are offered, they usually leave after fifteen minutes.

In one instance, the host asked them about Tom Tarter's rooster that disappeared the same night he heard they had a 'big scoff on.' One of the boys laughed while querying, "Is that right? Tom's rooster? First I heard tell of it." These mummers remained in the house about forty minutes, although mummers in this age group might remain longer if they were encouraged to stay with the offer of another drink.

Single girls in this age range will take more time with their costumes than the boys. Such a group was described earlier.

It is interesting to note that the girls did not often unmask even when the hosts guessed who they were. Single girls mummer to fool people; they cavort almost as wildly as the boys, adding more suspense to their mummering by not unmasking.

Type 7, Boys between Eleven and Sixteen; Type 8, Girls between Ten and Fifteen Boys in Type 7 favour "the fisherman" disguise. They also prefer to conceal their faces with a rubber mask, though others use a piece of flour sack. Households with several young children swap their rubber masks back and forth, using a different mask each time they mummer. A boy will often carry a stick on his rounds, although he does not use the stick as mummers formerly did, as defence against more aggressive mummers. They usually make a great deal of noise as they stomp up the back steps, thumping their feet and their sticks.

Among mummers of this age one boy usually acts as leader, knocking on the door of each house and asking to be allowed in. He does not, however, decide which house they will visit next. This decision is made in concert, each of the mummers suggesting where they should go. The group usually decides to go to the nearest house suggested. Sometimes these mummers are mistaken for big mummers because it is difficult to tell from the ingressed speech how old they are.

After they have been invited in, their behaviour varies according to the particular group of mummers and the nature of the household. Few people refuse entrance to adult mummers, although the response of householders varies: one household may actively participate in the fun regardless of their age; others will interrogate only the 'big mummers' enthusiastically, and a few households admit them, but without enthusiasm.

The boys stand together in the middle of the kitchen floor, or, if the householders do not respond to them immediately, will sit down on any chairs available. An adult of the household or an older child might begin by saying, "Let's see now, what have we here? I wonder who this could be?" as he tries to lift up the masks. They continue by commenting on their costumes, attempting to guess what family the mummer belongs to by his clothes. The mummers answer with a simple ingressed "No." They seldom elaborate or try to mislead the hosts, as older mummers might do.

Hosts may then ask the customary questions – can the mummers dance or sing? The chances of mummers dancing are always better if someone in the house plays the accordion. Mummers in Type 7, many of whom are just beginning adolescence, will not usually sing by themselves unless one is a recognized singer, in which case he is quickly identified. A number of young mummers might sing a song together in the disguised mummer's voice.

Boy and girl mummers between ten and sixteen do not usually unmask unless they have stayed more than twenty minutes in a house and have sung, danced, and generally enjoyed themselves with a participating household. Once unmasked, they resume their normal behaviour and may enter into conversation about whom they have visited and whether or not they plan to see certain friends and relatives that night. Or, when unmasked, children under sixteen may resume their children's roles. They sit watching and listening to the adults as they might on any ordinary social visit: the young girls giggling and the boys only speaking when spoken to.

Leaving a few minutes after they have unmasked, they rise in unison upon a signal by one of them: an almost indiscernible movement of the head or roll of the eyes toward the door. Children visiting a house on a Sunday afternoon rise in the same manner, as if they were all following the baton of a conductor. Mummers who have not taken off their masks will leave when signalled in a more obvious way: this signal will often be a verbal one. A mummer might say, "Time to go," or "We've been here long enough," or "Time to make a move." Every masked mummer wishes the household a Merry Christmas in an ingressed voice as he leaves.

One striking difference between mummering girls and boys of this age is that when the girls sit down on a day bed (a single cot-type couch found in every kitchen), they sit with their backs straight, fairly close to each other but not leaning on each other or tumbling over one another as do the boys. When mummering boys are standing, they hang onto each other, sometimes almost falling over one another, as opposed to the girls who manage to stand separately. Boys loll on one another when they have unmasked though not in the exaggerated, puppy-like piling on each other as they do when masked.

Girls between ten and fifteen usually mummer with girls of the same age. The girls are not as active in their 'carrying on' as the boys, and in some instances are almost shy, acting as if they thought the hosts knew who they were. These mummering girls do not usually visit very long, though they may remain in the house of an aunt or uncle longer than in other houses. Whether or not they unmask in a close relative's house might depend on the number of mummers in the group. In a few cases the girls who were related to the hosts unmasked, while those not related remained masked in the background.

Type 9, Children under Nine Children under nine often mummer in mixed groups. A nine-year-old brother may take his six-year-old sister and her friend, and be accompanied by his ten-year-old friend. Very often a nine-year-old sister in a large family will escort her three or more younger siblings.

Children under nine try to model their mummering style on that of adults and older children. If they remain in a house for more than fifteen minutes, they may slip out of the ingressed speech, as usually happens after the younger children begin to laugh when the hosts tickle them. All mummers, young and old, resume their normal speech when they have unmasked.

Young mummers, especially those who are five to seven years old and are mummering without an older sibling, will often be unmasked by the hosts regardless of their wishes. Four or five of these younger mummers will stand together in the middle of the floor, while the adults try to guess who they are. This becomes a learning experience for the little mummers as the adults, who already recognize them, go through the form of guessing the identity of the mummers who reply "No" in their ingressed voices at each wrong guess. This youngest group of mummers starts out after their supper around 5:00 to 5:30 P.M. and are usually back home by 8:00 or 9:00 P.M.

Type 10, Older Brothers and Sisters Escorting Younger Siblings There were many groups of mummers in which the older brother or sister who was responsible for the daily care of younger siblings shepherded his charges on the mummers' rounds. Usually this person was an unmarried girl of the household who might be from ten to twenty years old.

An older sister might suggest that the youngsters dress up, or younger siblings might pester their sister to take them around. If the children are younger than seven, they will usually receive help with their costumes. The only problem with older and younger children mummering together is that they are almost immediately recognized as a family group. This does not deter the 'little mummers,' some of whom would gladly mummer all twelve nights if they could.

Conclusion

A Christmas in Deep Harbour is something special. Every Christmas has a different rhythmic pattern, with the interlacing of various activities accelerating or restraining the tempo of the twelve days' celebrations. The climax of my first Christmas there was reached earlier than my second, apparently because several dances were held before Christmas.

Groups of men moving from house to house lend an air of anticipation to the night. Although they may not stop at your house, you may still watch them weave down the paths, for laughter and good times are contagious. The changing tempo of Christmas is controlled by the blending of all the events, and the influence of the social drinkers ranks highest. On an evening when there are no social drinkers singing and carrying on, the tempo and mood of Christmas is slowed and softened.

One of the best indicators that the climax of Christmas has been passed is that women begin to wish Christmas was over and men begin to return to their many chores. Attendance drops at various gatherings, and men spend more nights at home. As far as could be determined, few Christmas seasons sustain the same intensity throughout the twelve days.

The amount of liquor available is a prime factor regulating the number of social-drinking men and mummers. Several of the finest singers in the community are too inhibited to sing until they have had a few drinks. As one informant put it, "Everyone has a good time when there are lots of drinks on the go."

Christmas in Deep Harbour seems to an outsider a period when the community celebrates its identity, that is, as a group of people bounded by the physical limitations of the harbour, who think of themselves as 'belonging to Deep Harbour.' One criterion in defining the boundaries of a community is the number of people who are involved in a common pursuit. The men who went drinking together and the various types of mummers which I have described, have used the Christmas season to cement and reinforce the bonds established in their workaday lives. Mummering not only involves the community in an intriguing guessing-game; it requires identification of the people who are playing the game. The community takes stock of its members; many may not have visited any of the houses on the other side of the harbour since the last funeral or wedding; in particular, young children are named and their growth appraised. Christmas in Deep Harbour can be viewed, then, as an event in which the community reaffirms its identity.

The Mask of Friendship: Mumming as a Ritual of Social Relations

BY JOHN F. SZWED

In most of rural Newfoundland the Christmas customs and beliefs reflect the English and Irish origins of the majority of the population. But on the west coast of the Island, various historical factors brought about a mixed settlement pattern of French, Scots, and Micmac Indians, as well as English and Irish nearly all of whom had migrated to Newfoundland from Cape Breton Island after 1840. It is from these various ethnic sources that the custom of mumming appears in the villages in the southern part of the west coast of the Island. The background and description of this unique region is necessary to the understanding of mummers' practices.

1 The Village

The village of 'Ross' is located in the parish of 'Ross'[1] on a river a few miles inland from the Gulf of St. Lawrence in one of the few truly fertile areas of the Island. A railway and a ferry-boat from North Sydney, Nova Scotia, have for over half a century linked the parish to the outside world, and in recent years, the Trans-Canada Highway has passed near enough to bring tourists to its doorsteps. Ross itself is

1 / 'Ross' is a pseudonym for an "ideal" or "average" village among three observed by the author in 1962–64 while doing fieldwork as a Fellow of the Institute of Social and Economic Research at Memorial University of Newfoundland. I am grateful to Herbert Halpert, Francis L. Utley, and Melford E. Spiro for their helpful suggestions during the preparation of the manuscript of this paper.

connected to other villages of similar size by gravel roads and river frontage. Most of the settlements within thirty miles are Roman Catholic, and as a parish the area has a certain homogeneity. However, each village has its own school and, in most cases, a store of its own, so that some degree of autonomy is possible.

Approximately two hundred people live in Ross, and the average family has eight to ten children, although it is not uncommon to find a family of fifteen or sixteen offspring. Households are made up of a man and wife and their unmarried children. Each son (except the one inheriting the farm) either goes away to work in other areas, or marries and settles on a small plot of land given to him by his father, and continues to work at various labouring jobs. Unmarried daughters, too, leave home to work, but frequently their main concern is with finding marriage partners rather than simply earning a living.

The settlers of Ross and their descendants maintained a mixed cod-fishing and agricultural economy at the subsistence level until the 1930s when a decline in world fish prices shifted interest to the newly developing lumber and pulp wood industry to such a degree that fishing disappeared completely. For the first time money was in common circulation in the area, and the barter system began to weaken. The building of the US Air Force base in nearby Stephenville at the start of the United States' entry into the Second World War added greatly to the amount of available wage-labour opportunities outside the parish. After the war employment dropped off somewhat, but Newfoundland's Confederation with Canada in 1949 has brought a considerable number of jobs to the area in various public works programmes, although competition for them has remained high. Today agriculture is at best a marginal activity in Ross, and most villagers complain that they go for months without fish on the table, as fishing is now only a sport.

The people of Ross see themselves as very democratic, and they refuse to recognize anyone who comes from the area as 'high and mighty.' Individuals who attempt to better their circumstances far beyond those of their fellows are strongly discouraged by gossip, suspicion, ridicule, social satire (in the form of songs and imitations), and ultimately by withdrawal of aid and friendship. "There he goes, driving the car my money paid for," is a common observation heard in reference to a merchant or entrepreneur, and the enterprising individual is often pointedly reminded of a favour or help given him "before he was after making a fortune." The economic view in Ross is one that considers available goods and resources as limited, and sees one person's gain as a loss for the others.²

When people see themselves as equal, individual "contracts," not status, are the chief determiners of interpersonal relations outside of kinship groups: "Where all men are equal conceptually, the basis of their cooperation can only be reciprocal services; a voluntary reciprocity dictated by the mutual agreement of the parties, as opposed to the primary reciprocity of ranks."³ It is thus that in Ross each man attempts to establish social relationships with individuals outside his kin group through the voluntary and personal tie which has been called the "dyadic contract";⁴ when one person bestows a favour or "act of favor" upon another person, and the offer is accepted, a contract is created. Villagers in this way maintain a complex system of sharing meals and drinks with those people with whom they are aligned. But at the same time, a game of cards, the loan of a power-saw or a horse, sometimes even a piece of crucial gossip, all of these can act as the favours that initially link two persons together. Naturally, for a relationship to persist, this initial favour must be reciprocated, not necessarily in the same form or immediately, but some time in the near future. Any favour, then, "simultaneously repays past debt, incurs a future obligation, and reaffirms the continuing validity of the contract binding the partners."⁵ If an individual rejects an offered favour – say, an invitation for an evening of cards and gossip, or merely the sharing of a glass of 'homebrew' – the initiator is offended, for not only has his material offer been rejected, but his action of offering himself for a social relationship has also been turned down. But once a favour has been accepted, a dyadic relationship is on, and the recipient of the original offer must now reciprocate to express his faithfulness in the alliance and to show his willingness to have it continue.

A critical factor in dyadic contracts is the requirement that exchanges of favours be more or less equivalent. By this assured equality, the participants demonstrate their openness and "honesty" in the relationship, for it is this atmosphere of "friendliness" that surrounds

2 / See George M. Foster, "Community Development and the Image of the Static Economy," *Community Development Bulletin*, XII (1961), 124–28, for a discussion of the "static economy."

3 / J. A. Pitt-Rivers, *The People of the Sierra* (1954), p. 137.

4 / George M. Foster, "The Dyadic Contract: A Model for the Social Structure of a Mexican Peasant Village," *American Anthropologist*, LXVIII (1961), 1173–92.

5 / *Ibid.*, 1187.

all dyadic ties and ensures their continuation. All that can be known of a partner's motives in a contract is his willingness to continue the alliance; this he demonstrates by his actions of equal exchange, and by his friendliness in and out of the exchange situation. Beyond this fact, individual motivations and goals remain veiled. Thus, by the creation of a halo of effect and equality, continuity is granted to a relationship that is otherwise somewhat equivocal.

The fear of exploitation runs through any relationship and cautions the individual before he creates or accepts a dyadic contract. He must fear the partner who will maintain relations with others not so friendly or acceptable to himself, and thus expose himself to a flow of gossip that might be damaging. Again, he must be wary of a relationship in which he finds that he has accepted more favours than he can repay, lest he should find himself unable to restore the easy give-and-take of the symmetrical dyadic contract and in this way open himself to manipulation. It is these fears, then, that are modified by the illusions of equality and equal reciprocity. Illusions they are, to be sure, for real behaviour seldom conforms to this pattern; but they act to fill the gap between the known, surface facts of interpersonal relations, and the unknown, threatening mystery of individual motivations.

The maintenance of these illusions of equality is accomplished in Ross by the highly ritualized nature of interpersonal relations: the rules of etiquette surrounding the visiting of other persons; the rigid cordiality required of a host regardless of who his visitor might be – friend or enemy; the physical "openness" of the house to visitors (doors unlocked, no knocking required); and strong proscriptions on allowing interpersonal conflict to become overt. All of these contribute to the description of one common motif in interpersonal relations: caution. It is this caution that underlies even the most obvious of open relationships. It is a reserve that leads parents to warn their children of overzealousness in friendships at the same time as they advise them against making enemies and becoming involved in conflicts. Villagers go to great lengths to avoid direct hostile confrontations with each other, and hostilities may remain under cover for years, and perhaps never be revealed publicly. Outside of an occasional drunken brawl, or the rare sober exchange of hostilities, wariness pervades all relationships and ensures a rigid etiquette between persons of all ages. It is in the light of this theme of caution that the annual departure from normality signalled by the appearance of Christmas mummers strikes the observer as so startling.

2 Mummering

The twelve days of Christmas in the parish are celebrated by freedom from work, and by a high degree of social interaction in the form of house-parties and visiting. A month or so before the Christmas season large brews of beer are made and set aside in kegs to age. The women make many fruit-cakes and large batches of cookies, and open jars of preserved moose, chicken, jams, and vegetables. A cow or a pig is usually slaughtered so that all visitors can be given a meal or a 'lunch' – a late evening meal – of the highest quality. Hospitality and generosity are strikingly displayed.

Starting with the end of fasting at Midnight Mass on December 25, the holidays begin. On returning from Mass, food and drink are consumed in full quantity, as presents from one member of the family to another are opened. Adults go to bed quite late, and children wake in the morning to find more gifts, these left by Santa Claus. From Christmas Day through the rest of the days of Christmas, visiting continues. Whole families go together to other houses, beginning usually with their immediate relatives and moving next to the neighbours living in the same village. These visits begin somewhat formally, but frequently wind up in partial or complete drunkenness among the men. Even the women, normally quite hesitant about drinking alcohol, may take one or two glasses of wine or several hot rum toddies. House-parties, particularly, are scenes of drinking in great quantity with many men reaching a state of drunkenness. Although drinking occurs on some other festive days during the year's cycle, such as Easter, weddings, and so on, there is no period of greater indulgence than the Christmas season.

When boys and girls reach the age of sixteen or seventeen, or even slightly before, they may begin to visit others of the same age in their homes, and, depending on the parents involved, may be allowed to have a few glasses of beer. Certainly, by the age of nineteen or twenty, a boy will be expected to do a 'light bit' of drinking, if not more. Men and women too will visit from house to house in single sex groups, visiting others of their age group, much as they did before they were married. Most visits are made in the afternoons and usually end with a meal, although some individuals will also visit in the mornings and evenings. These visits are seen as signs of open friendship, and are looked forward to with great relish.

But the nights are another story. At nights, roaming from house to house, come groups of masked figures known as mummers. Mummers have always been known to go about at Christmas time in the parish, although no one has every heard of the mummers' play.

Mummers dress in household odds and ends: table cloths, burlap bags, hip boots, torn dresses, battered hats, woollen underwear, long coats, and gloves. Men usually dress as "generalized" women and women as "generalized" men. Shapes become blurred as the pile of coats, sweaters, table cloths, and padding reduce individual differences. Veils of various materials completely surround the head and are held in place by battered men's and women's hats. For mummers, a covered face is a necessity.

Mummers move from house to house in small groups of two to six, always after dark. Uninvited, they enter houses noisily without knocking, stamping their feet heavily as they approach the door and as they pass into the kitchen. Once inside, they begin a jogging, half-dance, half-shake that is the 'mummer's walk.' They often move about the room freely, and will sometimes even go into other parts of the house; they are aggressive, and may nudge or jostle members of the household, or begin dancing with them or other mummers. They may make jokes about the family. Frequently, the mummers bring musical instruments and may play guitars or violins, or beat on breadpans. One or two mummers might step-dance if asked to do so.

As mummers reverse their sexual roles in their dress, so they reverse their speech. On deep gulps of breath, words are swallowed in a rapid monotone of short phrases. Mummers will answer questions about themselves, but they usually sprinkle false clues to their identity among the true. Yet there are other means of determining mummers' identities. The over-all physical appearance of the mummer, though well disguised, is important in this process. The relative height of individuals and the appearance of hands (when they are exposed) are key determiners. The male-female inversion of dress acts as an indicator of sex. Articles of clothing, naturally, are used to identify individuals, although some attempt may sometimes be made to disguise these articles by mixing them and by using them in an unorthodox fashion.

This last point of identification implies yet another method of recognition: the make-up of the mumming group. The sexual make-up, physical characteristics, and number of mummers in a particular group are taken into account to relate the "unknown" group to a "real" social group. "If you guesses one right, boy, it's no trouble to guess the lot of 'em." Thus, in questioning mummers, particular attention is paid to who does the talking and the effect of the spokesman's statements on the group. In the same way, the questioner observes the general effect his questions and guesses have on the group, as when he watches for laughter accompanying his fixing names on the wrong persons, or the "inappropriateness" of his questions for particular mummers.

Since mumming is a "voluntary" social activity, persons who mummer together are normally co-actors in daily social situations. As a general rule, then, only friends and kin go mumming together. One young man who went mumming several years ago with a group of other young men from a village ten miles away said of their success, "Even my brother was after mistakin' me, sure!"

Although it is obvious that mummers go to some lengths to disguise their identities, it would seem there is usually no wish to stay completely unidentifiable. It is felt that there is no fun involved when there is complete failure at identification. It is significant, too, that in most cases mummers are eventually recognized by their hosts.

When identification is positively made, mummers are expected to 'strip' – to remove their masks. Not to do so is considered an affront to the hosts, and even fellow mummers may try to force a reticent masker to reveal himself. If a host fails completely to identify a mummer, he may try to remove his mask forcibly, often leading to a scuffle that may become quite rough. A host may offer a drink to the mummer he fails to recognize; but it is generally felt that an unidentified person should pass on to another house without accepting food and drink.

But once a mummer has been identified he ceases his aggressive behaviour and takes a seat along the wall, returning to the usual demeanour of normal social encounters. When children are mummers, the change of behaviour is even more noticeable, as their unmasking and identification causes them to return to their normal behaviour before adults, that is, a "seen-and-not-heard" manner that has them sit a distance away from the adults, carefully avoiding any position that could be construed as placing themselves on the same level as adults. Thus, children will not eat at the table with adults, and they avoid sitting on a day bed while an adult sits there.

Hosts are expected to offer unmasked mummers drink or even food. If these are not forthcoming shortly after the unmasking (an almost unheard-of possibility), the mummers soon become uncomfortable, and move quickly, and somewhat formally, on to the next house. Some houses have become known as 'good houses for mummers' for the quantity of food and drink that is given the maskers, as well as for the general atmosphere of hospitality that prevails there.

In recent years there have been very few changes in mumming practices among adults, except that nowadays fewer adults participate. On the other hand, many more children now go from house to house, even those only four or five years old. There has been some blurring between Hallowe'en and mumming for children, so much the same behaviour is found on both days. Within the last few years, then, a few younger mummers have begun to play pranks on their hosts, such as picking up small objects while they are in the house and leaving them in someone else's house. As a result, a few older people say that they do not welcome mummers, as they are 'too much bother.'

3 Interpretation[6]

In interpreting this ritual[7] of social behaviour, it is necessary to raise and answer a series of questions that present themselves as crucial to identifying its function: (1) Why should parish people go visiting, masked, at a time of the year when visiting is a formal gesture of reaffirmation of social and kin ties and is already prescribed? (We may contrast this with the French-Canadian pattern of mumming at Lent, when visiting is not normally expected.) What is the "value" for people who, as mummers, visit individuals whom they may have visited just a day or so before, or will visit shortly, in an unmasked state? (2) Why do mummers become aggressive and lose normal inhibitions once they have masked, and yet reverse their behaviour once they have been identified? (3) Why is it considered 'no fun' to go completely unrecognized on a visit, and yet also 'no fun' to be identified too soon? These questions, it seems to me, lie at the base of the mumming practices in the parish. To answer these, the ritual must be looked at more closely.

Mummers go visiting at night, a time when the surprise of visitors is at its maximum. As mentioned before, houses are always open to visitors and no warning of entry is considered necessary, yet children and dogs warn the householders of coming visitors almost without fail, thus allowing the family to 'see who it is,' and have a certain amount of 'preparation.' At night, however, visitors cannot be seen, and a

6 / The interpretation offered here is indebted to suggestions drawn from the writings of Melford E. Spiro, particularly "An Overview and Suggested Reorientation" in *Psychological Anthropology*, ed. F. L. K. Hsu (1961), pp. 459–92.

7 / "Ritual" here is broadly defined as largely symbolic activity, aimed towards controlling social relations.

visitor can cause considerable alarm if he comes unexpectedly. People say that "You can never tell who might come in at night," and the thought is worrisome. It is noteworthy that curtains are drawn only on the windows that face the drive that connects the house to the main road, the main approach to the house. In the village, privacy is the sense of preparedness for visitors, not the restriction or exclusion of them.[8]

The mummers' entry into a house at night, then, is a disconcerting event for the householders. The usual formal relations that surround the entry of non-family members into a house[9] do not apply: that is, a certain etiquette of greeting, of locating the guest in a particular chair (usually near the fire), of allowing the host to initiate conversation, of offering food and/or drink, and so on. The family must act and protect themselves as best they can. It is for them an uncomfortable situation as it is impossible for them to know what role or self to put forward.

For the mummer, on the other hand, this can be a great deal of 'fun.' It is a pleasure to see the hosts exposed – caught off guard – and to see them struggle with the situation. But perhaps more important to the mummer is the aggression which he can freely express towards his hosts, and yet be protected from the usual reprisals while he is in this "otherworldly" or (in Durkheim's terms) "sacred" state.[10] A mummer can get quite 'nasty' or 'mean' and yet be forgiven as he is considered to be just 'actin' like a mummer should,' and if the host were to act otherwise, he would be publicly labelled a 'bad sport.'

Mumming also presents an excuse for visiting those people whom one does not feel free to visit except in the context of a formality such as a business offer. In most cases, these are the people in another village, particularly those who live on the border of the mummer's own village. Mumming thus provides an opportunity to extend one's ties by artificially extending food and drink exchanges. Since it is considered bad taste not to offer a mummer a drink, the mummer puts

---

8 / Erving Goffman, *Presentation of Self in Everyday Life* (1959), p. 238.

9 / To a people who still maintain protective strictures on entering houses (such as "Always leave by the same door you came in or its bad luck," and "Count the four corners of the room when you come into a house you've never been in, and make a wish"), this seemingly simple act may be something of a territorial *rite de passage*. See Arnold van Gennep, *The Rites of Passage* (1960), pp. 15–25.

10 / That mummers express hostility and aggression is clear from the description of their behaviour towards their hosts, but even more so by the widely reported violence connected with mumming in various parts of Newfoundland. It was just such violence that caused mumming to be outlawed (see chap. x). For historical examples of violence during mumming in England, see chap. III.

himself in the position of having an opportunity later to invite this somewhat distant person for a reciprocal drink. Although, theoretically, there are no homes where a mummer will not visit, as a rule his activities are limited to his own village or those that border on his own.[11] In this way, the "mumming area" of a particular village tends to be coterminous with the area usually considered the "neighbourhood," the place in which constant renewal and affirmation of social ties is seen as most necessary.

Once the mummers have been identified and have unmasked there is laughter over the success of the deception, and the mummers take the customary visitors' seats. The host brings beer or rum for adults (candy or cake for children) and perhaps food. Mumming ceases and visiting begins.

Thus from the time of identification on, the atmosphere becomes that of all normal social encounters between members of different families, and is dependent upon the rules of such encounters. There is an easing of tension as the householder, no longer vulnerable to licensed aggression, returns to his "safer" (i.e., more predictable) role as host. For the mummer, too, paradoxically, there is an easing of tension, for although he has enjoyed his position as aggressor, by being identified he has been "recognized," returned to the group, as it were. He is aware that he is familiar enough to his identifiers to be recognized; this familiarity discovered through the host's eased manner and the offered food and drink (and thus an initiation of a drinking exchange) has enabled him to strengthen an otherwise uncertain relationship. The dyadic exchange has begun again – the ex-mummer must later reciprocate in order to maintain the relationship.

At the same time, by travelling in a group, the mummer has been identified (in two senses of the word) as a member of a group of friends and/or kin, as his house-to-house travels with the group affirms his ties with the members. All of these individuals are then bound together with the host in the same food-drink exchange, thus giving a multi-person dimension to the relationship. So it is that with the identification and subsequent unmasking of mummers and the sharing of food and drink a common framework is established – one that in effect says "We are not like mummers," and so the norms are reaffirmed and re-established.

11 / Some individuals will occasionally mummer in distant villages if they happen to have a very good friend or a kinsman there. In such cases, however, it is more common for a person to mummer with a friend or kinsman from that area.

But perhaps the meaning of the mummer ritual is most easily seen when a mummer is not recognized by his hosts. If not identified, he will leave without revealing his identity and thus without receiving food and drink.[12] This is seen by most mummers as 'no fun' and many feel that such a stop was a 'waste of time.' The mummer leaves with a sense of not being recognizable by his host, and the host remains with a sense of tension at not knowing who his 'tormentor' was: that is, he has been shown hostility with no sense of relief at the end, and no reaffirmation of friendship or norms.

It is thus understandable that in cases where very close friends or kin do not recognize a mummer, he will often unmask voluntarily. By the same token, taking mumming as a ritual of social reaffirmation also makes it clear why most mummers do not go to their own homes or to the homes of their kindred. For kin, reaffirmation of ties is handled in a different manner (i.e., in a corporate, rather than a dyadic manner): through the sharing of Christmas meals, attendance at Mass as a group, and the exchange of gifts. In addition, perhaps not to be recognized by one's own kin may be a particularly unpleasant experience.

But from another viewpoint, the family would not seem to require the expression of aggressive tendencies in its midst. The close emotional and economic interdependence of the family in the village both provides for greater expression of hostilities and reduces them by stressing common interest.[13]

Granting this interpretation of mumming, why all the fuss with old clothes, veils, and topsy-turvy behaviour?

For any social group to maintain control over its members (or really, for the members of a social group to maintain control over themselves in the name of the group), two techniques are available: (1) sanctions in the form of culturally provided punishment and reward; and (2) the development of the desire of individuals to seek goals that are themselves culturally approved norms. In other words, by absorbing cultural norms into the personality, individuals treat the norms as ends, rather than as means. In this way, social control tends to be provided by the individual personality (*super ego*) when sanctions are not

12 / Although, significantly for this analysis, a host will often try with the promise of drink to coax mummers to unmask.

13 / See Edward Norbeck, "African Rituals of Conflict," *American Anthropologist*, LXV (1963), 1254–79; Leonard Plotnicov, "Fixed Membership Groups: The Locus of Culture Processes," *ibid.*, LXIV (1962), 97–103.

easily provided by society. During socialization, each person acquires an awareness of social sanctions and at the same time becomes "norm-oriented."

Social control in the village is not always satisfactory: tempers do flare and fierce fights have broken out on rare occasions; weddings and parties are expected to produce discord; drinking encourages hostile outbursts; and conflict sometimes occurs at public meetings, where drinking is common. In-group aggression, then, does occur, despite the sanctions against it. The hostility that has been suppressed by community norms is still in existence. As Spiro has put it, "Although forbidden motives . . . may be *inhibited* by the fear of superego or of sanction punishment, the drives which activate these motives are not *extinguished*. On the contrary, they persist and demand gratification."[14] Thus, in looking for means by which forbidden motives are handled in Ross, one is led to look for methods of resolving conflicts between personal motives and cultural norms in ways that satisfy the individual and at the same time help maintain the total social system. Societal defence mechanisms (repression displacement and sublimation), analogous to the mechanisms of ego defence on the level of the individual personality, suggest themselves here.

In Firestone's analysis of mumming on the northwest coast of Newfoundland (chapter IV), he suggests that the practice there acts to utilize social and cultural materials in such a way as to cloak the forbidden motive of aggression so that it is gratified in a variant and disguised form. In other words, it allows for displacement of hostilities, but in a manner that shifts aggression (i.e., allows its gratification) from the in-group to the out-group by a "cognitive distortion of either its object and/or its agent – a distortion which is based on culturally constituted beliefs or behaviour patterns."[15] Thus, aggression is focused on mummers and strangers. But Firestone goes further when he suggests that the mummers themselves act to release aggression against the in-group in a manner that becomes culturally acceptable, while at the same time they may even increase their own "esteem" by doing so.

The patterns of mumming as described for Ross have many similarities to those described by Firestone. I feel, however, that although in Ross we see a displacement mechanism that distorts an otherwise forbidden motive – in-group hostility – and provides it disguised gratification, mumming here is an instance where a "forbidden motive finds

14 / Spiro, "An Overview and Suggested Reorientation," p. 480.
15 / *Ibid.*, 486.

direct gratification through a symbolic (ritualized) expression of the motive."[16] The deviation from norms so evident in mumming draws particular attention to the importance of the events occurring and gives them dramatic setting. Important, too, is the fact that the events that occur during mumming are not directed at particular individuals, and the aggression expressed is very broad and diffused. Therefore, despite the seemingly disruptive nature of mumming practices, the ritual culminates in a reaffirmation of ties that express a formal societal rejection of the sort of behaviour portrayed in the mumming.

Although similar rituals of displacement operate in many societies (such as in the form of witchcraft), not all provide for the "two-edged" function seen here, where hostility is expressed toward the hosts through the mummers' aggressive behaviour, while the hosts show similar hostility toward the mummers in the form of anxiety over the unpredictability of the situation. Through the aggression of both, the frustration is eased.

Rituals that seem to have a great deal in common with those seen here have been discussed extensively by Max Gluckman.[17] However, he has primarily described African rituals where rebellion is expressed against authority, and he has been led to argue that rites of rebellion exist only in societies where the social order is unchallenged and the social system stable.[18] But from the nature of the mumming ritual as we have seen it in Ross, it seems wiser to say with Norbeck that rituals of social hostility occur in societies where social life is highly organized: "Where other safety valves are inadequate, ritual expressions of hostility seem most expectable in societies that exercise firm control over the behavior of their members through highly formalized institutions."[19] Ross's highly structured system of social relations through dyadic contracts, mediated by the illusion of equality and caution in making alignments, allows for the cathartic expression of repressed motives on this one occasion of the year, one in which the deviant events themselves mark the importance of the occasion: the direct gratification of forbidden hostilities through ritual means and the subsequent recreation and renewal of the social order.

16 / *Ibid.*, 488.
17 / See Max Gluckman, *Rituals of Rebellion in South-East Africa* (1954); *Customs and Conflict in Africa* (1959); *Essays on the Ritual of Social Relations* (1961).
18 / *Rituals of Rebellion in South-East Africa*, p. 30.
19 / Norbeck, "African Rituals of Conflict," 1274.

118 The Mask of Friendship

Rituals of social reaffirmation mark Newfoundland communities off from the larger part of Western complex society; whereas the urban-oriented world rejects and denies social conflicts and repressed hostility, groups such as those found in Ross are able to utilize this same material in open expression to limit the strength of conflict in the group. The fact that in Ross adult interest in mumming is waning, the practice passing into the realms of children's play, is only another sign of the village's gradual merge with modern society.

One note of apology should be made in conclusion: the sober, long-faced treatment that this paper has given Newfoundland mumming should not be allowed to create the impression that this time of masking is exclusively a period of serious crisis for all involved. Far from it. There is a great deal of fun had in mumming, and both mummers and hosts bemoan its passing from the scene. On the other hand, we should not be allowed to ignore the fact that humour, too, can be a device for maintaining equality in human relationships, as Freud has shown, and by the same token it has its own cathartic role to play in human relationships.

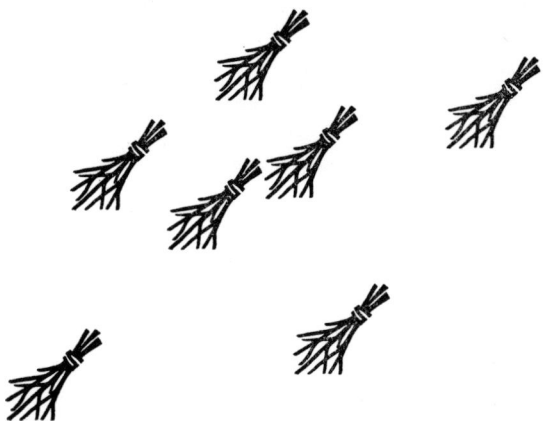

The 'Naluyuks' of Northern Labrador: A Mechanism of Social Control

BY SHMUEL BEN-DOR

Makkovik, a Labrador coastal community, is inhabited at present by two ethnic groups, the Eskimos and the "settlers."[1] The Eskimos are, ironically, the newcomers to Makkovik. These original residents of the Labrador coast were living in the northern village of Hebron until 1959 when the Newfoundland government, under a centralization programme, resettled the Hebron Eskimos in three other communities. About half the Hebron population was resettled in Makkovik. The English-speaking settlers, on the other hand, are the descendants of Europeans who settled in northern Labrador in the mid-nineteenth century: storekeepers and traders, trappers and runaway sailors. The Moravian Mission is the third element responsible for the cultural configuration of northern Labrador. The first post of this Protestant sect was established in Labrador as early as 1771 and in subsequent years it became the *de facto* government of the northern part of the coast, exercising its authority over both Eskimos and settlers. The Eskimo mummers, the 'naluyuks,' seem to owe many of their characteristic features to the teachings of the Moravian Mission.

The 'naluyuks' appear in the village once a year on the night of Epiphany, that is, Twelfth Night or January 6. The Eskimo term 'naluyuk' means a non-believer or heathen, and its proper plural form is "naluyuyit." The settlers and English-speaking Eskimos, however, anglicize the plural form by adding final 's' to 'naluyuk.' In this way the local form 'naluyuks' has come into existence. The term is used to

[1] / The fieldwork on which this paper was based was conducted under a Fellowship of the Institute for Social and Economic Research of Memorial University of Newfoundland in 1962–64.

refer both to the semi-legendary pagan Eskimos of the past and to the costumed figures who visit the houses on January 6.

The 'naluyuks' are widely discussed on the days before their arrival. Adults wonder who the 'naluyuks' will be this year, and parents reiterate to the children the "rules of the game." Throughout the excitement adults are cautious not to let the children hear that real persons play the role of the 'naluyuks.' The persons assuming the role of the 'naluyuks' gather in the evening in one of the houses. These roles are acted by several men (in 1962 and 1963 there were respectively three and five 'naluyuks') who are relatively young. In selecting a house for the initial gathering great care must be exercised that children are not present, and therefore a childless household is most desirable. The custom, the Eskimos say, is for the sake of the children and the secrecy surrounding it reminds one of similar behaviour by adults in non-Eskimo Western communities in connection with Father Christmas or Santa Claus. There is no doubt that the 'naluyuk' image is very real to an Eskimo child and if we may judge by the present behaviour of adults, the image does not fade when the facts are finally realized.[2]

The purpose of the pre-performance gathering is to transform mere flesh-and-blood individuals into the formidable 'naluyuks.' This physical transformation is achieved by the use of a three-piece costume: a cover for the body, for example, bearskin, coarse sacking, or an oversized coat; a paper, cloth, or commercial mask to cover the face; and a stick. One or more of the 'naluyuks' are equipped with bags. During the turmoil which accompanies this dressing up, Eskimo parents come with wrapped packages containing gifts, mostly sweets, for their children. Some parents are overtly reluctant to come, but if so they send their gifts by others. Those who deliver the packages stay only long enough for the name of the child to be written on the package and then are quick to depart. With the costumes completed and the gifts stowed in the bags, the 'naluyuks' are ready to start their rounds.

Parents and children wait for the 'naluyuks' in their houses, but a small crowd of adolescents, unmarried persons, and several inquisitive settlers anxiously linger outdoors. The very cold temperature at this time of the year does not discourage this crowd from its long vigil, but

---

2 / The association of costumed individuals with the fearful image of the 'naluyuks' was clearly evident in the school Christmas play. Although the children knew in advance about the costumes and witnessed the change of clothes, several Eskimo children burst into hysterical sobs when the disguising operation was partially completed.

occasionally the cold prompts a few individuals to take a brief and warm refuge in one of the houses. At last, the 'naluyuks' emerge to the shrieks of the small audience. The sound carries to every household in the community and everybody thus learns that the 'naluyuks' have arrived. Since the 'naluyuks' are traditionally expected to come from the east, the disguised figures walk eastward onto the harbour ice, turn around and begin their formal trip to the first home.

The procedures in each house are similar. The members of any household are well aware that the 'naluyuks' are approaching. The commotion which accompanies the short walk from house to house and the streaming into the house of visitors in advance of the 'naluyuks,' tell the children that their nerve-wracking anticipation is nearing its climax. For days they have practised for this moment and from the beginning of the evening have not deserted their lookouts at the windows. Now they take their seats on the chairs or benches usually placed for this purpose. In some homes, other seats, facing the children, are prepared for the 'naluyuks.' The parents sit by the children and invariably embrace them in a protective manner. The suspense and fear which lead to this protective gesture are understandable if we remember that the 'naluyuks' are the most prominent of the Eskimo bogey-figures. The 'naluyuks' are regularly used to discipline young children and are said to take bad children away. The annual visit of the 'naluyuks' reinforces the image.[3]

The 'naluyuks' enter the house and face the children. At this point the children are expected to sing a hymn or a Christmas carol to which the 'naluyuks' respond noisily by pounding their sticks on the floor. The observer might think that the 'naluyuks' are demanding more, but the explanation given by the Eskimos is that they are expressing their satisfaction in this way. The pounding, however, seems to increase the children's anxiety. Often a child becomes choked with fright and cannot utter a word; others bury their faces in their parents' laps; and some seem on the verge of tears. But all usually complete the carefully rehearsed hymns. The parents share the anxiety of their children and the audience too exhibits signs of concern. Often, an older person in the crowd interrupts the proceedings with a loud 'taymak' (enough), which sometimes ends the performance.

As soon as the singing part ends, the 'naluyuks' proceed with a

3 / There are clear parallels between the 'naluyuks' in this capacity and the giant Katcinas of the Hopi Indians. We may safely assume that the reaction of an Eskimo child is similar to that described from his own recollections by Sun Chief. See Leo W. Simmons, ed., *Sun Chief* (1942), pp. 45–47.

series of questions. These questions are asked in a disguised voice and are usually answerable with the simple 'ah' or 'auk' (yes and no respectively). The questions are not crystallized formally but left to the individual 'naluyuk.' Yet the range of inquiry is limited by the one topic of interest – the behaviour of the interrogated child. "Are you a good boy?" "Are you lazy?" "Do you help your mother?" The youngsters whisper their answers. The questions and answers constitute the second part of the visit. To the relief of the children the 'naluyuks' now proceed to the final stage. They browse in the gift bag, locate the right package, and hand it to the child.

The parents and visitors who crowd the little houses exhibit signs of restrained amusement with which is mingled apprehension and fear. The dominance of one over the other varies from individual to individual. Adolescents seem to be apprehensive; adults more amused. Yet, in the only house without children which was not skipped altogether, the two older women who sang the hymns did not demonstrate any signs of amusement. A possible correlation might be found between the degree of anxiety and the duration of association with Christianity. Among the persons who were asked in advance about the nature of the custom, the only ones who stated their fear without indicating some of the amusing aspects were those who had accepted Christianity only in their adult years. These individuals, who were, by definition, "naluyuyit" (i.e., heathen) until their conversion, seemed to exhibit more anxiety than others. It is difficult to measure a degree of anxiety and therefore hard to substantiate this correlation, but it should be noted that in addition to their verbal answers, the former "naluyuyit" do not, as a rule, participate in those aspects of the seasonal activities which they can avoid. These activities take place outside the houses.

The two elements which characterize adult behaviour, apprehension and amusement, are clearly expressed during the short walk taken by the 'naluyuks' from one house to another. The crowd accompanying the 'naluyuks' increases as they move along the rows of houses. Persons whose homes have already been visited join in the merriment although their children, without exception, stay indoors. As soon as the gathered audience spots the 'naluyuks' emerging from one of the houses, it scatters in all directions, screaming and shouting with excitement. The excitement turns into terror when the 'naluyuks' turn with their sticks on one of the crowd. The individual who is singled out escapes rapidly while the others watch, shout, and cheer. The 'naluyuks' play up their part and they seem to enjoy it – a raised stick, a dash at one, a poke at another, a sudden and unexpected turn followed by a short chase, or a persistent harassment of one individual by one 'naluyuk.' Each one of these actions breaks the crowd into many fleeing individuals. Each member of the crowd maintains a safe distance from the 'naluyuks' and tries to avoid their path; but occasionally a daring adolescent deliberately attracts the attention of the 'naluyuks' and publicly demonstrates his ability to outrun these clumsily costumed figures. Should this individual accidentally stumble and fall, his outwardly courageous appearance gives way to marked fear and an appeal to be left alone. The crowd watching a chase offers deafening support to one of the two: some encourage the chased person, others cheer on the 'naluyuk.'

At times this exuberance carries into the houses. The boldness of the 'naluyuks' gains momentum as the crowd increases in size and the effectiveness of their antics is assured. Occasionally they may even turn on one person in the house while watching a child performing his part. The slightest gesture on their part sends the spectators running outside, and many of them will stay outdoors during the visit to the next place. This overly boisterous behaviour by the 'naluyuks' is welcomed by some but not by others. In 1963 the village headman addressed the 'naluyuks' during the proceedings and told them that proper 'naluyuk' behaviour required that they sit down and listen quietly. This address restrained the 'naluyuks' while indoors but did not affect their pattern of behaviour once the performance was completed and the gifts handed out. The alternating indoors-outdoors behaviour is kept up until the last house is visited.

The origin of the 'naluyuk' day and its associated practices offers an interesting challenge to the student of history. There are three probable sources. The terms referring to the masked and costumed figures, "naluyuyit," and the date of the event point to the Moravian Mission as a possible source. For the Mission the significance of Epiphany lies in the Christian tradition of the Wise Men, representing the pagan world, who discover the truths of Christianity. Their arrival from the east, the bag of gifts, and even the sticks, which are commonly seen in pictures of the three Wise Men, are additional elements which favour this source. A second possible source, also of European origin, is the traditional appearance of the mummers who travel from house to house at Christmas time. This custom is still alive in Newfoundland as described elsewhere in this volume. A Newfoundland-settler route is always a possibility. Some of the older settlers recall the existence of a similar tradition in Makkovik, although it has not been practised for many years. Alternatively, the Moravian missionaries could have introduced various versions or elements of mumming based on their own national (usually German) origin. Some of the features, however, of the 'naluyuk' day in its Hebron-Makkovik costume and form must be attributed to a third source – the Eskimos themselves. What seems likely is that the Eskimos of Labrador have fused into a new form elements of their own native, pagan tradition with a European-derived Christian colouring.

Whatever its derivation, the custom in its present form may be assumed to answer some needs of the group in question. The use of mythological bogey-figures has been recorded in other Eskimo societies,[4] and their function is, of course, not limited to the Eskimo culture. It is obvious, however, that the 'naluyuks' are more than merely fearsome figures for disciplining children. The release of accumulated tensions which they afford after a long Christmas season in church attendance cannot be ignored. This function is closely linked with the elements of entertainment which are embodied in the 'naluyuk' complex. In addition, the custom in its present form is an institutionalized way for releasing hostility and is also a mechanism of social control. The 'naluyuks' are in the most obvious position to take advantage of their veiled identity and express their repressed hostility towards specific individuals without inviting later reprisals. The observers also may, and do, express their hostile feelings through the 'naluyuks.' This explains in part the anxiety and apprehension shown by both adolescents and adults. The persistent harassment of some individuals and the mixed reaction of the observers, who shift their support from 'naluyuk' to victim and back again, support this argument. The crowd is likely to turn the wrath of the 'naluyuks' on those persons who are regarded as public nuisances. When I observed the proceedings, the support of the crowd was almost entirely behind the 'naluyuks' in two instances, each involving a teenager. Both of the harassed individuals were strongly resented though for different reasons. One had assumed a self-righteous attitude since his confirmation, preaching against drinking, and had even forced several persons

---

4 / Professor Herbert Halpert has drawn my attention to the following: Henry Rink, *Tales and Traditions of the Eskimo* (1875), pp. 47 and 64; Franz Boas, *The Central Eskimo* (1888), pp. 620–21; Knut Rasmussen and W. Worster, *Eskimo Folk-Tales* (1921), p. 137, n.; C. E. Gillham, *Medicine Men of Hooper Bay* (1955), pp. 80–87.

to pour out their 'homebrew' at gun point. The other had neglected his senile father who had thus become a burden on the rest of the community. The 'naluyuks,' encouraged by the loudly expressed consent of the crowd, increased their pressure on these two teenagers until both of them retreated to a safe distance; one of them never dared to enter the houses with the 'naluyuks' lest he should be further punished. The 'naluyuks' had clearly expressed society's disapproval.

Mumming in an Outport Fishing Settlement: A Description and Suggestions on the Cognitive Complex

BY JAMES C. FARIS

At least three of the contributors to this volume have discussed the place of the mumming complex in Newfoundland and Labrador in functional terms. It has been interpreted as a means of social control in the Labrador Eskimo 'naluyuks' (chapter VII), as a cathartic mechanism having implications for both the disguised mummers and undisguised hosts in 'Ross' (chapter VI), and as a device for the release of in-group aggression and hostility in the area of the Straits of Belle Isle (chapter IV). It is the aim of this paper[1] to consider in more detail not the purpose of mumming – that is its functional aspects – not its antecedents or particular form, but the complex of mumming from the point of view of the people themselves. What *are* mummers, conceptually? How do mummers see themselves, cognitively? In other words, where does the mumming complex 'fit' in the way in which people of the community order their experience? How is it articulated in the social structure? This paper will not, then, be concerned with what mummers *do* in the outport community, but what mummers *are*, and will offer a non-causal explanation. This is illustrated paradigmatically. The suggestions are, to some extent, speculative and untestable, but are based rather closely on informants' statements, and I submit they reveal a fundamental structural logic operative in 'Cat Harbour' social life.

1 / The research on which this paper is based was generously supported by the Institute of Social and Economic Research of Memorial University of Newfoundland. Data are from fieldwork from January 1964 to March 1965, and are from one community, 'Cat Harbour.' I should like to acknowledge the helpful comments of Adam Kuper, Sue Drucker-Brown, Archie Mafeje, and particularly Melvin Firestone. Indeed, it is on Firestone's discussion of the similarities between mummers and strangers that the present essay elaborates, though from a different focus.

1 Mumming in Cat Harbour: Description

Mummers, 'janneys,' or 'Dark Ones' as they are sometimes called, are the disguised individuals who visit from house to house during Christmastide.[2] People in Cat Harbour also sometimes refer to the young people who come around at Hallowe'en (a recent introduction) as mummers, and I have heard men say of someone with his parka-hood up (which hides the face), "Here comes the Old Mummer hisself."[3]

People never 'janney' alone. As few as two may go together, although more often groups of four, five, or six are encountered. People report groups of fifteen or twenty going from house to house in the past. A nucleus, perhaps two or three people, usually based on friendship, kinship, or residential association, will decide to 'janney up' and meet at the house of one of the participants, or go around in turn to pick up each of the participant actors. Usually, however, this nucleus will add others as it makes its rounds, often from completely divergent cliques, and thus people who rarely interact otherwise will sometimes 'janney up' together. This is considered an ideal arrangement, for it confuses those hosts who, on establishing one mummer's identity, are tempted to guess the others on the basis of their knowledge of the social networks which exist in routine daily life.

In Cat Harbour adult mummers of opposite sex will band together. Children, who are also said to mummer, though none were encountered during my period of research, 'janney up' separately. The aged do not mummer because it is usually quite cold out and mumming involves rather strenuous activity. A group will usually start at one end of the settlement and continue to the other, perhaps reserving for last a house where, anticipating a dance, they hope to stay longest.

It is said that in former times men would sometimes wear women's clothing, such as bridal gowns and dresses; and women would wear oilskins and 'Cape Anne's' (oilskin caps), thus specifically changing sexual roles. Today, blankets, quilts, or borrowed coats are used to cover normal clothing, and sex is simply disguised. A woman, for

---

2 / Christmas in Cat Harbour is from December 25 to January 6. People attempt to 'get in twelve days' wood and water' so as to have nothing to do during the Christmastide but celebrate. During my stay mumming was from January 1 only.

3 / I wore a beard during the period of field research, which effectively frightened many small youngsters. Parents would explain "They think you're a mummer." I was also used by many of the same parents to threaten children: "We'll let the old whisker man get you," and "We'll let Mr. Faris carry you away," and "Do you want us to let the stranger get you?"

example, may wear her son's pants and boots, and a man may borrow his brother's boots. Hands are covered with mitts and gloves, both as a protection from the cold and to disguise recognizable characteristics. The headgear for both men and women is usually an out-of-style hat or stocking-cap, under which hangs either a thin silk scarf or a woman's slip covering the face and neck. Since these may be quite transparent, some will add a nylon stocking stretched over the head or a commercial rubber mask. Mummers generally blacken their faces and add moustaches. Anything which disguises the head is called a 'false face,' and this is regarded as the essence of the disguise. One will hear, "Get your false face on and come with us," and mummers are considered unfrocked, undisguised, determined, if their 'false faces' are removed. The disguise is complete when one gets a 'split' (a small piece of wood used for domestic fires) with which to knock on the doors of houses visited.

Mummers stoop to disguise their height, and walk swaying from side to side. They may make waving motions with their hands and arms, and they sit bent over, weaving slowly from side to side.

Mumming is always late in the evening, perhaps as late as 12:00 or 1:00 A.M. Usually only two mummers will go up to knock on a kitchen door;[4] the others linger back out of the light or around the corner of the house. They bang loudly on the door with the split, and when it is answered, ask in reverse speech (i.e., inhaling), "Mummers allowed?" If the host admits them, they signal to the others to come, and the entire group enters at one time. Sometimes the two mummer spokesmen are asked how many there are, to which they reply, again in an inhaling voice, "Just us!" This technique is said to have derived from former times when many more went mumming and people were reluctant to admit large numbers of mummers at one time. The query "Mummers allowed?" has relevance in Cat Harbour, for some houses will not admit mummers. There are, as well, some houses mummers do not usually visit at all, such as the homes of the Jehovah's Witnesses, an austere, millenarian sect, who say they do not admit mummers because they are part of Christmastide, which the sect does not acknowledge. One of the local leaders of the Jehovah's Witnesses told a group of mummers, "Come back after Christmas, boys, anytime you like, but not now – we don't believe in Christmas." It was the institution of Christmas, not the mummers, that was rejected. In other houses

4 / Houses are always entered through the kitchen, where a fire is kept and where most visiting is done – the living room door often having neither handle nor even steps leading to it from the outside.

(with United Church members) it is the uninhibited behaviour of the mummers that is regarded as sinful.

Once the mummers are admitted, people say, "Anything can happen." They mean just that, for the role deviation sanctioned by the 'false face' is practically unlimited. I was told that formerly mummers 'got pretty rough' when making their rounds, and socially peripheral people in the settlement, those most offensive to the general moral order, were often beaten if caught out by the janneys. The behaviour of mummers today is quite uninhibited. I witnessed a mummer (a female disguised in male clothing) engage in mock copulation with one hostess. The woman's reaction was slight embarrassment and some protest, but also laughter, and this appeared to be a consistent reaction to the general frolic in which the mummers engage. In another instance, a mummer (again a female) grabbed a married woman, visiting at the house when the mummers arrived, and danced with her into the prohibited 'inner part' of the house. The 'inner part' is the parlour, living room, and bedrooms, and it is an absolute breach of conduct to go into this section of the house without specifically being invited by the householders.

Although undisguised females are largely the 'victims' of the mummers' antics, the mummers themselves are by no means the only ones allowed licence. In determining the identity of mummers, the hosts are sometimes allowed to explore with their hands the upper torso, head, and face of mummers in an effort to 'find them out.' Undisguised men, for example, often single out an obviously female mummer and proceed to dance a few steps with her, then 'feel her up.' It is said that this 'feeling up' must always be 'above the waist.'[5]

Mummers will not usually unmask until they are sure you are not randomly guessing their identity. I have been told that formerly janneys sometimes would not unmask even after they were identified and their 'false faces' had to be removed by force. Any undisguised person in the house may guess, and all usually participate. If small children are still awake, they are held by a parent or older sibling. They often break into tears and have to be comforted – frightened as

5 / While I was talking with a group of men in a shop one night (shops in Cat Harbour are often open at night, especially during Christmas), four mummers came into the shop and the shopkeeper announced he was going to 'feel up' one small mummer, who was a married woman. On 'feeling' the woman's breasts, he immediately announced who he thought it was, which brought roars of laughter from both the mummers and the undisguised men in the shop. When the mummer finally unmasked, the shopkeeper had been wrong. Later, in discussing the incident, I was assured this would not be 'allowed normally.'

much by the violent, quick, and unexpected actions of the mummers as by the disguises. Children are also pre-conditioned to fear the mummers from the threats made by parents.

Mummers do not say much, and usually answer questions with a nod or shake of the head. If they do speak, it is in the disguised inhaling voice. Mummers may be asked to dance a jig or do something active so that people may catch some characteristic gesture or movement peculiar to an individual. People will say, "Do something for us, mummers," or "Dance a few steps, mummers." In this way, activity is assured, for "It's all part of the fun." After the mummers are identified and have unmasked, a 'lunch' or 'some Christmas' is served. This usually consists of pastries, cakes, cookies, pies, and tea. The janneys may decline this offer if they have already eaten at several other houses. Drinks are then offered, chiefly to the men. This means 'berry-ocky' (a hot drink of berry juice, usually with rum added), rum, a homemade berry wine, or beer. After the 'lunch' and drink are consumed, the mummers replace their 'faces,' perhaps engage in a few more quick antics, then leave.[6] If it is the last house to be visited, they will persuade the host to 'get a fiddler' (i.e., get someone's accordion) and have a dance. In Cat Harbour, the visiting itself is secondary to the general sanctioned deviation – the frolic and the drinking – called locally 'times.'[7]

2 The Conceptual Logic Behind Mumming: The Stranger as a Cognitive Category

Elsewhere in this volume, Firestone states, "I do not mean to imply that people of the straits consciously feel that mummers symbolize strangers or feel that the two categories necessarily have anything in common. However, they are functional equivalents." (Chapter IV)

---

6 / On one occasion, after the mummers had unmasked and consumed their 'Christmas,' all present tried to no avail to get one shy woman to step-dance. She persistently refused, until people were getting ready to leave, then suddenly grabbed a quilt one of the mummers had been wrapped in, threw it over her head, and began to dance, kicking up her heels in a most uninhibited manner. Note the change in role-façade necessary for her to accomplish this.

7 / The significance of 'time' in Cat Harbour is interesting. Essentially, a 'time' is an occasion of sanctioned deviation – thus, mummers mean a 'time,' and drinking (frowned upon except at sanctioned occasions, such as weddings and Christmas) means a 'time.' If a wedding, for example, did not have much 'brew,' people will say, "We didn't really have a time, did we?"

Quite apart from their functional equivalence, Firestone has, it seems to me, convincingly demonstrated the conceptual similarities. What I should like to do is to enlarge on this point, and show how, at least in Cat Harbour, the cognition of the stranger, symbolized in the mummer, has rather wide and significant structural implications.

In Cat Harbour, as in other small outports with a marked lack of social change, the confluence of social networks, kinship, religion, economics, residence, and so on, over a period of time has meant that role expectations are largely congruent; hence behaviour is, with considerable assurance, predictable.[8] This is only the case, however, *within* the settlement and for people who 'belong to the place.' The behaviour of the stranger, the outsider, cannot be predicted with surety, regardless of the ostensible reason for his presence in the settlement. The hundreds of small Newfoundland coastal fishing communities are 'closed' societies, and long years of isolation and a series of brief, unfortunate encounters with the outside world has meant that the outsider, the stranger, is unpredictable, unreliable, not to be trusted, deviant, and, especially in former times, potentially dangerous and malevolent. In Cat Harbour today, the category 'stranger' is edged with suspicion.

Though today a community of strong Protestant tradition, 'Cat Harbour' was first settled by Irish Catholics some time before the end of the eighteenth century, or perhaps earlier. The earliest settlers were probably deserters and fugitives from West Country vessels or from vessels from Conception Bay opening the Labrador and northeast coast fishery, for evidence exists that some changed their names, possibly to escape apprehension. Certainly the choice of Cat Harbour itself would indicate some attempt to be left alone. The water is shallow and rough at all times (thus prohibiting the landing of larger vessels), there is no shelter, and through the first quarter of the nineteenth century Indians were often a threat.[9] Moreover, there was the competitive (and sometimes destructive) presence of the French fishermen until 1783, and the repressive activities of the British Navy

8 / Relevant here are two theoretical concepts: *mutual steering*, whereby the performance of one role guides and conditions the performance of another, having the effect of maintaining norms; and *role knowledge*, the process over time of one actor adjusting, learning, and preparing for the adoption of another role with which he is, on adoption, thoroughly familiar. The similarity to the rigidly structured system of roles in 'Ross' (cf. J. Szwed, chapter vi) should be readily apparent.

9 / Records document Indians raiding Cat Harbour around the turn of the nineteenth century and stealing, among other things, 'canvas' (sails). Cf. J. Howley, *History of the Beothucks* (1915), pp. 276ff.

and West Country vessels even later, until settlement was officially sanctioned in 1824. Prior to that it was illegal and actively discouraged. (See chapter II.)

From the beginning, then, anyone from the outside, any 'strangers,' even representatives of legal authority, were potentially hostile. There was of course no resident clergyman; even after the 1830s Cat Harbour was only visited two or three times each year by the Anglican missionary based on Greenspond.

The first Protestant migrants to Cat Harbour whose arrival is documented were from the Harbour Grace area of Conception Bay. They began to arrive around 1800. Most had recently come to Conception Bay from the west and south of England – Devon, Cornwall, and Jersey – although others were the descendants of some of the earliest English settlers in Newfoundland. The original Catholic inhabitants were soon outnumbered by the Protestant arrivals who continued to come until about 1850 when the migrations ceased. The *Census* of 1869 lists 112 Anglicans and 31 Roman Catholics. Apparently religious animosities similar to those in Conception Bay continued (cf. chapters II and x), so that in 1884, the year following the Harbour Grace Affray,[10] the Catholic portion of the population was forced out of Cat Harbour, and moved further 'down' the shore to Fogo Island where their descendants may be found today. One Catholic woman who married into the community after that date was regarded as almost monstrous, as a witch, malevolent, and was used to threaten children. The Catholic in Cat Harbour became a sterotype 'stranger,' potentially dangerous, polluting, evil, and even today one can hear Catholics referred to as 'pretty dark.' The significance of this symbolism will be indicated below.

Experience in the past with political and mercantile representatives has reinforced the general adage that "You can't trust strangers." Political representatives, whether provincial or federal, have often been strangers to the area both in the past and even today. Frequently presented from a slate of complete outsiders, often St. John's lawyers, businessmen, or those in political favour, they have often shown little or no interest in the welfare of the constituency. Cat Harbour was also exploited, as were many other Newfoundland outports, by foreign

10 / The Harbour Grace Affray was a skirmish at Harbour Grace in late 1883 when a group of Catholics fired upon, and killed, several parading Orangemen. Cf. (Mrs.) E. Senior, *The Origin and Political Activities of the Orange Order in Newfoundland, 1863–1890* (1960). There is evidence that both Catholics and Protestants of Cat Harbour had kinsmen involved in the Affray.

entrepreneurs and by profiteers in fish marketing. Many dealings with 'outside' institutions, especially economic ones, have resulted in failures.[11] Inasmuch as Newfoundland salt fish is placed on the international market, the people have been subject as well to world economic fluctuations over which they have no control, but from which they have endured hardship.

Today strangers, such as the Mountie, the doctor, and other local representatives of the outside institutional structure, have specific roles in the community. But these 'introductions' are relatively new in Cat Harbour, and although they are there ostensibly to help the outport, they remain 'strangers.' Parents even threaten children with, "Do you want the Mountie to get you?" and "We'll let the doctor carry you away."[12]

Another 'stranger' with a specific role is Santa Claus. When the community sought a man to play Santa Claus this year (1964) I was contacted. When I refused, using the excuse that I wouldn't know what to do or how to behave, I was told, "But you'd make a good Santa Claus; you're a stranger, sure." Although the custom of having a Santa Claus is not a recently introduced 'outside' institution but continues back into the dimmest memory of the settlement's oldest inhabitants, nonetheless Santa is also placed in the generalized 'stranger' category.

There is an annual 'Christmas Tree' held in the local Orange Lodge Hall at which Santa Claus hands out gifts. Most of the Christmas gifts in the community are distributed in this way. Children are often afraid to go forward to receive their gifts when Santa calls their names, for apart from his 'false face' and the costume (note here the similarity to

---

11 / One example will suffice. The settlement 'fell hard' for the promises of William Coaker and the FPU (cf. J. Feltham, *The Development of the Fisherman's Protective Union in Newfoundland* [1959]) even to the extent that the minute book of the local FPU council closed each meeting early in the Union's history with 'God Save Coaker,' and on his occasional visits placed mats on the beach so that he would not have to walk on the sand, proclaiming him 'The Saviour.' But, "as you expects of strangers," the FPU collapsed, and recorded in the local minute book during the late years of the Union are expressions of bitter cynicism and disappointment.

12 / The RCMP and the government doctor have served the area since Confederation (1949), although they rarely come to Cat Harbour. The nearest nursing station is twenty miles away, the nearest RCMP in Gander, eighty-six miles by road. The road linking the community to Gander was completed in 1961, and access is now much easier. Rural electric power arrived in late 1963. Still, however, in the minds of most of the older people and the young children, the doctor somehow means sickness, and the Mountie somehow means crime.

mummers), parents admonish children to be good or "Santa Claus will put you in his bag and take you away." Adults, however, are also quite reluctant to go forward and receive their gifts; some absolutely refuse to go, in spite of pleas from other adults, "He won't hurt you," "Don't be afraid," and "You know it's only Lloyd." In one case an adult woman refused to go forward though she knew that the Santa that year was her own brother-in-law. When an adult did go forward to receive his gifts, 'all hands' applauded and cheered; when I queried this display, I was told, "It takes some guts to meet Santa Claus, so we always blow them up and clap." For his part, Santa's behaviour is also 'stranger-like.' Like the mummers, he is allowed certain physical freedoms, and will often grab someone and dance a few steps, or pinch, kiss, or hug one of the adults.

As a consequence of the rigidly virilocal marriage and settlement pattern in the outport fishing community[13] women are most often the 'strangers' in Cat Harbour. In 65 per cent of the marriages they are outsiders who have married into the community. The clearest manifestation of their 'strangerness' is found in the use of "formal" affinal terminology,[14] and in accusations of witchcraft. Only an outsider can be guilty of witchcraft. People will often say "Only women can be witches"; when presented with a case of a male witch, one person announced, "Yes, but he was a stranger." Perhaps congruent with this is the fact that men are usually associated with an 'all good' category, that of 'doctors' or 'wizards,' those capable of curing, 'charming' (i.e., stopping) blood, and other good works.

Witchcraft in Cat Harbour is viewed as the power to hex, 'jink,' or call evil for purposes of revenge, spite, or wanton malice. It can be, in rare cases, sold; that is, a person not possessing the power can 'hire' a witch to hex for him, but most commonly it is used by the witch personally. Witchcraft can be learned by either men or women. I have

---

13 / Statistically in Cat Harbour, only three uxorilocal alternatives occur in a universe of sixty-two cases. (Note also this pattern in the Northern Peninsula – see Firestone, chapter IV.) This statistical universe is composed of the marriages of which at least one partner is living in Cat Harbour today. It ignores those (both male and female) having married out, and is thus purely from the local perspective.

14 / That is, the use of "Mr. and Mrs." terms of address and reference for parents-in-law and respected elders, as opposed to the familiar terms for parents-in-law and honoured elders, 'aunt and uncle.' Women (and men) marrying into the community usually adopt the formal terminology, whereas a local girl marrying a local man most often uses the familiar terms. This terminology is normally maintained throughout the lives of the actors. Formal terms are also applied to outsiders – I was, for example, Mr. Faris, during the major portion of my research.

data, however, on but two male witches. It is more precisely regarded as being inherent in the personality and character of one class of individuals – strangers.[15]

Since everyone in a closed virilocal society such as Cat Harbour is "placed," the rare man who marries into the community from the outside is inevitably in an uncomfortable position. He is always consciously a stranger. He is often referred to by his wife's maiden surname. One of three such individuals now living in Cat Harbour, a man just over sixty years old who has been in the settlement for over forty years, recently confided to me, "I'm just like yourself; I'm a stranger here too." Men formerly admonished their sons, "You don't want to marry too far; you can't trust them," that is, do not marry a girl from too far away, too much of a stranger. In Cat Harbour, "once a stranger, always a stranger" holds and women who have been in the settlement thirty years are spoken of by true-born natives as 'strangers': there is no case where assimilation is ever complete.

Associated with the concept of the stranger in Cat Harbour is a general black/white symbolism operative in the community. The archetype stranger, the Devil, is the 'Black Man' or 'Blackie,' and things dark by nature, such as the crow, have evil associations and are regarded as malevolent omens ('tokens'). In Cat Harbour, one would seldom, even in jest, call someone a Devil, especially a child. It is regarded as cursing and usually circumlocutions are used, such as 'Black Man,' 'the Old Mummer,' 'Old Nick,' or perhaps, in my case, 'the Old Whisker Man.' My four-year-old daughter, who after a period of several months became totally acculturated, here furnishes a significant example. One of her favourite games was that often played by her outport age-mates in an attempt to scare each other: they would threaten each other with "I'm the Black Man, I'm coming to get you," or "I'm a stranger, I'm coming after you." She was particularly successful in the latter, and would comment at length on the excellence of her 'black looks.'

I have noted earlier that Catholics are referred to as 'pretty dark' and mummers as 'the Dark Ones.' Witchcraft is sometimes referred to

---

15 / No more than one in four adults in Cat Harbour today take witchcraft very seriously, but during the period of my research, interest was revived with the success of a local witch in hexing a sealing vessel. This was of sufficient consequence to merit the use of two traditional witchcraft cures, neither of which appeared to have worked. During the summer fishing voyage, three additional witchcraft accusations were made, two stemming from fishing failures, the other from a persistent illness.

as 'black magic,' and people overtly fear the night and darkness, using it to threaten children. A particularly saintly individual, who must, of course, 'belong to the place,' is spoken of as 'pure white'; and, other things being equal, a white sled-dog or horse is regarded as more dependable, trustworthy, stronger, and worth more than a black one.

When two men get too far into a heated argument, they are said to be 'getting black.' There is in Cat Harbour a strict avoidance of physical conflict, of overheated arguments, and of overt emotional expression in general. There are seldom fights, and in its long history no cases of homicide. Conflict and hostility must be avoided or at least repressed in so small and isolated a community where the social networks are so totally entwined. But more important, when exposed emotionally one is in a polluted state, as it were, not in possession of the protective formal façade normally maintained. Behaviour cannot be predicted and one is subject to exploitation; one is in a *dangerous* state, in a *sacred* state in Durkheimian terms. It is understandable why such expression is labelled 'black.' When news of some type of conflict permeates the outport, such as the assassination of President Kennedy, people shake their heads and say, "That's what you'd expect with all those strangers." One old man, 'vexed' at his neighbour, shook his fist at him and shouted, "If I were in the outside world, I'd really smack you one." Note the similar avoidance of conflict in 'Ross' (cf. chapter VI).

The logic behind the symbolism in its application to the outsider can be seen most clearly in a conversation between two men who had not seen each other for some time: "I hadn't seen you for days, you're a proper stranger." "Yep, I'm just as black as the Devil!" In fact, if one wishes to make reference to a stranger with whom everyone is not familiar, such as myself, someone directly from the outside, as opposed to a 'stranger' who has been in the community for many years, he will speak of a 'black stranger' or 'blackest kind of stranger.'

This symbolism and the structural logic by which it is articulated extends further: at funerals, those classed as 'mourners' – the closest kinsmen of the deceased – wear black ribbons, and are regarded as being in a state of ritual pollution. They are *mourning* – a highly emotional (and therefore dangerous/sacred) situation. They are seated separately in the church, 'parade' separately in the funeral procession, have a special and exclusive ceremony in the house of the deceased, and do not touch the corpse or coffin, dig the grave, or handle any of the logistics of burial. Instead, a category of persons (and things) wearing white ribbons – *close outsiders* in a kinship sense (kinship is the singular factor in defining 'mourners') – take care of all the physical arrangements of the funeral. In this category are included the pall-bearers, the horse and sleigh (or now, in good weather, a pick-up truck) used to pull the bier, and the officiating minister or lay reader. Each of these displays a white ribbon, and is necessary in a very real way to *make hot things cool*.[16] Those in the black ribbon category, those *closest* to the deceased in normal social intercourse, are ritually removed, as it were, from active social participation during the specified mourning period. Their *outsider* position, that is, their *abnormal* behaviour, symbolized in colour, is structurally similar to the peripheral position of the stranger – the stereotype *abnormality*.

Some behavioural items traditionally associated with the mumming complex, specifically, knocking and hospitality, are conceptually relevant to the general notion of the stranger. Firestone's paper has pointed out the hospitality lavished on 'strangers.' "Covert fear and overt friendliness are complementary. The more you find out about an outsider, what he is up to, and what he is like, the less of a threat he is." (Chapter IV) This, apart from the fact that here the stranger is never fully incorporated, is exactly the situation in Cat Harbour. It is usually articulated as 'respect for strangers.' When people entertain those who 'belong to the place,' they 'have people in,' but when entertaining outsiders, they 'have strangers.' One doesn't entertain 'guests,' one 'has strangers,' and much more opulent hospitality is extended to the outsider, some people even having a different table 'for strangers.' Strangers are usually taken into the little-used and otherwise prohibited 'inner part' of the house. (Note also that the mummer is offered special food and drink.) Finding out who the outsider is, what he is up to, helps one understand the threat he may pose; but hospitality is also an attempt to put one's self in good stead with someone potentially dangerous. People go out of their way to please a witch, not to 'cross' her; it is the same with strangers. Strangers are expected to sit at the 'first table' (the table of close kinsmen and honoured guests) at a wedding; and if for some reason this is not done, those responsible worry over the apparent affront. People give up their own comfort so that the stranger may enjoy himself. One does not want to offend the malevolent outsider.

Again as in the Straits of Belle Isle, mummers and strangers both knock before entering. In Cat Harbour, however, the general cognition

16 / The use of *close outsiders* (i.e., local people, but not close kinsmen) and *make hot things cool* (i.e., dispose of the corpse, *hot*, burial making things *cool*), both idioms of African mortuary ritual (cf. Jack Goody, *Death, Property and the Ancestors* [1959]) is deliberate – the striking parallels cannot be ignored.

of the 'stranger' is so broad that there are other stranger-*like* relationships which may require local people to knock. One, for example, is the case of specific financial transactions, such as canvassing for a charity, or buying and selling something on the spot. Children who would normally run in and out without any warning whatsoever would knock to be admitted if they had papers, calendars, seeds, or cod's tongues for sale. This brief cash-for-merchandise (or service) type of relationship is an *outsider* one, foreign to the outport which until recently did almost entirely without cash. It is the type of dyadic relationship one has with a shop clerk in St. John's or Gander – a short, specific contract finished on the culmination of the sale and without the usual obligation and credit aspects characteristic of financial transactions in the traditional outport setting. A person in the community who wishes to establish one of these 'stranger-like' relationships will signal this by knocking, just as the outsider and the mummer do.

As in the straits, adults will knock on a table or wall to distract misbehaving children and say quickly, 'the janneys' or 'the Dark Ones.' Children know a knock means 'strangers.'

3 Conclusions

It would be misleading to leave the impression that the conceptualization of the stranger and its implications are of paramount importance in everyday life, that witchcraft is rampant, that children are terrorized, that mumming is not enjoyed, or that, regardless of its motivation, hospitality in Cat Harbour is not very real. It is only that I have concentrated on structural contrasts and attempted to illustrate a general logic: the cognition of an entire complex of somehow *unnatural* or *abnormal* behaviour and belief defined by Cat Harbour people. In so doing I have of necessity left unstated the warmth and essentially gay nature of the people in everyday life. It is also true that, with the completion of the road to Gander in 1961 and the arrival of electric power in 1963, urban values and attitudes (where one is in constant interaction with outsiders and where one's neighbours and closest friends may be 'strangers' in the Cat Harbour sense) are coming into the community. In the class structure of the settlement, those who are looking upward are in essence looking outward – into the world of contemporary Western values and goals. People are becoming more familiar with strangers; more strangers are coming into the settlement; and local people have become more mobile. The physical isolation which existed previously is going, and now the social isolation is breaking down. Some feel an apprehension about this; they fear a general moral disintegration since, after all, strangers and outside attitudes are polluting and dangerous. But others, especially the young educated adults, are rapidly adopting urban attitudes and values. People say, "You don't see so many mummers as there once was," and "It don't seem people is as scared of strangers as they used to be." But despite such changes, conceptual categories are slow to shift in an isolated outport. They lag behind *reality*. The cognitive associations and implications of 'strangers' and the logic by which they are articulated in traditional Cat Harbour society have therefore not yet altered significantly.

But how does all of this fit together? How does it make sense? I suggest we are now in a position to consider a model with which to illustrate the structural logic behind the data presented. Cat Harbour, as well as other communities discussed in this volume, is normally characterized by rather rigid and formal role expectations. But 'people who belong to the place' sometimes let down their hair, and sanction *deviation*, even reversal, from these rigid and formal role expectations. Such occasions are the 'times' – the periods of sanctioned licence. Mourning, just like the 'time,' is a behaviour somehow contrary or *deviant* from routine daily life: a polar opposite from the gaiety and licence of the 'time,' but importantly, a quite different sort of behaviour than that normally characterizing the community, a reversal, as it were. Both are, in a Durkheimian sense, *sacred* or *polluted* states, and opposed to the normal, everyday *profane* or *secular* behaviour and expectations.

Leach has, it seems to me, made very fruitful use of this: "In these puritanical days explicit role reversal is not common in our own society but it is common enough in the ethnographic literature and in accounts of Mediaeval Europe. You will find such behaviours associated with funerals, or with *rites de passage* (symbolic funerals) or with the year's end (e.g., in Europe: Saturnalia and the Feast of Fools)." Further, "*Role reversal* . . . is symbolic of a complete transfer from the secular to the sacred; normal time has stopped, sacred time is played in reverse, death is converted into birth. This Good King Wenceslas symbolism is something which has a world wide distribution because it makes logical sense independently of any particular folklorish traditions or any particular magical beliefs."[17]

We have, from Cat Harbour, quite explicit and specific reversals in the occasions of licence – the mummer's reverse speech, behaviour,

17 / E. R. Leach, *Rethinking Anthropology* (1961), pp. 132–36.

	'PEOPLE WHO BELONG TO THE PLACE'		'STRANGERS'	
	I: Secular Cat Harbour, "normal"	II: Sacred or polluted Cat Harbour, "abnormal"	III: 'Those we have something to do with'	IV: The outside world
BEHAVIOR/BELIEF	no knocking	knocking ----→		
	inhibited behaviour, taboo on physical freedom, taboo on drinking	controlled "uninhibited" behaviour, "allowed" physical freedoms, drinking at 'times'	←----	totally uninhibited behaviour & physical freedom, indiscriminate drinking
	work	no work		
	"familiar" address terminology		'formal' address terminology	
	peace and cordiality	arguments ----→	←----	violence and fighting
	white (general symbolism)	dark, darkness,	getting black,	black
	dominant Protestant majority	---- Catholics ----		the Devil
ROLES/RELATIONSHIPS	people (esp. women) born in Cat Harbour	←----	people (esp. women) marrying into Cat Harbour	people (esp. women) elsewhere
	obligation, credit, debt →	cash transactions ----	←----	RCMP, doctors, politicians ---- crime, sickness, sin
	'helpers,' pall-bearers	mourners		
		Santa Claus MUMMERS		
		---- witchcraft ----		----

FIG. 1. Paradigm illustrating the structure and logic of the cognitive categories 'strangers' and 'people who belong to the place.' Traditional Cat Harbour society (and the young children) would tend to push categories II and III to the right and blur divisions *cd* and *ef*. Contemporary and future Cat Harbour will tend to push categories II and III to the left and blur divisions *ab* and *cd*. There is a tendency, in other words, to merge categories. In terms of the individual's life cycle, cognizance of *ab* occurs earliest, then later *cd* and *ef* are articulated.

change of sex, disguise, and so on; and we have the English word 'time' significantly used for such occasions. Similarly, mourning behaviour indicates a role reversal in the specific prohibitions surrounding intercourse with the deceased, one with whom the 'mourners' were in close interaction in life.

In Cat Harbour, however, there are other implications. For what does all this have to do with colour symbolism and the 'stranger'? A central theme of this paper is that there is a very powerful impetus in human affairs to define experience, to order existence. This statement is neither original nor unique.[18] But my thesis is that any *deviations* from the limited role alternatives available locally must be within the conceptual scope of the outport individual. That is, if one is to adopt, even briefly and ritually, a *deviant* or reversed role, then such a role must be defined in some way by the experience and tradition of the individual adopting it. Role reversal, then, is culturally defined. It is structurally significant in that 'times' are role reversal; but to show how this makes sense of many Cat Harbour phenomena, we need to look at just what the culturally defined criteria of role reversal are. Conveniently, in Cat Harbour, black is the reverse of white; but my point is that it need not be in all societies.

What I am suggesting is that in the *reverse* state, the 'times' (or in mourning), one can expect to find behaviour, expectations, and belief that are culturally defined as *reverse* or *abnormal*. And I suggest Cat Harbour people draw their cognition from the symbols, the behaviour and belief they regard as characterizing the stranger – the most *abnormal* or *deviant* category with which they are familiar. I find it plausible and, under the conditions, to be expected that the dangerous *sacred* or *polluted* extremes of Cat Harbour society should partake of the behaviour and symbolism thought to mark the stranger. There are, of course, *real* strangers, and in addition strangers with whom Cat Harbour people have experience – those with whom they must (by virtue of the exchange of sisters and daughters for wives, if nothing else) interact. But the beliefs and the relationships surrounding these latter individuals only serve to mark them as representative of the *real* outside world. As I hope I have shown, there is a tendency to associate conceptually behaviour which is ominous, unpredictable, and uninhibited, potentially dangerous and polluting, with this state. This, then, quite apart from its various functions in specific circumstances, is the fundamental essence of mumming in Newfoundland and Labrador.

18 / Cf. John Beattie, "Understanding and Explanation in Social Anthropology," *British Journal of Sociology*, X (1959), 45–60.

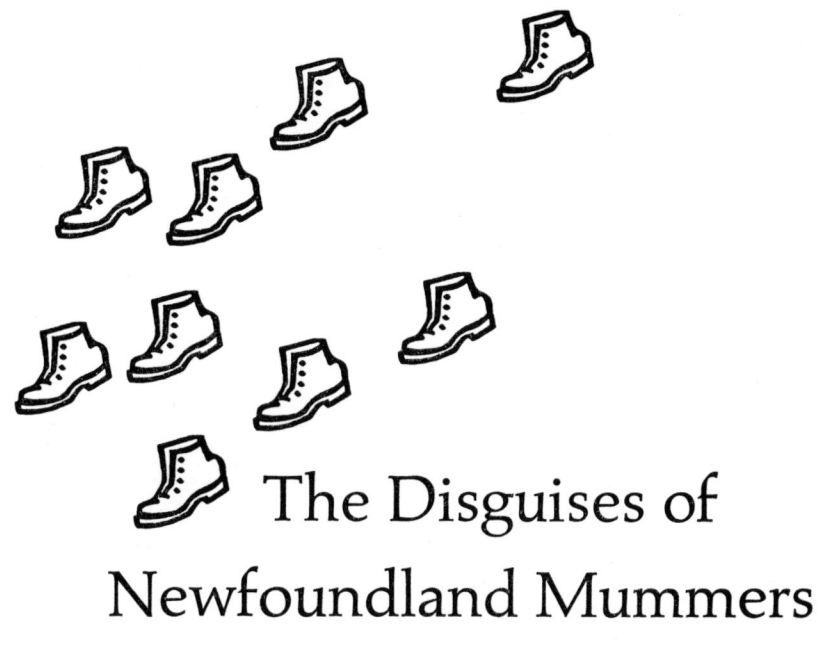

The Disguises of Newfoundland Mummers

BY J. D. A. WIDDOWSON
AND HERBERT HALPERT

Disguise is a central element in Christmas mummering throughout Newfoundland. This paper describes some specific disguises used by Newfoundland mummers, and makes a partial analysis of the data assembled up to the spring of 1965. No attempt has been made here to discuss the sociological or psychological implications of the custom; some of these are treated in other essays in this volume. Nor is there any attempt at comparison with British and Irish analogues, much less with European parallels. The material presented supplements and reinforces the observations and reports by Chiaramonte, Faris, Firestone, Szwed, and Williams.

This account of some of the mummers' disguises is based on reports from one hundred communities, concentrated mostly in the eastern half of the Island, but including a few representative areas on the west coast, the south coast, and the coast of Labrador.[1] The information comes largely from two sources: transcriptions from a large number of field interviews and tape recordings (designated as T),[2]

---

1 / Subsequent investigations, through fieldwork and specialized questionnaires, have elicited further evidence that mummering with its attendant masking occurs in a very large number of communities other than those dealt with in this essay. It seems safe to say that up to a few years ago, the patterns of disguising described here were general throughout the Island.

2 / All transcriptions were made by J. D. A. Widdowson and, except where omissions are indicated, are verbatim. The tape recordings, written reports, and related material collected in this survey are on file in the Folklore and Language Archive of Memorial University, together with relevant biographical details of the informants. We are deeply indebted to the many people, too many to name individually, who took such pains to answer our questions either in the field or through written replies to our questionnaires.

148 The Disguises of Newfoundland Mummers

and written responses to a questionnaire which was part of a general survey of frightening figures.

The mummers, who are also widely known as 'janneys,' practise broadly similar customs over the whole area covered by the survey, although the reports show that there is considerable local variation in details. The activities involve both adults and older children and normally take place during Christmas, sometimes continuing on each of the twelve nights of the Christmas season. Although Christmas mummering still continues, the tendency in recent years has been for younger children to take an increasing part, and in many areas the disguising now seems to be more common at Hallowe'en (October 31) and on Bonfire Night (November 5) than it was formerly. This newer, and perhaps less elaborate, pattern is centred on the custom of asking for a 'trick or treat' at the houses visited. This is now common in St. John's and other urban centres where the older type of adult mummer at Christmas has become rare. Nevertheless, the older custom still persists in many 'outports' where the mummers often dress in fantastic costumes and in this disguise visit homes in the community. They often entertain by dancing, singing, or telling stories, and may receive some form of refreshment. The custom of guessing identities is a central feature of the visit, the mummers usually unmasking if their identity is guessed.

1 Masks, Veils, and Headgear

The facial disguise adopted by the mummers is perhaps their foremost concern. They take particular care to disguise their faces and heads, usually obscuring the face and hiding the shape of the head. Reports from ten communities state that faces were often blackened. At Port Blandford, Glovertown, and Coachman's Cove, stove-polish was used for this purpose.

An informant from Glovertown described this old-fashioned stove-blacking:

[They] ... used to buy it in cakes, you know, and put it in water and melt it ... and they'd put that into the water and make the water black like ink; put it over their face. It would all wash off again, you know. [T]

Burnt cork was also used for blackening:

Cork, burn the cork and get the black and put on them. My, they used to be dark! The real darkies. And they'd spend some time when you'd get them back, washing them and cleaning them up. [T Nipper's Harbour]

... a gentleman ... made hisself up with burnt cork, and he made such a job of himself that I wouldn't have known him. I saw him after in somebody else's house and I didn't know he had made himself up. I wouldn't have known him, and he'd altered hisself that much; made a complete job of it with burnt cork. [T Eastport]

At St. Mary's, in St. Mary's Bay, soot, oil-pencils, and even tar were used. There too, faces were sometimes painted with "any kind of paint that you could rub off inside of a few days"; at Nipper's Harbour cocoa was used to make faces appear brown or red. In many parts of Newfoundland mummers who dressed as ghosts completed their disguise by whitening their faces.

Also common is the use of semi-transparent materials to disguise the face. Some of the mummers wear veils which hang down loosely before the face and are usually either fastened behind the head or held in place by the headgear. These veils are made from muslin, lace, net curtain, cotton, or any other thin fabric:

... you has a little cloth over your face; why, you see through all right but the other fellow couldn't see.... 'Tis a kind of muslin, bit of muslin or something or other.... [T Salvage]

Some would put on what they used to call muslin, you know. Muslin or scrim, window scrim [a thin curtain material], you know, like you'd have for a curtain; you could see out through it, you know. It wouldn't open enough to make out the features of anybody.... [T Glovertown]

Oh, just a handkerchief or anything like that, any piece of cloth, you know.... that's right, some thin stuff, you see. And then of course when you go in the house you'd just pull down the veil. When you'd leave of course you'd just lift it, you see. [T St. George's]

Veils were also made from ladies' nylon, silk, or cotton stockings, as in this description from Joe Batts Arm: "Sometimes the upper part of a lady's nylon hose was used. This was sewn up at one end, then pulled down over the face." (T) The old-fashioned black stockings, thicker than modern silk or nylon ones, were a famous disguise at St. George's on the west coast, and had some characteristics of the mask, obscuring the face more than thinner material would. Eyeholes had to be cut in them. This type of disguise is also reported from Badger's Quay.

The coloured or painted veil, as remembered in Sop's Island, shares characteristics of both the veil and the mask:

Mostly they wore just veils or sometimes painted ones and sometimes not. ... a piece of curtain or anything that you could see through.... Oh, it would be painted with crayon or dye or anything at all that would make it look colourful and grotesque. [T]

An elaborate facial disguise, a curious combination of veil and mask, was described by an informant from St. Mary's:

I only saw one of these once. 'Twas a mess of old fish bones and everything, and they're all hooked together, and they looked pretty good too, and he could lick the bones when he was out at night. [T]

Very often the mummers wear true masks, or 'false faces' as they are usually called, which they make themselves. Many of these homemade masks are frightening and a considerable amount of time may be spent on making them as hideous as possible. Not only do the masks often arouse fear in small children, but even adults have expressed a strong dislike of encountering anyone whose face is so covered.

Masks take many different forms. The commonest are made from cardboard or paper, or from cloth of any weight and thickness. The degree of elaboration of these basic materials varied considerably.

You could make your own false face, yes. Well, they'd get paper and mix up a bit of flour into a pan; now if they wanted to make a good hard heavy one, you know, they'd paste the paper together, and sometimes they used to use house-paper [i.e., wallpaper] ... them days you'd get house-paper with old pictures on it, faces of people ... and big noses and big stuff like that ... away back in them days.... And they'd go to work then and they'd make their face.... They'd cut out a big nose and glue it on, and fit themselves up. [T Glovertown]

The masks were normally painted with bright colours, but in a few instances were painted black or merely decorated with lipstick and crayon.

Some of them would make those false faces, you know and they'd ... paint it whatever colour they wanted, red or black or blue or whatever colour ... would make it funny, you know. Paint the big moustache, curling away up here.... [T Glovertown]

More recently, masks have been store-bought:

They'd have all kinds of faces on, and queer old faces; dogs' faces and cats' faces and . . . you know, they'll be the false face, see. They get all kinds of shapes. . . . [T Nipper's Harbour]

. . . what they calls false faces, you know. Oh we used to have them here for sale. . . . I don't know what they're made of but . . . 'tis very warm work mummering you know, because you got on a lot of clothes, you see. . . . Sometimes those false faces melt. [T Baine Harbour]

But when there'd be a crowd of janneys they'd have on the false faces and . . . they used to be ugly false faces in them days. My! just like the old people, two or three hundred years back . . . big crooked noses and they were all bony and sticking up, you know. They'd buy them. [T Glovertown]

In fact you could wear what they called a false face, you know, paper faces . . . with the nose shape and all; just a scale drawn over your face, put right over it. The eyes would be there, and a mouthpiece, but you wouldn't see the face, you see; you'd just see the eyes. Some would be black. You could buy them in St. John's, you know, the false faces. [T Baine Harbour]

Sometimes just a small strip of black cloth was used to cover the area round the eyes, but usually the masks covered the whole of the face.

Efforts to disguise the shape of the whole head are seen in several reports. In St. John's and Aguathuna (opposite sides of the Island), mummers sometimes wore paper bags, such as small sugar bags, over their heads, with holes cut out for eyes and mouth. In St. Joseph's, Placentia Bay, an informant described the wearing of cardboard boxes with eyes cut in them and a big face drawn on the box. Pillowcovers were also worn, or a large sheet might be draped over the head, with holes cut for eyes, nose, and mouth, and with the face decorated with lipstick and crayons.

From Fortune Harbour comes an account of masks made from birch bark:[3]

You could have them round. Round would be the most easiest way to have them, for you'd slide the bark right off of it. You get the piece of birch so

---

3 / Normally called 'birch rind.' Birch rind, 'malldow,' and hay (the latter two mentioned later) are the only instances so far reported of plant materials in mummers' disguises. Although sticks or 'splits' (pieces of kindling wood) are often carried when mummers go their rounds, there seems to be little traditional use of such available materials as evergreens or other plants.

long ... if it was cold, or 'twasn't in season or anything, you'd put it over steam. You'd warm the wood and then you'd slide the bark off.... Well you have them just the size of your head or a little shade bigger. Then you'd trim it and cut eyeholes in it.... [T]

Frequently the head disguise was elaborated by addition of makeshift hair (especially whiskers) of various lengths and kinds. One report from St. John's refers to rope being draped over the head to represent hair. Such additions were also helpful, of course, in concealing the shape of the head.

Sheep's wool or various kinds of fur were common materials:

The sheep's wool [mask] was usually made on a piece of cardboard, and had the wool for eyebrows, big shaggy eyebrows and whiskers, and usually down on the throat so that a person could not look in behind the mask and see who it was, because you couldn't let anybody see who you were when you were out with the mummers. [T St. Mary's]

They'd have an outfit they'd made and they'd decorate it with wool. Maybe go to the trouble of dying wool to have different colours.... [T Fortune Harbour]

... Whiskers ... well they'd probably have ... the tail of a sheep ... someone killed a sheep and skinned the sheep and well they'd save the tail and use it for a whisker ... could be rabbit fur or probably the fur had come off a ... coat or something or other like that, you see, or as I said before, a sheep's tail. Why I refer now to a sheep's tail, I made [whiskers out of] one myself one time. [T Salvage]

They'd have rabbit skins, like; now they'd have those for a whisker. The whole rabbit skin would be hanging out further down for a whisker. [T Fortune Harbour]

In Harbour Grace, Heart's Content, Wesleyville, and Glovertown the strands of a moss called 'malldow,' which grows on fir and spruce trees, was used for the whiskers. It was usually stuck onto the mask or directly on the face with glue, molasses, or gum from the trees.

... big beards, you know. I tell you what they used to make the beards out of now, most of the people I've seen making them. They used to go in the woods and get ... what they used to call the malldow off the trees. You could see it on trees – just like hair or like whiskers – grows down on the trees. You get off big handfuls of it, and they used to bring out that and glue it on and glue the moustache. That would be light grey, and some would be brown, and different colours according to the way it would turn with the sun, on the trees. [T Glovertown]

A Wesleyville informant associated this wearing of whiskers particularly with the activities of the mummers on Bonfire Night (November 5) in that area. At Winterton, strands of a black malldow were occasionally used, but black sheep's wool was the more usual trimming.

Masks were not only trimmed with fur and sheep's wool, but some were actually made from animal skins. At St. Anthony, where mummering is still very much alive, the mummers make masks from muskrat skins, cutting holes for eyes and mouth. Masks of skin and leather were also worn at Fortune Harbour.

A striking form of the mummers' face and head disguise, and one frequently reported from areas where skins were in use, was the adoption of animal heads and horns to complete the mummers' headdress. Sheep heads and goat heads were most commonly worn by mummers in Fortune Harbour, Salvage, Burnt Islands, Winterton, Old Perlican, and St. Joseph's. There are particularly good reports from Fortune Harbour.

Some of them had a ram's head skinned and used the head of the ram, the skin; put it over their face, horns and all on it. [T Fortune Harbour]

But they'd have horns you know. They used to use horns . . . skin a lamb or a ram or something. [They'd just put the horns on their heads?] Yes. They looked ugly-looking, just like Old Nick. [T Fortune Harbour]

An elderly woman also from Fortune Harbour recalled a costume used by mummers at Hallowe'en. The costume was black and the horns of the headdress were painted the same colour:

More of them would have black, all black tights, like, and all black; two big horns out of them. They'd get them off a ram, you know, a sheep; that would be a male sheep, and they'd have those great big horns out, some of them, you know, and they all out like this, some of them. Well, they'd get a set of these, and put on these, and they'd do them over, you know, paint them or something on there; make them black. [T]

Other skins with heads attached were also used. The use of moose heads is reported from Grand Falls and Portland Creek; at Conche a seal's head was used. More frequently the head of a bull, cow, or calf was used.

Well now, they'd have calf skin that would come down along their necks, just the whole thing ... and the horns would be sticking there, you know, stuffed with ... wire or something to keep them [in position]. They used to take a lot of time, a lot of pride in making them. [T Shallop Cove, French tradition]

Sometimes a mummer would put the dried head of the bull or cow over his own head and wrap himself in the hide.[4]

What must have been an impressive variant of the custom of wearing animal skins and heads was given in a taped interview:

Well, your Christmas times – we used to call 'em mummers, you know. Some people they rig up and they get the old uniforms, and right down – I was generally at Port Ann. ... I suppose 'twas Burnt Island then – they had this eagle. ... They caught [it] ... out on the island ... took it out the nest, you see, and they grew it up and finally they killed it in the Fall; something got wrong with it and they had to kill it. And they skinned it and made a costume out of it: uniform for mummering. Over the head, they had the white over the head, the head over the head, you know, and 'twas large enough to go right down over your body. I imagine them birds must be eight or ten feet long, and you wouldn't know if it was the Devil were there or something was coming, see. [T St. Joseph's]

The use of a bald eagle as a costume is the only account so far received (1965) of the use of the skin and feathers of a bird as a disguise.

With the last two masking disguises we are already dealing with the full-length costume of animal skins. This will be illustrated further in the second section of this account, but an interesting variant of this type was found at St. George's where a woman went mummering

... one night with a paper mask, and a hen's head tied onto her neck and the two claws down by her ears. The head of the hen was hanging down here [i.e., round the neck], and the two claws were hanging from her ears. ... That's only about ten years ago. [T]

Mummers frequently concealed the shape of the head by hats and caps of all kinds, but especially large old-fashioned headgear, such as women's large hats with feathers, or high beaver hats.[5] The mummers would sometimes decorate their headwear elaborately.

4 / Descriptions of such animal figures as the "Christmas bull," the hobby horse, and the "Derby Ram" are not included here. Also omitted are the costumes used with such Christmas customs as "Hunting the Wren," "Shoeing the Horse," and so on. Our many reports on these are receiving separate study.

5 / Reports from later fieldwork indicate that in a few areas the cut-off sleeve

I've seen some of them getting around in a great big crowned hat...
and they'd painted it... different dabs of crayon, you know, on it, coloured
crayon around it and so on. They'd have their hats decorated, of course. Well
they'd probably put the wing of a bird or something or other like that, and
probably the feathers of a bird, and they might have them decorated with
... any such thing as rabbit skins or anything like that, you know, whatever
they could come across. [T Salvage]

A report, unusual for the present day, is a Bay Bulls description of
the model of a ship used as a hat decoration. (Cf., however, the older
printed descriptions in chapter x.)

It will be observed that the wearing of such high headgear not only
conceals the shape of the head, but effectively enhances the costume
disguise by increasing the person's height.

2 Costume

Since the disguise of his identity is one of the mummer's chief aims,
elaborate preparations are often made long beforehand. Mummers
dress in any costume which will effectively conceal their identities and
many choose unusual and fantastic garb. Sometimes there is a deliberate
striving for humorous effect, but often the costume is part of an
elaborate disguise which makes the wearer appear grotesque or
frightening.

Since a person can be most easily identified by his facial features,
the mask may perhaps be regarded as the most essential element of
disguise. Once the face is obscured, however, attention will be concentrated
on the disguising of other individual traits by which people
are usually recognized. These are treated elsewhere in this book, and
include both voice disguise and the disguise of habitual gestures and
gait. In this section we shall describe how mummers deliberately
distort their normal physical appearance by the use of costumes and
'rig-outs.'

Since an individual's normal weekday or Sunday clothing will easily
identify him, mummers rarely wear their habitual clothing; they may,
of course, intentionally borrow some items of the ordinary dress of
other members of the community. "You must be so-and-so; I knows
them boots, sure." Turning one's normal clothes inside out was a ready

---

of an old oilskin jacket is pulled down on the head like a hat, with the tapering
cuff on top. In Change Islands, Notre Dame Bay, it was the custom for mummers
to make tall hats out of cardboard and decorate these with tinsel and ribbons.

means of disguise when other costumes were not available, or when a person away from his home community suddenly decided to go mummering and had no time to prepare a more elaborate disguise.

There is great individual variation in the creation of costumes. Old-fashioned clothes, such as those left by grandparents unused in attic trunks for many years, provided one of the most common types of disguise.

And they'll dress up ... in old costumes; that's what they generally go for ... or what they try to get. Most mummers these days ... go back and get something very, very old. For instance I saw a mummer a few years ago with a black, beaded dress on that was over a hundred years old, one of the long black dresses, and by the way they weren't short to their knees then. ... this dress was dragging on the floor. So that's what they generally do in those little settlements here now.... they'll get something ... as much out of vogue as possible. [T Eastport]

Now he had a wonderful lot of clothes, all kinds of it: long-tailed coats and old dressed hats and everything. And they used to go down there; bring a bale-full up the gardens. Everybody could go there and dress then. All kinds of clothes there. [T Nipper's Harbour]

Costumes might be adapted, or even made especially for the occasion. In a few cases, including one report from Old Perlican, new clothes that the neighbourhood has not yet seen, particularly fine silk dresses, were used.

In many of the communities covered by the survey we have reports of deliberate attempts not only to dress in finery but also to spend a considerable amount of time and care in trimming costumes with ribbon and braid:

New Year's Night you'd be dressed up like the Queen of England, with ribbons of all descriptions, and white shirt, and striped pants and fancy shoes.... [T Conche]

... you'd make fancy clothes, you know, if you could.... braid; used to braid up your pants, see. [T Badger's Quay]

They'd wear a nice decent suit of underwear or something, and pants and coat or some different kinds outside, you know, trimmed up and all ... and even their shoes and everything, boots, like that, they'd have a different kind of boots from what they used to wear every other time, all rigged up. [T Fortune Harbour]

Although the wearing of old-fashioned clothes, finery, and other people's clothing, are frequent modes of dress, mummers in a number of areas also dressed in old clothes, patched garments, or rags which flapped loosely about them.

Several informants, asked about the costumes worn by mummers, stressed that they represented extremes from everyday wear by a reply such as: "Sometimes you'd dress in fine clothes, sometimes you'd dress in rags, you know. Whatever there was around."

I used to dress up myself and go out. Sometimes I'd have an old patched dress, patches sewed on, you know, old patches, and dressed up like that. [T Coachman's Cove]

They have the mumming suit on, see; so much of it would be plain and rags and one thing and the other. They dresses up with all the rags, you know; some of their clothes were torn and all this kind of stuff, you know. . . . [T Salvage]

Oh most of them dressed up in rags, so you wouldn't know their clothes, you know. If they were dressed in their own clothes, you know, you'd know them by their clothes. But they dressed up in rags, and they'd turn them wrong side out, see, so you wouldn't know them. [T St. George's]

The more radical disguising of a person's shape could be achieved by the wearing of capes, dressing-gowns, or other loose-fitting garments; or, more frequently, by draping sheets, blankets, or quilts over the shoulders. A number of informants emphasized the fact that such disguises were often chosen so as to make the wearer appear as grotesque as possible. The effect was usually amusing but sometimes frightening. The change of shape was frequently achieved by stuffing pillows, cushions, or sometimes even hay, beneath the costume. If pillows were put under clothing on the mummers' backs, for example, this both disguised their shapes and gave them the appearance of hunchbacks.

Well, the ordinary costume would be oversize clothes that were stuffed with pillows and things to make you look as if you had humps on your back or a big stomach or something or another like that. And usually the whole thing would be covered over with a blanket of some sort, and maybe something all in rags. . . . yes, but underneath there would be those stuffings, you see. You'd be really stuffed out of shape and hardly able to get along, some people would. [T Sop's Island]

They'd have everything, they'd even go to the clothes lines and take the men's one-piece [underwear], you know, and get into them. Get a cushion somewhere and put it up here, a big lump on their back, into those tight underwear, and maybe another one on their chest or somewhere else. [T Fortune Harbour]

Details of this custom were collected from Port Blandford, Winterton, New Perlican, and Green's Harbour.

... the menkind mostly are dressed and ... full up the back with a big hump, like a camel, and something out here too [indicating stomach]. [T Fortune Harbour]

They'd dress up every shape. ... They'd have perhaps a big pillow like that up on top of their back here; make out they was round shoulders, or a hump on their back. [T Glovertown]

The hunchback effect could also be obtained by wearing or carrying something outside of the clothing on the back. The carrying of a 'brin bag' or a knapsack is reported from Port Blandford.

The brin bag is large and bulky and would be held over the shoulder. It was not usually removed even when the mummer came inside the house. Both the bag and the knapsack would serve the dual purpose of concealing the shape of the wearer and of frightening the children. Children were told that the mummer would put them in the bag or knapsack and carry them away if they did not behave themselves.

The mummers often made up stories that they had travelled a long way by sea from outside Newfoundland – "from Hottawa," or "from the North Pole," for example, or that they had been shipwrecked. On the Northern Peninsula janneys usually say that they have "come from Harbour Le Cou," a comparatively distant settlement on the southwest coast. They emphasize the distance they have travelled, or their imaginary privations, to bring out their need of food and drink, and thus invite the hospitality of the host.

It is not surprising that shipwreck figures so often in these imaginary voyages since fisherman's oilskins are frequently used as mummers' disguises. From among the oilskins which are usually left hanging in the (fishing) 'stage,' mummers would borrow old and well-used oilskins belonging to other people, preferably choosing parts of different sets. Since oilskins, even when well-used, are stiff and bulky, they effectively conceal the shape and disguise the bodily movements of the wearer.

Sometimes long sea-boots of rubber or leather were worn. Since boots can be easily recognized, someone else's boots would be borrowed or sometimes even one boot from two different people. At Winterton the wearing of an unusual pair of boots by a mummer is widely remembered with great amusement:

> He made a pair of boots and he called 'em 'come-aheads-and-go-astarns.' They were made two ways, see. A pair, and another old pair of boots nailed to the back of them, see, and you couldn't tell which way he's going by his tracks, because they were going ahead and going behind, you see. . . . that's why they call 'em 'come-aheads-and-go-astarns,' you see. [T]

At Shallop Cove, Bay St. George, boots of a type called 'shanks' were often worn by the mummers. Caribou shanks were cut off and skinned, and the skin was dried and dressed before being fitted to the foot and leg of the wearer.

Sometimes they disguised their shapes in even more unusual ways.

> . . . they used to work theirself from all shapes. They have a couple of pillows up their back and another one on their stomach, all round, and some more get down in the flour-barrel: take the head out and bottom out of it and walking around [in] a flour-barrel. Cut the holes and put the two arms out through, wearing a flour-barrel. Maybe some fellows would get those hoops . . . you call them water-hoops, and put un into a large sack, we used to call it, what you call a hay-bag, we'll say, for bringing hay in out of the field. And they put that hoop in, they have to stick un on their edge to get in the doors, but when they get in the house they'd be all round. . . . You never know his shape then, that way. [T Winterton]

This type of disguise is reported too from Sop's Island and also in these two accounts:

> . . . they dressed up like that lots of times, you know, dressed up in a barrel and with brin clothes on, dress made out of bags; yes, lots of times. [T Coachman's Cove]

> Yes, they've done that at home time after time. . . . barrels over their heads. Yes, they have it over and have little holes cut through, see, for their face and eyes to come out. . . . Big enough one to go down: a flour-barrel; and then they'd have an old shirt or pants on or something, you know, besides. [T Nipper's Harbour]

According to a woman, also from Nipper's Harbour, dresses were made from brin bags, with hoops underneath to change the shape of the wearer.

Still another means of disguising the shape of the body was by the use of animal skins, particularly bulky ones. Frequently, as mentioned in part one of this account, the skins used were attached to the dried or skinned head of the animal, providing both a mask and enveloping cape.

> Oh yes, they had sheepskins; they'd have everything on, you know, wear everything they get.... They put their arms through where the legs was cut off, see, where the legs come out, see, you know; it had a hole through there and the neck part will be hanging down.... And the head of the sheep where he was skinned out, see, you haul over your head, see, and the arms through the fleece.... the arms come out where the legs came out. [T Salvage]

A sheepskin costume is also described in this account from a fifty-seven-year-old man at Winterton:

> I was dressed out once in a sheep's fleece, yeah, had a sheep's fleece on, but that's all I had. I never act as a sheep [nor] nothing like of that. I dressed up in a sheepskin. I had it wrapped around me, that's all. I never had the head on, and the tail was down on the back... and I had all except the head around me. All the legs was on, as well. [T]

The same informant also gave us our first report of mummers taking live animals with them on their rounds: in his community, Winterton, they used to take goats with them and milk them in the houses they visited. An informant from Change Islands also remembers a goat being taken along by the group when he went mummering there as a boy about forty years ago. Goatskins were used frequently at St. Joseph's (Placentia Bay), and at Winterton; deerskins [presumably caribou skins] and sealskins were used at Conche; dressing up in bearskins is reported from one community – Avondale.

A unique imitation of the animal skin costume may perhaps be mentioned at this point. An Englishman who lived at Winterton for many years is still remembered for the singular costume he wore, described in a tape recording as follows:

> He dressed up in a ... cat's rig. He was a heavy man ... and that man put on a cat's rig and he was dressed [as] a proper cat and he [was] bawling like a cat when he'd come in 'cross the house. And people used to ask, 'What have you got there?' 'Oh, it's just a cat.' Some fellow'd say, 'Is she any good for mice?' 'Yes, she's able to catch mice where there's no mice to.' That was a good thing, wasn't it? He'd come in, he'd jump up on a chair like of that, and he'd turn round just the same as a cat and put his paws on the chair.

How ever he used to make hisself so small! Put his two paws on the table, and he'd jump up on the table and turn around and purr and all of it. Proper cat, see. And he'd train – he must have been trained for it, otherwise he'd never have done it. Had his costume out of the cat's cloth, we'll say, and pinned up his ears, took his ears and tied 'em together and put whiskers on him and all of it, [with] a long tail on un.... That's the kind of rigs they used to wear. There's none of that today, though. [T]

Mummers did not, apparently, dress to impersonate other individuals. Certain distinct types do, however, recur. Dressing up as a ghost, completely in white, was frequently reported in the replies to the questionnaires. A long white sheet draped over the head and body was effective. A variant was the wearing of long white underwear as an external garb. In Joe Batts Arm a mummer wore a completely white outfit, including long white underwear, white hat, gloves, and boots, and a whitened face. It might be worth noting here that in a few areas mummers placed static white figures where they would be easily seen in order to scare passers-by.

Costumes representing witches, goblins, and skeletons are usually reported in the questionnaire replies by younger informants and may represent a more modern development. A student from Wesleyville mentions that the mummers there dressed as witches and goblins at Hallowe'en and on Bonfire Night. The questionnaire replies also include a few references to skeletons.

Other specific types are described by an eighty-one-year-old man at Catalina:

Mummers were really something when I was a boy. If you wasn't afraid of them, you wasn't afraid of nothing when you was four or five. They used to dress up fierce like Eskimaws and Heathens, and bawl and carry on with a lot of crazy stunts. When we watched them comin' down past the cemetery we could have swored it was the Second Coming. I can still hear 'em moaning and roaring. [T]

There are a few reports of specific types not necessarily used to frighten. A mummer dressed as a doctor carrying a doctor's bag is mentioned by an informant from Fortune Harbour:

... they'd be a crowd, you know, and they'd have one for a doctor, see. ... and they'd have a sick fellow, you know, and he'd be calling the doctor and he'd be, you know, giving un medicine and pills. [T]

Since a fragment of a mummers' play text has been recorded in this community there is some possibility that the doctor figure recalled was a character from the play.

Mummers at Exploits, in Notre Dame Bay, sometimes dressed as doctors, nurses, and pirates. At Fortune Harbour, besides one flower-girl costume, there is a more detailed description of a nurse:

And they'd make nurse's [costume] . . . they'd have the nurse, and a child in her arms and the bottle and all, and little aprons on, you know. They'd make all those outfits themselves. [T Fortune Harbour]

From Coachman's Cove we have a description of both a scrubwoman and a doctor.

Sometimes they'd come in with an old mop and a bucket . . . make out, you know, that they were going scrubbing, and sometimes they'd come in as a doctor, with a suitcase and take out all the things, all the bottles and, you know, make out they were a doctor. They'd have everything, everything that was going. [T]

From Nipper's Harbour comes the only report of a mummer disguised as a shepherd:

He was dressed up, you know, and he was like an old shepherd. Well I nearly died. . . . He was like one of those old shepherds: you used to see them. . . . years and years gone by, and he certainly looked cute that night going off. Oh yes, he was dressed right up with the old stick and everything, you know, the crooked stick. They'd rig right up, whatever kind of a shape they want to get in. [T]

More modern costumes reported alongside the older disguises include service uniforms, ice-hockey clothing (presumably with padded shoulders and knee pants), and even the woman's cape and fur hat of a typical town dweller. All of these would be unusual in a small settlement.

I've been mummering myself. Oh, dress up in everything. Old women's dresses, you know, an old pair of knitted drawers on. In them days, you see, in the First World War . . . there were some fellows in the Navy and Army from here, you see. Well the girls, when they came, the girls would get their suits and put [them] on, you know; some women wore navy clothes and that's the way we used to have it. [T A man from Baine Harbour]

A friend and I dressed. . . . I dressed in a hockey suit and she dressed up in . . . just an ordinary fit-out with a cape over her shoulder. I remember we went into people's houses and everybody would ask her where she bought her furs, and things like that, and she had a sort of a pussy-cat thing [mask] on her head, or an owl. We used to go into the houses and somebody said to her I remember in one house, 'What is this you got here? A horned owl or a pussycat?' And everybody wondered what hockey league I belonged to, and all that sort of thing. They tried to guess who we were and of course they didn't. Everybody would want us to stay and have tea just to see who we were. We really had a lot of fun over it. [T Two young women from Eastport]

Most of the costumes described so far have been of individuals who come as an unrelated group. Group disguise, where the costumes are related, seem less common. We have descriptions from four areas (Fortune Harbour, Port Blandford, Coachman's Cove, and Avondale) of mummers being dressed as bride and groom. The Avondale group describes a whole wedding party.

the men. . . . have big things sticking out of their ears, you know. . . . a suit like that. . . . was something like a clown – [only] a bit different. Anyway they used to have a black suit and they'd have a big long tail out of it, you know . . . dragging on the ground, and the women used to have somebody to keep up their dress, you know, the great big old black dress. You'd have all colours: red, white and blue, and roses hanging off you. The bride and groom had roses all down on and all colours of paper tied around, and a hat . . . all furnished up, you know; done up grand with ribbons . . . and walking-canes. And some [would] be smoking the pipe, and then they'd be – the old man and the old woman'ed be smoking the pipe, and cutting the baccy up with the knife and – yes, act the whole wedding out. Dance and get in and have the wedding, you know – we're married 'fore we go, see. That's the way we used to plan it, and the bride's mother and the bride's girl'ed be dressed different, see, and we'd go in the house and ask 'em could we have a dance for the wedding. [T]

We have reserved for separate treatment the costumes of the mummers' plays, which are, of course, most related to the group disguise just given. The play costumes are set apart from those of the ordinary house-visit not merely because of their elaboration and ingenuity but also because they are connected with the specific roles of the individual characters. We should observe again that the normal house-visit costume is rarely specialized.

In treating the varieties of masks and costumes worn, this paper tends to emphasize the odd and unusual since for the informants these are the most memorable. Most people seem surprised when asked about the ordinary disguises and suggest there is nothing especially remarkable about them. If questioned further, they give the clear impression that most costumes are comparatively simple, just odd combinations of ordinary clothing, or ordinary clothing worn in extraordinary ways.

The central aim of the disguises of Newfoundland mummers is to conceal their identity by whatever means are at hand. The documentation in this paper reinforces the general anthropological points about role-changing treated by other contributors to this volume.

Mummers in Newfoundland History: A Survey of the Printed Record

BY G. M. STORY

A historical account of mumming in Newfoundland can begin with Sir Humphrey Gilbert and his celebrated voyage in 1583 because the mummers, when they emerge in the Island, continued some of the customs familiar in the west of England communities from which, like Gilbert and his crew, the majority of the early settlers derived.[1] Appropriately, too, Gilbert, when he set sail from Plymouth with his five ships, took with him "Morris dancers, Hobby horses, and Maylike conceits."[2] He intended them partly for the "allurement of the Savages," but also "for solace of our people."

Possibly the entertainments he had in mind were similar to those condemned by the contemporary Puritan divine, Stubbes, who, in *The Anatomie of Abuse* (1585), wrote angrily about the heathenish Christmas, May Day, and Midsummer Day rites of the people of rural England. Stubbes describes how it was the custom to select a Lord of Misrule who would march with his followers in procession, "their handkerchefs swinging about their heds like madmen, their hobbie horses and other monsters skirmishing amongst the route."[3]

---

1 / I have two particularly heavy debts to acknowledge: the first is to the Gosling Memorial Library in St. John's whose staff, working in cramped quarters, courteously assisted me in consulting newspaper and periodical files; the second is to Herbert Halpert who found for me much material that I had overlooked. I have no doubt that further reading, especially of local newspapers, will reveal additional references and descriptions.

2 / "The Voyage of Sir Humphrey Gilbert," (Haie's *Report*), in Richard Hakluyt, *Voyages & Documents*, ed. J. Hampden (1958), p. 250.

3 / *The Anatomie of Abuse*, 3rd ed., quoted by Katherine M. Briggs, "The Folds of Folklore," *Shakespeare in His Own Age: Shakespeare Survey 17*, ed. A. Nicoll (1964), pp. 178–79.

The effect of Gilbert's entertainments on the English, Spanish, and Portuguese fishermen in St. John's is not recorded; and after a brief stay, during which he claimed the land for the English Crown, he sailed to his death by drowning on the return voyage to England, a transitory yet not insignificant figure in the Island's history. He founded no permanent settlement and his departure left Newfoundland as it had been for a century before he arrived: a summer fishing station for the maritime nations of Europe. Yet Gilbert's voyage was (if Ireland be excepted) Britain's first overseas colonial effort, and it had a sequel: domination of Newfoundland waters by British naval power, and thereafter the establishment of organized plantations.

Elsewhere in this volume (chapter II) I have sketched the rise of the English settlements on the Island and pointed out the difficulty of reconstructing, in any kind of significant detail, life in the early communities. It is not to be expected, therefore, that the institution of Christmas mumming should be documented in the earliest Newfoundland records, least of all in Gilbert's era when the Island was without permanent settlers. Nor do the seventeenth-century sources provide any evidence relevant to this essay. Yet some seasonal customs there must have been, and in the eighteenth century we begin to find descriptions of a few practices even in remote places. Thus, in 1770 George Cartwright, an adventurous Englishman in charge of a trading and fishing station on the coast of Labrador, recorded the proceedings of his men on December 24:

At sun-set the people ushered in Christmas, according to the Newfoundland custom. In the first place, they built up a prodigious large fire in their house; all hands then assembled before the door, and one of them fired a gun, loaded with powder; afterwards each of them drank a dram of rum; concluding the ceremony with three cheers. These formalities being performed with great solemnity, they retired into their house, got drunk as fast as they could, and spent the whole night in drinking, quarreling, and fighting.... This is an intolerable custom; but as it has prevailed from time immemorial, it must be submitted to.[4]

Cartwright's irritation, it should be noted, was caused partly by his fear that the traditional burning of the Yule log (or 'back-junk' as it

---

4 / *Journal of Transactions and Events ... on the Coast of Labrador* (1792), I, 74. A century later, another visitor to Labrador noted the special importance of Christmas visits and celebrations to the isolated inhabitants of the coast: W. A. Stearns, *Labrador* (1888), p. 160.

was also called) would set fire to his premises, and partly, as he disclosed on another similar occasion, because the rum and brandy for the two day saturnalia were provided at his expense. The universality of the custom was also noted a little later by the Rev. L. A. Anspach.[5]

Anspach had come to Newfoundland towards the end of the eighteenth century to take charge of a new grammar school which had been established in St. John's.[6] In 1802 he was appointed by the Society for the Propagation of the Gospel to supervise the Anglican Mission of Conception Bay, with headquarters at Harbour Grace. He set up schools at Harbour Grace, Bay Roberts, and Brigus, and eventually became a Justice of the Peace and a Judge of the Court of Civil Judicature of Newfoundland; he left the Island in 1812. His history of the country, which appeared in 1819, was therefore written from considerable firsthand knowledge of some of the east coast communities. It is this book which contains the earliest record that has so far come to light of Christmas mumming in Newfoundland. The description is very brief. "Men and women," Anspach writes, "exchange clothes with each other, and go from house to house singing and dancing, on which occasion Christmas-boxes are expected, and generally granted previous to the performance, in order to get rid of them."[7] The "Christmas-boxes" he describes as "presents, not in coin, for this is not in common use there, but in eatables, from a turkey or a quarter of veal or mutton, or a piece of beef just killed for the occasion, down to a nicely smoked salmon."[8]

Commenting on the custom Anspach raises the question of the antiquity and the early distribution of the practice of Christmas disguising in Newfoundland. "The Author must," he went on, "in justice to the *native* inhabitants of Conception-Bay, observe, that frequent attempts have been made to introduce this practice among them, but they have been generally resisted and publicly reprobated.

---

5 / *A History of the Island of Newfoundland* (1819), p. 475: "The ancient British custom of the *Yule*, or Christmas log or block, is universally observed by the inhabitants of Newfoundland. On Christmas-eve, at sun-set, an immense block, provided on purpose from the adjoining woods, is laid across on the back of the fire-place, to be left there till it is entirely consumed: the ceremony of lighting it is announced by the firing of muskets or seal guns before the door of each dwelling house. This, among them, is the prelude to a season of joy and merriment."

6 / The biographical notes are from H. M. Mosdell's *When Was That? A Chronological Dictionary of Important Events in Newfoundland* (1923), p. 2.

7 / Anspach, *History*, p. 477.

8 / *Ibid.*, 476.

If the character of the natives of Newfoundland, in general, agrees with that of those of Conception-Bay, which he had greater opportunities to appreciate during a residence of upwards of ten years among them, no where can a race be found more remarkable for indefatigable industry, for contempt of danger, for steadiness of temper and of conduct, sincerity and constancy of attachment, and a strong sense of religious duty."[9]

The problem is twofold: to determine to what extent Anspach's desire (natural, perhaps, in a man who belonged to the Anglican "Establishment") to present Newfoundland to English readers as an eminently respectable and orderly society led him to minimize the prevalence of Christmas mumming and the period of its introduction to Conception Bay; and to determine also whether his half-confessed unfamiliarity with more distant settlements makes his generalization reliable.

These problems can be raised, but not, perhaps, answered. D. W. Prowse, however, at the end of a note on outport festivities, recorded the following tradition which relates to the era before 1820:

> From Mr. Daniel Ryan, of King's Cove [Bonavista Bay], and from other sources of information, it appears that sharemen were always clear of service by 20th September; after that there was dancing, drinking, and card-playing every night from house to house in the out-ports, often ending in a fight; when the Hibernian element was present, generally a faction fight. . . . There was always a carnival of dancing, mumming, and, of course, drinking, from Christmas to Twelfth day.[10]

But whenever the custom was introduced to the Island, by the fourth decade of the nineteenth century descriptions of unusual fullness and interest begin to be recorded, especially accounts of the practices of the mummers in St. John's.

The first of these detailed references to Christmas mumming in the capital occurs in one of the most interesting books written by a visitor to the Island. J. B. Jukes, a Cambridge geologist, was retained by the Legislature in 1839 and 1840 to conduct a survey of mineral resources. He was much struck by the custom of observing a general holiday during the latter part of December and all of January. It was an interregnum between the conclusion of the cod fishery and the start of preparations for the seal hunt. Merchants closed their books and

9 / *Ibid.*, 477–78.
10 / *History of Newfoundland* (1895), p. 451, n.

the upper classes amused themselves with a general series of dinner parties, dances, and amateur theatricals. Jukes continues:

The lower orders ceased work; and, during Christmas, they amused themselves by what seemed the relics of an old English custom, which, I believe, was imported from the West of England, where it still lingers. Men, dressed in all kinds of fantastic disguises, and some in women's clothes, with gaudy colours and painted faces, and generally armed with a bladder full of pebbles tied to a kind of whip, paraded the streets, playing practical jokes on each other and on the passers by, performing rude dances, and soliciting money or grog. They called themselves Fools and Mummers.[11]

An even more detailed account of these Christmastide observances, including the earliest reference so far found to the mummers' play, was given by Sir Richard Bonnycastle, who visited Newfoundland a year or two later than Jukes:

There was, and still is a sort of saturnalia amongst the lower classes, in St. John's particularly, which lasts three days, commencing at Christmas, with boys [i.e., young men] only.

The mummers prepare, before the New Year, dresses of all possible shapes and hues, most of which are something like those of harlequin and the clown in pantomimes, but the general colour is white, with sundry bedaubments of tinsel and paint. A huge paper cocked hat is one favourite headpiece, and everyone, among the gentlemen, excepting the captain or leader, and his two or three assistants, is masked. The ladies are represented by young fishermen, who are painted, but not masked. Some of the masks are very grotesque, and the fools or clowns are furnished with thongs, and bladders, with which they belabour the exterior mob. Much ingenuity is observable in the style of the cocked hats, which are surmounted with all sorts of things, feathers in profusion, paper models of ships, etc.

They go to the Government House first, and then round to the inhabitants; and it has been customary to make the captain a present of money for a ball, which is given at the end of the carnival, if it may be so styled.

They perform, at those houses which admit them, a sort of play, in which the unmasked characters only take a part, and which is very long and tiresome after once hearing. It is a dialogue between the captain and a sailor, and commences with Alexander the Great, and continues down to Nelson and Wellington. They are both armed with swords, and a mock fight goes on all the while, till one is supposed to be slain, when the doctor is called in to bring him to life again.[12]

11 / *Excursions in Newfoundland* (1842), I, 220–21.
12 / *Newfoundland in 1842* (1842), II, 138–40.

A text of the Mummers' Play current in St. John's in the 1840s was taken down in 1885 from an elderly Newfoundlander living in Boston, Massachusetts, and printed in that year in the Christmas number of the St. John's *Evening Telegram*.[13] But whether it is the same version witnessed by Bonnycastle is doubtful: the "Alexander" in this version is not "the Great," but "the Czar of Russia," and neither Nelson nor Wellington appear in it, though its abbreviation by the transmitter may be responsible for their omission. It is apparently of Irish provenance. Possibly more than one version was current, for the performance in St. John's, about mid-century, of a text similar to some current in the Torbay-Dartmouth area of Devonshire was reported by an eyewitness in 1874.[14]

[13] / December 24, 1885; reprinted December 21, 1962. The text is printed in chapter XI.
[14] / R. J. King, *Sketches and Studies* (1874), p. 367, quoted by Miss Theo Brown, "The Mummer's Play in Devon and Newfoundland," *Folk-Lore*, LXIII (1952), 34.

Still a third fragment, unlocated, from this period is recorded in the *Christmas Review* (1892):

> I am Father Christmas,
>   Welcome or welcome not:
> I hope Old Father Christmas
>   Shall never be forgot.

The opening lines are from the old pantomime that in days of yore was played under the mummer's mask, while the Yule log was trailed through the most important highways of the fairly well-populated settlements scattered around the coasts of Newfoundland. The old Christmas pantomime, no doubt, owed its origin to the West Country pantomime of the sixteenth and seventeenth centuries. Imagination can throw each one of the younger amongst us back to the times when the characters of St. George, the Dragon, Santa Claus, St. Patrick, Dr. Foster, the host Piscator, Mephistopheles, and so on, were impersonated by Newfoundland fishermen. Fancy the sealing-gaff giving place to the crozier, the 'sculping-knife' to the sword, and the hundred and one other incongruities of this *olla podrida*. This was in the "forties," and Christmas was then a twelve days' Saturnalia; for all the crops of the sea had been gathered in, and the population, at that time almost all fishermen, abandoned themselves to pleasure. Here is part of the pantomimic rhyme that has floated down to us:

> I am the good St. George, from Albion's cliffs I come,
> That beauteous Isle of smiling fields – the fairest in Christendom.
> I fought the Hydra-headed Snake – led Dragon to the slaughter,
> I slew proud Egypt's lordly King, and wed his royal daughter.
> I am the brave St. Patrick, from Erin's fairy vales,
> Across the broad Atlantic I spread my whitening sails;
> I tune my harp to merry song; with open heart and hand
> I greet the sons of fog and ice in friendly Newfoundland.
> And I, the bold St. Andrew, of Scotia's heathered shore,
> Of money I have little; of brains I have a store.

The text of the extant St. John's play was preceded by a long and nostalgic introduction, written by William Whittle, recalling seasonal customs in the capital between 1840 and 1865. His account of the behaviour of the mummers provides a remarkable eyewitness record of the custom, by far the fullest that we have from Newfoundland documents of the nineteenth century, and therefore worth extensive quotation. Whittle's opening words suggest the important function the custom had in the hierarchic society of the period:

What made the intervening days between Christmas Eve and Twelfth Day more enjoyable, was the fact that the humble received no rude check from those to whom knowledge had opened her stores and wealth her coffers.

And all this had good effect, for nothing so harmonizes the differences between the poor and the rich as a reciprocal kindness of feeling on such occasions. The laboring classes in those days had enlarged privileges granted them, if not by positive law, at least by well-established custom. So folly was, as it were, "crowned and disorder had a license." The younger generation remember the "Fools." Their time of appearing out was from Christmas Day to Twelfth Day. . . .

I remember, some years ago, just about Christmas time, one of my brothers, who was quite a genius in that line, making a full-rigged brig, and giving it to a person who was to be a "Fool" on New Year's Day, to be used in the decoration of his cap, with the understanding that the brig was to be mine at the end of the day. Well, bright and early on New Year's morning I presented myself at the door of the "Fool," fully two hours before the hour came for him to dress. Finally out he came "dressed to kill," or "mash," as the saying goes now. His milk-white shirt sleeves were literally covered with ribbons, his pantaloons were of the heaviest broadcloth; and his cap [was] surmounted with my coveted prize – the full-rigged brig.

Down Lunekiln Hill[15] he went with the fleetness of a deer – and there was method in this, as he was anxious that few should know where he emerged from. And down I went after him. Up Playhouse Hill[16] he ran until his eye lit on someone, who, like himself, was swift afoot. Then

---

    The lake of crystal water, the brown and rugged hill,
    With memories of the Highland lands my Scottish soul doth fill.
    And I your host, old Piscator, cradled on Neptune's breast,
    Who at this blessed Christmas-tide doth seek the season's rest.
    From whatever clime, whatever land, your weary feet may roam,
    In Newfoundland, and with her sons, you'll always find a home.

15 / Probably what is now Lime Street.
16 / Now Theatre Hill.

commenced the chase, up lanes, "across lots," down lanes, in and out of the crowd, until the person chased sought shelter in some hallway.

Yet, his haven was not secure, for, with his shoulder against the door, the "Fool" was determined that it should yield. Then for I saw an impending danger to the spars of the brig: then came the cry and he obeys the command, the door is forced open, the victim secured, a few friendly taps on the legs, and they shake hands and walk out together. . . .

How well they kept from each other the knowledge of what each one was to wear! Odd costumes were discussed for weeks on street corners, at firesides, and at friendly parties, but each one kept his secret in regard to his own dress. And it is safe to say, no belle ever dressed for the "Irish ball"[17] that had as many come to criticise her taste or admire her appearance as a "fool" had.

"Munn" Carter, I remember, was always a conspicuous "fool," and one who could handle himself well, for Munn was a fellow whom every would-be boxer did not want to tackle. Davey Foley was always the owner of a stylish rig, while his friend, Masey Murphy, appeared, I think, as an "Owenshook."[18] The "Owenshook" was always a terror to encounter, for he rarely was merciful to any one who made him draw upon his wind, and woe to the man who disputed his right of giving a sound castigation for the trouble incurred.

I must hasten to speak of the most important of these sports and ceremonies – the "Mummers." Those who did not live previous to the "Fire"[19] never saw this grand celebration, when some two or three hundred of the most stalwart fellows that ever trod the deck of the ship, donned their silk dresses, their costly bonnets and rich laces, and, marshalled by their escorts, promenaded the streets calling upon the governor, the clergy and the mercantile fraternity. So important were these celebrations deemed by our ancestors, and such was the earnestness bestowed upon their preparation, that the most costly garments were loaned from the wardrobes of the "finest ladies in the land" for the purpose. . . . The "fools," escorting the ladies, were attired in blue trousers, with gold or red stripes on the sides, their white shirts completely covered with artificial flowers and ribbons, while from their sides, hung swords which were loaned them from the barracks for the occasion. Young men and boys, dressed as ladies, often extravagantly, were

---

17 / Probably the annual St. Patrick's Day dance, still so-called by the St. John's Irish.

18 / Joseph Wright's *English Dialect Dictionary* records from Ireland *oonshugh*, a foolish woman. The variant forms *oonchooks* and *eunchucks* also occur in the Newfoundland documents.

19 / The 'Great Fire' which destroyed St. John's in 1846.

thus escorted through the streets. One of the older customs was to draw a yule-log along with them. The procession invariably started from the Custom-house,[20] in recent years, and after marching through the principal streets, put up at the house of Bill Cody, who lived in the direction of the Riverhead bridge[21] for dinner, where the wassail-bowl was drawn upon and many a bumper drank to Father Christmas!

General confirmation of Whittle's description is provided by a number of shorter nineteenth-century accounts which also give further details of the appearance, behaviour, and route of the St. John's mummers. One of these, by a prominent local journalist, A. A. Parsons, includes a reference to the hobby horse vividly recalled from his childhood; the account also mentions the characteristic disguised speech of the mummers:

A weird figure bearing the head of a horse, nodding and gesticulating wildly to his companions, who were attired in all kinds of fantastic dress, paraded Water Street and halted at the foot of Market House Hill, where now stands the new Court House,[22] the oddly garbed figures meanwhile capering in amusing fashion around the hobby-horse – as I found the centre figure was called – chasing people and striking them with whips at the ends of some of which were attached inflated bladders. Father Christmas was easily recognizable whilst St. George of Merrie England indulged in rough horse-play with his companions. All the characters wore masks; several of them were clad in feminine apparel, but it was easy to determine by their ungainly antics and loud meaningless talk, that they were all of the opposite sex.[23]

A still later account, especially valuable for its description of the mummers' dress, is given by the Rev. G. J. Bond (d. 1930), a brother of a celebrated Newfoundland Prime Minister; it is either an eyewitness account, or derived from firsthand sources:

The Fools were one of the great Christmas institutions in the city, as persistently perennial as the season itself. For the time being they held right of way on Water Street, Middle Street,[24] and the streets uniting them.

20 / On the site of the present Sir Humphrey Gilbert Building on Water Street.
21 / Now the Long Bridge. Mr. E. B. Foran informs me that Cody lived at the junction of what is now Hamilton Street and Patrick Street, near "Cody's Well," a public resort.
22 / Between Water Street and Duckworth Street. It was opened in 1904.
23 / "Memoirs of Christmas – How the Great Festival Used to be Celebrated," *Holly Leaves* (1917), pp. 19–20.
24 / Duckworth Street.

In processions and in detachments they made things lively for other pedestrians, whom they banged over head and shoulder with inflated bladders. The fools wore masks or thick veils. Their heads were crowned with triangular hats made of cardboard and covered with wallpaper, or gigantic cocked hats adorned with a profusion of glittering metallic spangles and gaily coloured ribbons, and terminating at the top in two or three points from which issued plumes. Sometimes a small model ship took the place of points and plumes, and quite an amount of ingenuity and artistry were expended in designing and decorating this extraordinary headgear. They usually wore white starched shirts and no coats, the shirts being plentifully bedecked with ribbons. From before Christmas till Old Christmas Day, called Twelfth Day, they held high carnival.

Joined with these gaily bedecked Fools were a small number of veiled men in women's garments. They bore the appellation of Oonchooks, and were perhaps more persistent and punishing in their thrashing of people than their more spectacular companions. But they had their place in the procession, and were recognized as a quite legitimate part of the show. Oonchooks and fools were doubtless representatives and survivals of customs brought to this country by the early settlers.[25]

It is apparent from the descriptions of mumming so far cited that the custom, among the more sober classes, was regarded with some disapprobation (witness Anspach's comment that the *native* inhabitants of Conception Bay – by which he possibly means the old-established merchants and planters – gave Christmas-boxes to the house-visitors "in order to get rid of them"); obvious too that public mumming in St. John's was habitually boisterous. Some measure of violence was apparently associated frequently with the ritual – notice particularly the fearful joy with which the spectators regarded the 'oonchooks.' Nor were the Fools' 'swabs' merely decorative: William Whittle records that "many a time have I seen a 'Fool,' whom the mob tried to 'run,' pull off his cap, take the handle of his 'swab' and clean out some two or three hundred persons."[26] Turbulent behaviour of mummers was not, of course, peculiar to Newfoundland: Sir Edmund Chambers documents the violence which led to the statutory prohibition of masking in fourteenth-century London,[27] and other parallels are noted elsewhere in this volume. (chapter III) That disguises could be

25 / "Old Christmas Customs," *The Book of Newfoundland*, ed. J. R. Smallwood (1937), II, 259.
26 / "The 'Fools' and the 'Mummers,'" *Evening Telegram*, December 24, 1885.
27 / *The Mediaeval Stage* (1903), I, 393–94.

adopted for far from entertaining purposes is illustrated by the murderous attack on Henry Winton near Harbour Grace in 1835. (chapter II)

The social, economic, and religious conditions in the larger east coast communities in the nineteenth century made violent incidents explicable. Some St. John's mummers, at least, were Irish, and brought with them to Newfoundland the local feuds and rivalries of their native towns and districts. These they continued with stick and fist, though not usually with fatal results. The historian Pedley (d. 1872) gives a good description, in a very disapproving tone, of these street-corner brawls of the St. John's Irish factions.[28] Judge Prowse (1834–1914), recalling the St. John's he knew as a schoolboy, supplements Pedley's account, and explains the association of these highspirited encounters with the Christmastide celebrations of the mummers and fools:

> The faction fights went on for many years.... "Yallow-belly Corner," on the east side of Beck's Cove,[29] commemorates the spot where the wounded in the melee used to be washed in the little brook flowing into Beck's Cove. The Tipperary "clear airs," the Waterford "whey bellies," and the Cork "dadyeens" were arrayed against the "yallow belly" factions – the "Doones" or Kilkenny boys, and the Wexford "yallow bellies."[30] There were besides the "young colts" and a number of other names for the factions. They fought with one another "out of pure devilment and divarsion," as an old Irishman explained it to me. Besides these scrimmages there were plenty of fights when the "fools" or mummers came out from Christmas to Twelfth Day. These men were dressed up with high paper caps of a triangular form, ornamented with ribbons. They wore white shirts, sewn all over with ribbons and streamers. A good "rig-out" cost both time and money. The "swabs" were made of a bladder, covered with canvas or a switch, made sometimes of a cow's tail fastened to a stick. Some were dressed as women, with long garments, known as "eunchucks." They were all masked, and ran at passengers with an Indian yell, and spoke in a falsetto voice. Men were often beaten badly for old grievances by the fools. I remember, as a boy, how

---

28 / *History of Newfoundland* (1863), pp. 294–96.

29 / On Water Street. On the peculiar St. John's usage of *cove*, see William Kirwin, "Lines, Coves, and Squares in Newfoundland Names," *American Speech*, XL (1965), 163–70.

30 / So-called from the sashes or badges they used to wear in athletic games in Wexford: see P. K. Devine, *Ye Olde St. John's* (1936), p. 137. The Hon. Dr. J. M. McGrath recalls *yellow belly* used in a non-pejorative sense by the Irish in St. John's as late as the 1920s (oral communication).

proud I used to be to shake hands with a fool, and to know what "rigs" Noah Thomas or Mick Toole were going out in. Each company had one or more hobby-horses, with gaping jaws to snap at people. The fools had to be put down by Act of Parliament.[31]

The general cause of the banning of the mummers, to which Prowse refers in his last sentence, was a series of incidents which occurred in 1860 and 1861 in St. John's and certain large communities in Conception Bay. These incidents were of varying degrees of gravity. In December 1860 there was a street row between mummers, the fools, and the spectators: the latter were worsted in the clash and, on the order of a stipendiary magistrate, Mr. Justice Carter (d. 1871), posters were issued prohibiting the appearance of the maskers on the streets of St. John's.[32] The fracas does not appear to have been of a deeply serious nature; but as the values of the burgeoning middle class made themselves felt, the increasingly stuffy tone of the capital was no longer congenial to traditional festivities. This change was applauded by a correspondent writing to the press the day after the ban in St. John's was announced: "Every well disposed citizen must be gratified at the proclamation issued by the Police Magistrates to suppress 'mumming' with its disgusting attendants, – rioting, drunkenness, and profane swearing."[33]

Within a few days, a more serious incident at Bay Roberts, a Conception Bay community with some 2,400 inhabitants, led to the statutory banning of mumming throughout the colony. A Protestant named Isaac Mercer was murdered, supposedly by Roman Catholic mummers, and the incident was followed by riots. The disturbances spread to other Conception Bay towns and the widespread turbulence, exacerbated by denominational rivalry and a failure of the fishery, continued for some time. Influential voices were raised in the St. John's press demanding prompt measures to put down the disorders: the Anglican Bishop of Newfoundland, Edward Feild, wrote a strongly worded letter to the editor in which he used the St. John's Christmas disturbances and the murder of Isaac Mercer as evidence of the "generally disordered condition of the Colony."[34] An editorial in the

31 /*History of Newfoundland* (1895), p. 402.
32 / William Whittle, *Evening Telegram*, December 24, 1885; confirmed by *Notable Events in the History of Newfoundland* (1900), p. 234: "1860, December 21st. Posters first issued forbidding mummers (commonly called 'fools') in the city." Dr. E. R. Seary drew my attention to this second reference.
33 / "Mumming Suppressed," *Times* (St. John's), December 22, 1860.
34 / "Letter to the Editor," *Telegraph* (St. John's), February 9, 1861.

Newfoundlander,[35] replying to these and other strictures, argued in vain that "the death of the unfortunate man ... was but an accidental result of the sport of Christmas 'mumming,' and not of any deadly intent"; an aroused Legislative Assembly, on June 25, 1861, passed "An Act to make further Provision for the Prevention of Nuisances" (24 & 25 Vic., c. 3), chapter vii of which read as follows:

Any Person who shall be found, at any Season of the Year, in any Town or Settlement in this Colony, without a written Licence from a Magistrate, dressed as a Mummer, masked, or otherwise disguised, shall be deemed guilty of a Public Nuisance, and may be arrested by any Peace Officer, with or without a Warrant, and taken before any Justice of the Peace, in the District or Place where such Person may be found; and on conviction, in summary manner, before such Justice, be committed to Gaol for a period not exceeding Seven Days, unless he shall pay a fine not exceeding Twenty Shillings; such Licence to be numbered, and a corresponding Number worn by the Person so licensed, on a conspicuous part of his Dress.

The Act (which, incidentally, has never been repealed) was legally effective throughout the colony; but the extent to which it was enforced varied in proportion to distance from the capital and the availability of "Peace Officers." In St. John's, it put an end to Christmas mumming in its elaborate, public, processional form through the streets: William Whittle, writing in 1885, recalled its inglorious end when "some years after the mummers and fools had ceased to operate, one came out on the 'Cross'[36] on Christmas Day. He struck right and left, and finally ran into the arms of a policeman who locked him up."[37] But folk customs die hard, and in the form of the house-visit in disguise, mumming was still being practised by adults in the capital as late as the 1920s.[38]

Nor, despite the legal ban, was the custom less tenaciously maintained on the Avalon Peninsula outside St. John's, though again not in its most public form. In the social history of individual communities, the documentary sources record its continuing significance. From

35 / February 25, 1861.
36 / Rawlins' Cross.
37 / *Evening Telegram*, December 24. An editorial in the *Newfoundland Express*, December 29, 1863, noted the altered tone of the season in St. John's: "The unseemly practice of mumming having been put down by Legislative enactment, our streets have been quieter than we have ever seen them previously at Christmas."
38 / See, for example, "When Jennies Went Calling," *Evening Telegram*, December 24, 1956; *ibid*., December 24, 1964; and confirmed by several senior University colleagues.

Harbour Grace, for example, in the late nineteenth century comes the story of a doctor who organized a mummers' entertainment in the days when "mummers were in bad repute, as with masks on, they often waylaid innocent folks, and for a grudge would sometimes handle them very roughly."[39] In this instance, nothing more was involved than the capture of the local constable, who, locked in his own handcuffs, was delivered to a surprised magistrate.

Sometimes the tricks played by the mummers were very elaborate. An example is given in a story from "the old days," reported from a community not far from St. John's:

Uncle John Smith was a very crusty old gentleman who lived alone and who would not let the mummers into his house nor offer them any Christmas cheer.... One teenage "mummer" whom we shall call Peter Jones, decided that he would play a joke on the old man for his refusal to admit the mummers to his home.

Peter had an unusual costume designed for the mummers' parade. It consisted of the hide of a young bull which his family had killed just before Christmas. Peter decided that he would take the hide, head and horns and play the part of Satan. Then he would visit the old man. Then he would play his grim joke.

Uncle John's trusty flint-gun was hung as usual over the high fireplace. He kept it loaded and primed and ready for use at all times. Peter, indeed, everyone in the little settlement, knew this and always avoided the old man's house. So, on the morning of Boxing Day when Uncle John went for a walk, brazen Peter got into the old man's house and removed the leaden ball from the gun.

That night the mummers were out in force again and Peter was there dressed like the devil. He told his friends what he was going to do and they went close to the old man's house to watch. Peter entered the yard of the stern recluse and advanced up to the door. He hammered loud and long. Uncle John shouted from the inside, "Be off with you. You are not allowed to come into this house." Peter knocked again ... louder and longer. Again the old man told him to go away. "I have come for you, old man," shouted Peter; "Get ready to meet your end." There was footsteps inside as the hermit got out of bed and went for his gun. He hurried to the door and opened it. Peter had retreated a few yards out into the garden.

Uncle John could make out the satanic form dancing and calling him.

The old man raised his gun, took aim at the devilish form dancing in the

---

39 / *Daily News* (St. John's), December 20, 1956.

moonlight and pulled the trigger. But the dancing, singing figure kept calling, "Old John, I have come for you," and the old man fainted.

The other mummers rushed to the side of Uncle John. They carried him into his house where he revived after a few minutes. One of them told the nearly hysterical old man the joke Peter had played on him.

Instead of being angry, Uncle John invited the mummers to stay and have tea and buns and he laughed and danced with them. He never acted Scrooge again and until the day he died he and Peter Jones were the best of friends.[40]

At Brigus, Conception Bay, fifty miles by road from St. John's, mumming was still a well-established part of the twelve-day Christmas holiday, with adults participating, in the late nineteenth century. Captain Nicholas Smith, for example, records in his autobiography the return from the Labrador fishery in 1888 when "we moored the schooner in winter quarters and had a few holidays during Christmas enjoying ourselves with the boys mummering and dancing."[41]

Nevertheless, the disrepute into which adult mumming, especially when it involved public processions, fell during the 1860s, appears to have led to a transference of parts of the traditional custom to other forms of secular ceremonial. The activities of fishermen's fraternal societies, for example, began to play an important part in the Christmas holiday period. Thus, the Star of the Sea Society (founded by Roman Catholic fishermen in 1871), with headquarters in St. John's, held its imposing parade on New Year's Day. The (Protestant) Society of United Fishermen (founded in 1862, reconstituted and enlarged in 1872) soon had no fewer than forty-two lodges, and on January 1 in each settlement with members it too held its annual parade, a colourful affair with flags, sealing-gaffs, and emblems borne in procession, ending with a 'soiree' (supper and dance). Equally important was the Loyal Orange Society, introduced to Newfoundland in 1863. In the fishing communities, the height of the inshore fishery and the Labrador voyage coincided with the customary July 12 celebration of the Battle of the Boyne, and the ceremonial parade was (perhaps uniquely to

---

40 / "When Santa Called for Uncle John," told by Mr. L. E. F. English to Don Morris, *Evening Telegram*, December 24, 1956.

A St. John's resident describes with excellent detail his own participation in mumming "in a distant outport," c. 1860. *Christmas Greeting* (1893), pp. 17–20 (communication from D. G. Pitt).

41 / *Fifty-Two Years at the Labrador Fishery* (1936), p. 45.

Newfoundland) transferred to the Christmas period. On St. Stephen's Day (December 26) outport members used to march in procession.[42]

With a few exceptions, the remaining documentary references to, and descriptions of, adult Christmas mumming refer either to an indeterminate period (probably around the turn of the present century), or are the more recent recollections of living persons. Though most of the evidence refers to the custom as practised in the communities of the Avalon Peninsula, the documents occasionally record its occurrence elsewhere on the Island.

From Trinity, in Trinity Bay, for example, come two accounts. In one the voice and costumes used for disguise are listed: 'claw-hammer coats,' hats, bonnets, cloaks, ulsters and caps, kid gloves, fancy vests, beaver hats, pearl-gray spats and a high falsetto voice.[43] Another account records that the elaborate disguises were the subject of keen competition, with prizes for the best 'dress up'; and continues: "On one occasion . . . the old Constable of the place had occasion to seize one of the mummer gang of young men, to take him to jail for safe keeping. That noble virtue of *esprit de corps* took possession of the rest of the gang and they insisted that if one went to jail they would all go to jail." On their release next day, the mummers "dressed as they were in all kinds of inner and outer garments, in order to get home had to run the gauntlet through the swarm of delighted youngsters who pelted them with snowballs."[44] The same account also records that the different groups of Trinity mummers often had distinctive names, one group, for example, being known as "the Hurdy Gurdy mummers." A further piece of information, tantalizing to students of folk plays because it is so brief, records that it "was not uncommon for some to prepare a 'skit,' and perform it from house to house to the enjoyment of all."

From Port Union, also in Trinity Bay, comes an account of mumming, with a hint of a tradition of fear and violence, in the year of Newfoundland's Confederation with Canada:

42 / The fishermen's fraternal societies are described in the following: William F. Graham, "The Star of the Sea Society," *The Book of Newfoundland*, ed. J. R. Smallwood, pp. 196–97; C. T. James, "The Society of United Fishermen," *ibid.*, 192–95. There is a detailed history of the Orange Society in Newfoundland by Elinor Senior (Memorial University History thesis, 1960). Joshua Stansford's *Fifty Years of My Life* (1950), which records the author's life at Grates Cove, Conception Bay, between 1904 and 1950, has many references to the Christmas activities of the Protestant societies.

43 / "Mumming at Christmas," *Daily News*, December 28, 1955.

44 / "Mummering at Trinity," *Daily News*, January 3, 1955.

The mummers are out on their rounds again. They beat on our doors, tramp through our kitchens, sit in our rocking-chairs, giggling behind their masks; and altogether make so much commotion that old and sober folk are inclined to grumble at having their quiet evenings disturbed [by people who] disguise themselves in a couple of flour-sacks and an old night-gown. ... Quite recently in some parts of the country, there have been rumours of masked men lurking in dark corners to scare the passersby.[45]

In the same year (1949), the custom of 'janneying' was described in an unidentified, but probably northeast coast, community in terms very similar to those found in the accounts of the contemporary practice recounted elsewhere in this volume.[46] It is the same practice – the disguised house-visit by janneys – described from the northern coast in a document in the Vaughan Williams Library at Cecil Sharp House, London.[47]

The west coast, the last part of the Island to be settled, provides a quite early reference to Christmas mumming. At Sandy Point, Bay St. George, the Rev. Henry Lind recorded in his diary, on January 6, 1858: "I am sorry to find that the majority of the young people (& some of the married ones) are busy in dressing up to act as 'Mummers,' commonly & properly called 'Fools.' "[48]

From the south coast there are fewer references in the printed literature; but a recent short article by Mr. Harold Horwood, accompanied by photographs of the mummers at Burgeo, is among the more interesting of the newspaper accounts.[49] Such newspaper descriptions have, in recent years, reflected the gradual decline of adult mumming at Christmas in all but the more remote settlements, and the increasing restriction of the practice to children.

This is, perhaps, the place to mention a report which is unusually interesting, but which at the same time poses some perplexing problems. From "the isolated villages along the north shore of the Gulf of St. Lawrence, from Natashquan to Blanc Sablon, where Quebec cuts across the southern edge of Labrador," we have a very full account of

45 / "Mummering," *Fishermen's Advocate* (of Port Union), December 23, 1949.

46 / Elizabeth V. Melchen, " 'Janneying' in Newfoundland," *New York Folklore Quarterly*, VII (1951), 272–74. See also the article by Cassie Brown, "Some Old Christmas Customs in a Newfoundland Outport," *Daily News*, December 24, 1965.

47 / This item was drawn to my attention by Dr. E. C. Cawte.

48 / Manuscript Diary of Rev. Henry Lind, 1857–1864, Memorial University Library, Nfld., B, L 64. I owe this reference to Dr. J. F. Szwed.

49 / *Evening Telegram*, December 22, 1964. See also Farley Mowat, "Will Ye Let the Mummers In?," *Weekend Magazine*, XVI, no. 52 (1966), 6–9.

the Christmas house-visit by disguised mummers, with details which closely parallel the Newfoundland custom.[50] We must presume that the custom derives from one of three possible sources: from French or French-Canadian tradition; from the contiguous English-speaking settlements of Newfoundland Labrador, from some of which janneying has been reported in replies to questionnaires; or directly from the British Isles.

There are a number of accounts of the performance of the mummers' play in this century, and two of these (from Change Islands, Notre Dame Bay, and Salvage, Bonavista Bay) are printed in the following section of this volume, together with the complete texts of the plays themselves. Two fragments of the play from other parts of the Island have also appeared in print, both communicated by Miss H. Faith Mercer of St. John's.[51] The first is part of a speech by "Jack Tar," one of the characters in some versions of the folk play:

Sailor (sings)
>
> Here come I, Jack Tar
> With my knapsack on my back, sir.
>
> ....
>
> Now what think you of me, sir?
> To my whack fi-di-diddle fi-di-dee
> To my whack fi-di-diddle fi-di-dee
> To my whack fi-di-diddle die-dee.

The fragment was recorded in Twillingate, Notre Dame Bay, from an old woman who may have come originally from Herring Neck, a settlement on the eastern end of Twillingate Island. Miss Mercer reported that "A Christmas Masque" used to be performed at Herring Neck. She also contributed part of the Doctor's rigmarole in the play, a fragment handed down through three generations in Burgeo, on the south coast:

Doctor. I have here in my satchel a little bottle of hectum spectum of high generosity ... mixed up with a hen's tooth and a cat's feather [and guaranteed to cure]

> The itch, the stitch, the palsy and the gout,
> All pains within, all pains without;
> If the devil is in I'll root him out.

50 / Bruemmer, Fred., "The Mummers," *The Beaver: Magazine of the North* (Winnipeg), outfit 297 (Winter 1966), 24–25. I owe this reference to (Mrs.) Violetta M. Halpert.

51 / To Miss Theo Brown, "The Mummer's Play in Devon and Newfoundland," *Folk-Lore*, LXIII (1952), 34–35. Additional details were communicated by Miss Mercer in a letter to Herbert Halpert.

The play, described in general terms by Mr. M. F. Harrington in an essay published in 1957,[52] was once a common feature of Christmas mumming in many parts of the Island. Its imagined passing more than half a century ago was mourned by that indefatigable local historian, folklorist, and antiquarian, the late P. K. Devine:

> The utilitarian spirit of the age deals with those old customs and traditions with a ruthless hand. Many of the old customs that our forefathers of Newfoundland observed at Christmas, in the days of the open-fireplace, are looked on by their descendants with ridicule, if not with contempt. *Cui bono?* After a hard season's work at the fishery, the harmless sports and relaxation of the Christmas season made new men of them.... Phlegmatic and silent fishermen, who had not a word to say all the year round, now blossomed into Grand Knights of St. Patrick, St. Michael and St. George, Hector, Alexander, etc., and gave out their heroic speeches in verse as they went in fantastic mumming costume from one neighbour's house to another. At the village of Vocksinge,[53] the last of them passed away to his eternal reward a year ago. Alas! old age and hard work had shrivelled him up to unheroic proportions. But "poor old Tommy Holland" once stood on the floor on Christmas night, a veritable hero, as he recited:
>
> > "Here come I, Hector, the renowned Hector,
> > King Priam's only son."[54]

It is a charming passage; yet it was a premature elegy on the passing of a very striking part of the Christmas celebrations of the Newfoundland Christmas mummers. For the recent recovery of additional texts, and numerous fragments, of the mummers' play suggests that it must have been more widely diffused, and begun its retreat somewhat later, than is commonly supposed. Their discovery by fieldwork in 1964, 1965, and 1966 provides further evidence of how deeply imprinted in Newfoundland are the traditional practices documented in the historical accounts of Christmas mumming with which this essay has been concerned.

52 / "Newfoundland's Old-time Christmas," *The Atlantic Advocate*, XLVIII, no. 4 (December 1957), 22–23.
53 / Probably an aural error for Boxey, a community on the south coast (communication from W. J. Kirwin).
54 / *Christmas Bells*, no. 10 (1901), 4.

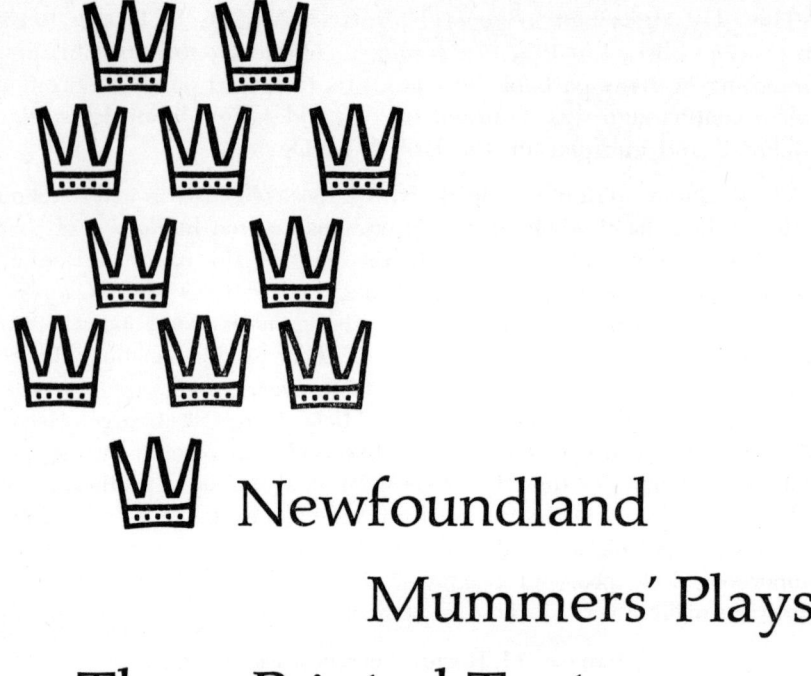

Newfoundland Mummers' Plays: Three Printed Texts

EDITED BY
HERBERT HALPERT AND
G. M. STORY

1 Introduction

The three Mummers' Play texts reprinted here appeared originally in St. John's newspapers, of Island circulation only, in 1885, 1949, and 1950.[1] Unknown to scholars outside Newfoundland, they are presented in this section both to make them available to students of folk drama and to complete the record of the various forms of Christmas mumming in Newfoundland.

All three texts – the St. John's Play, the Change Islands Play, and the Salvage Play – belong to the Hero-combat form; as yet we have found no Newfoundland texts or reports of either the Wooing Play or the Sword Dance Play. These three varieties of English folk plays are discussed in some detail in section 5 of chapter III. There too will be found a discussion of the quasi-dramatic action of the Hero-combat type; we merely repeat here that there is, normally, a presentation, a combat between at least one pair of heroic antagonists, a death followed by a revivification often humorously treated, a conclusion in which various characters not involved in the main action are often presented, and finally the taking up of a collection.

The enormous possibility for variation in the Hero-combat Play, even when, as with these texts, St. (or King) George is one of the constant figures, can be clearly seen. The action follows the same basic pattern, but there are wide variations in length, distribution of characters, and,

---

1 / We wish to repeat here acknowledgement of our debt to Mr. Leo Moakler for putting at our disposal newspaper clippings of both the Change Islands and Salvage texts which he originally edited for the *Newfoundlander*. We are indebted also to Mr. Alex Helm who commented on an earlier draft of this introduction in a private communication which he allows us to quote.

of course (as in all orally transmitted texts), curious similarities and differences in wording. Within this latter variation, however, the recurrence of common rhyme patterns will be observed – evidence of the importance of rhyme in assisting memory. All three plays are written in a strongly marked jog-trot metre, but again there is considerable variation within the plays, and the verse is frequently interrupted by prose passages. The plays are respectively 68, 101, and 130 lines in length. The brevity of the first (the St. John's Play) is apparently the result of shortening through deliberate omission by its nineteenth-century transmitter, William Whittle. Despite its brevity, however, several of its nine characters do not appear in the other two plays. The Change Islands Play has eleven characters, the Salvage Play has twelve, and they are not all the same.

In commenting briefly on each of the three versions, we draw particular attention to the occurrence of certain unusual features of these texts and discuss a few parallels with versions from Ireland, Great Britain, and the United States.[2]

In the St. John's Play, Father Christmas is the Presenter who calls for room, but makes no effort to introduce the characters, most of whom introduce themselves. St. Patrick fights and wounds St. George, who thereupon calls for a Doctor to come to his aid. The Doctor, without describing his usual travels and training, cures him with one of the familiar whimsical mixtures. St. George then engages in inconclusive combat with the Turkish Knight. The appearance at this point of Alexander, labelled by Whittle, "Czar of Russia," is a feature of some interest. He is a static figure who plays no part in the action; yet his bragging speech is of the kind one expects of one of the combatants. Though King Alexander, or Sir Alexander, figures in northern chap-books and in versions of the Scottish play of Galatians, the character of his speech in the Newfoundland text is completely different, and the figure is unique in the versions of the folk play available to us. Mr. Helm notes that the Czar of Russia appears in Wexford versions which we have not seen. Since our text refers only to "Alexander," an identification with Alexander the Great, conqueror of the ancient world, and also famous in mediaeval legend, is possible.

2 / The versions available to us in the Newfoundland Folklore and Language Archive are far from exhaustive. They include, however, virtually all the printed texts listed by E. K. Chambers, *The English Folk Play* (1933), pp. 236–44; the texts printed by the (English) Folk-Lore Society, as listed by Wilfrid Bonser, *A Bibliography of Folklore* (1961), see especially pp. 85–86; and nearly a hundred printed texts not listed in the above, as well as a few manuscript texts.

For here Alexander is juxtaposed with the Emperor of China, the Mogul Emperor of India, one of the Hanoverian line (possibly George I), and Louis XIV of France – warrior figures spread over two continents and many centuries.

We have been unable to identify the character Frederick Galloway. A musician who appears in the play, Bradley the fiddler, may very well have been a local St. John's performer. The character Valentine appears in a few Dorset, Hereford and Isle of Man texts as Prince or General Valentine; but in none of these is there any association as here with Orson, "the wild man of the wood." We suggest tentatively that Orson and Valentine may have been introduced from a chap-book, such as the eighteenth-century *The History of Valentine and Orson*.[3] Their appearance in the St. John's play is apparently unique. Dan Donnelly, "the wight of Dublin city," who "conquered nations with my mighty fist" is also, apparently, unique to this version. He is probably Dan Donnelly (1788–1820), the hero of the Irish street ballad "Donnelly and Cooper."[4] Born in Dublin, he defeated Cooper the Englishman in an eleven-round pugilistic encounter on the Curragh of Kildare in 1815. In the fight he broke his opponent's jawbone. With but few exceptions, St. Patrick is found in Irish versions; and the combination of St. Patrick and Dan Donnelly naturally suggests an Irish provenance for this text. Mr. Helm suggests to us that the omission by the Doctor of an account of his travels also points towards an Irish origin.

The Change Islands Play is opened by Roomer, a hypostatized request for performing space especially common in West Country and Irish versions, where he often appears merely as "Room." He introduces Father Christmas who should be the Presenter. Father Christmas, however, in a confusing speech mentions a figure who never appears: "old Johnny Jack, my wife and family on my back," a personage who, chiefly in British south and West Country versions, usually serves as the Collector at the end of the play. He concludes his speech by calling for King George. King George then describes

3 / See John Ashton, *Chap-Books of the Eighteenth Century* (1882), pp. 109–23.

4 / See Colm O Lochlainn, *Irish Street Ballads* (1939), pp. 52–53 for text and tune, and n. p. 221. For some other texts, see *Wehman's Irish Song Book*, no. 1 (1887), p. 120; Manus O'Connor, *Irish Com-All-Ye's* (1901), p. 27; Wehman Bros. *Six Hundred and Seventeen Irish Songs and Ballads* (n.d.), p. 38; Daniel O'Keefe, *The First Book of Irish Ballads* (1965), pp. 23–24. For a tune and one line, cf. George Petrie, *The Complete Collection of Irish Music*, ed. Charles Villiers Stanford (1905), p. 79. The ballad is not reported in any of the Newfoundland folksong collections.

himself in heroic terms, in a pattern repeated by most of the following characters, and calls for his successor.

The combatants, or potential combatants, are such well-known figures as King George, the King of Egypt, the Valiant Soldier ("Slasher is my name"), and the Turkish Knight. King George and the Turkish Knight strike one another down in turn, with King George emerging as the final victor. To revive his slain son, the Turkish Knight, Father Christmas calls for a Doctor. Again, as in our first text, the Doctor does not mention his travels; there is little by-play about the fee he is to charge, and only a brief description of his medical ability and his nostrum. After the cure is applied to the "crackbone of his heart," the fallen combatant revives. We are then given a parade of characters.

The first two who appear, Pickedy Wick and Beelzebub, are collectors. Beelzebub, of course, is found in many texts. Pickedy Wick, however, is apparently a unique collector-figure, though there may be distant echoes of the Paddy Whack in a Cheshire text, and the old figure of Pickle Herring, found in the (suspect) Revesby Play as well as in a Kentucky version. But these collector-figures, instead of ending the play, suddenly call on two additional characters. The first is Bold Hercules. We have been unable to locate a parallel to him in the play texts; nor are we able to trace the derivation of the concept of Hercules as a weather-controller. Once again, we suspect a chap-book, or perhaps a broadside ballad, as a source. The second figure, Jack Tar, is usually found only in northern plays, particularly the Pace Egg Play, where he is a very common figure in the Pace-egging song. We must reckon with the possibility that the English schoolmaster, Justinian M. Dowell, who introduced the play to Change Islands, may have been responsible for the intrusion of Jack Tar.[5] In this play, we have, finally, a musical conclusion in which the ensemble sings a nonsense song, apparently to the tune of the nineteenth-century minstrel song, "There's one more river to cross."

In our final text, the Salvage Play, Beelzebub enters first and introduces Father Christmas. Beelzebub is normally a collector-figure belonging at the end of the play. As in the Change Islands Play, however, Father Christmas, who we would expect to be the Presenter, merely presents the next character, Dim Dorthy; and thereafter each character introduces his successor. Dim Dorthy is presumably the male figure in female clothes who is Dame Dorothy in West Country

---

5 / At the same time it is worth noting that we have a fragmentary song by Jack Tar recorded on a neighbouring island (see chapter x).

and Kentucky texts. She calls on Sir Guy, presumably Guy of Warwick, famous in at least one chap-book[6] as the slayer of a dragon thirty feet in length, but in legend and ballad (as well as in another chap-book) the slayer of the gigantic Dun Cow, whose huge bones are reputed still to survive at Warwick.[7] This legend of the Dun Cow is known in at least three British counties. In Ireland there is a similar legend of a cow which gave an inexhaustible supply of milk.[8] While there are possible references to Sir Guy in four mummers' texts that we have seen, the reference to 'Duncow' is apparently unique to this Newfoundland version.

As in the St. John's Play, the Salvage Play has two fights. In the first of these, King George fights with, and slays, the Grand Turk; but immediately afterwards he calls for a Doctor to treat his dead brother-champion. The Doctor in this version has a somewhat fuller role than in the other texts, boasting about his skill, mentioning his travels, and finally, after elaborating on his nostrum, effecting the revivification. In the second fight, the Valiant Soldier fights with and wounds the Turkish Knight, apparently a double of the Grand Turk. But he spares the life of his antagonist, scornfully commanding him to return home with news of the champion "old England bears today."

Unexpectedly, Valiant Soldier then calls for Oliver Cromwell. Although Cromwell appears in a few English texts, he is more commonly found in the Irish versions, evidence of the imprint he left on the Irish consciousness. Cromwell in turn calls for the Captain of the Play and his Wife, normally associated with the beginnings of such plays. Again unexpectedly, the Captain summons a figure called the Wren, who promptly sings the standard St. Stephen's Day song, usually sung by the men or boys who carry the Wren in a "collecting procession." According to E. R. R. Green,[9] the Wren appears in two texts (neither of which we have seen), one from Co. Donegal, the other from Co.

6 / See Ashton, *Chap-Books of the Eighteenth Century*, p. 148.

7 / See C. Hardwick, *Traditions, Superstitions, and Folk-Lore* (1872), pp. 109-11; Thomas Percy, *Reliques of Ancient English Poetry*, ed. Henry B. Wheatley (1887), III, 107-13.

8 / See W. G. Wood-Martin, *Traces of the Elder Faiths of Ireland* (1902), II, 127-30. For other references see Tom Peete Cross, *Motif-Index of Early Irish Literature* (1952), under Motif D 1652.3. *Cow with inexhaustible milk.*

9 / E. R. R. Green, "Christmas Rhymers and Mummers," *Ulster Journal of Archaeology*, 3rd ser., IX (1946), 3-21; see especially pp. 11-12. For mention of additional Irish appearances of the Wren, see Alan Gailey, "The Folk-Play in Ireland," *Studia Hibernica*, VI (1966), 114. Alex Helm reports that the Wren appears only occasionally in English versions (for example, in Yorkshire).

Tyrone, both in Northern Ireland. Green has some interesting comments on the relation between the mummers' play and the St. Stephen's Day custom of Hunting the Wren. Although the Newfoundland Folklore and Language Archive possesses a large, and growing, body of data on the practice of the latter custom in the Island, the Salvage Play provides our only example of a direct connection with the mummers' play.

As with the Change Islands Play, this version ends with the singing of an irrelevant song, "My Bonny Light Horseman."[10]

The frequent confusion, inconsistency and apparent dislocation in these Newfoundland texts will be readily seen. These are not, however, features which are peculiar to these versions; on the contrary, they are consistent with similar orally transmitted plays in the British and Irish traditions. The comparative scarcity of Newfoundland interpolations is, indeed, a phenomenon to be noted. At the same time, they strike the ear of Mr. Helm as having a non-English flavour. It may be that the intensive study of all the surviving texts and fragments will, as Helm suggests to us, demonstrate that they have a regional character.

In editing the three texts which follow, we have adhered closely to the conventions of the copy text, except that the placing of the speech designations has been regularized, the run-over of lines in narrow newspaper columns abandoned, contractions have been expanded, and the typography standardized. Each text is preceded by a brief preliminary note giving, in the words of those to whom we owe the preservation of the plays, information about the location, origin, and performances. The line-numeration has been added editorially and refers only to lines of actual text. The texts, with one exception, are taken from the earliest print. The exception, the St. John's Play, appeared originally in an article entitled "Rambling Thoughts about Christmas" by William Whittle which was printed in the special Christmas number of the *Evening Telegram*, December 21, 1885. This number is not to be found in the newspaper collections of the *Evening Telegram*, the Gosling Memorial Library, or the Provincial Archives; we have therefore based our text on the 1962 reprint. Editorial annotation has been kept to a minimum. We have been able to give

---

10 / According to Barrett, this song has been frequently reprinted in Britain as a broadside ballad since 1790. Texts and tunes are found in W. A. Barrett, *English Folk-Songs* (n.d. [1891?]), pp. 50–51; Frank Kidson, *English Peasant Songs* (1929), pp. 42–43; Helen Creighton, *Songs and Ballads from Nova Scotia* (1933), pp. 143–44.

some information on a few persons but others have still escaped us. Information given in this introduction is not normally repeated in the notes.

2 Texts

I. *The St. John's Play.* Date, c. 1840. Source, William Whittle,[11] The *Evening Telegram*, December 21, 1885; reprinted December 21, 1962, p. 23.

But what I most particularly wish to speak of is the "Tragedy of St. George," which was also another of the sports of the season of Christmas. It is an understood thing in dramatic life that a man assuming a character must, for the time being, divest himself of his personal identity, and make himself believe that he is really and truly that which he represents himself to be and by so doing, it goes a great way in persuading others into the same belief. So it was not a little amusing to see those noble fellows, who, perhaps, all the week were "culling" or "stowing" fish, stride and strut as King George, the Turkish Knight, Valentine and Orson, and other characters of the tragedy. Acceptably well, too, as I am informed, they read [i.e., recited] their lines.

Old Newfoundlanders, who have lived here in Boston 40 or 50 years, will repeat the lines of the tragedy today with as much fire and pride as Edwin Booth[12] would the lines of "Richard the Third." More power to them! One of them said to me, a few days ago, as his head shook with age, "Ah, these were the times! Lots of money; lots of fun!" and his good heart warmed and his weak yes [eyes] brightened as he recalled them. "Mickel Dreeling," said he, was "Captain of the Mummers" for many years previous to my leaving St. John's, and always rode a fine horse. Bob Daley used to be the "Doctor" in the "Tragedy of St. George." Sir John Harvey[13] was the last governor before whom they appeared; then came the 9th of June – glory be to God! – that left us homeless and penniless. In 1847, the year after the fire, came Sir Gaspard LeMarchant.[14] That year I left St. John's."

He told me the history of the "hobby-horse," and described the combat in the Tragedy. He repeated most of the lines; those he did not remember, I jogged his memory, for from childhood I had heard it repeated every Christmas time. The Doctor he considered the most conspicuous figure in

11 / Whittle was a St. John's–born emigrant to Boston. He was active in raising funds for the relief of those who suffered in the fire which swept St. John's in 1892. See D. W. Prowse, *History of Newfoundland* (1895), p. 529.

12 / Edwin Booth (1833–1893) the celebrated American Shakespearean actor.

13 / Governor of Newfoundland, 1841–47.

14 / Governor of Newfoundland, 1847–52.

the troupe, and with his marvellous cures and empirical gibberish, was a noted personage....

These performers were richly dressed, generally with white trousers and fancy suspenders showing their shirtsleeves which were profusely decorated with ribbons, high caps, made of pasteboard and covered with the costliest of wall paper from which also flowed yards of the richest ribbon.

Much the same as the "Fools" of more recent times, Father Christmas was personified as a very old man, whose face was completely covered by a mask. Each character in the play differed in dress, to describe which would consume too much valuable space.

The following was the cast of characters: – Saint George; The Doctor; St. Patrick; Turkish Knight; Dan Donnelly; Father Christmas; Valentine and Orson; Alexander, Czar of Russia, &c.

THE TRAGEDY

Enter Father Christmas.
  Make room, make room my gallant boys,
  And give us space to rhyme;
  We've come to show St. George's play,
  Upon this Christmas time.

  (*The Fiddler stands up and all stand around him.*)

Enter St. Patrick.
  Here am I, St. Patrick, in shining armor bright.
  I'm a famous champion besides a worthy knight.

Enter St. George.
  Yes, St. Patrick, you are a famous champion, besides a worthy knight.
  But you are not fit St. George to fight.
  What was, St. Patrick but St. George's stable boy,
  Who fed his horse seven long years on oats and hay,
  And after that he ran away.

St. Patrick.
  I swear by George, you lie, sir!

St. George.
  Pull out your sword and try, sir!
  Pull out your purse and pay, sir,
  For satisfaction I will have before you go away, sir!

St. Patrick.
>Satisfaction you will have;
>The satisfaction that you crave;
>Before ten minutes are at an end
>I'll have your head tumbling in the grave!
>So now the fight is between you and I; 20
>I will conquer and you must die.

(St. George falls wounded and calls for a doctor.)
>Five pounds for a doctor!
>That won't do.
>Ten pounds for a doctor!
>That won't do.
>Twenty pounds for a doctor!
>That will and must do.
>Is there a doctor who can be found, who will cure your champion of his deep and deadly wound?

Enter Doctor.
>Here I am. I can cure the itch, the palsy, and the gout,
>And if the devil is in him I can root him out! 30

St. George.
>What is your medicine?

Doctor.
>I have here a little bottle in the waist-band of my breeches called hectum spectur high generosity, minced up with a hen's tooth and a cat's feather.
>Put this into a bottomless skillet, boil it over a slow turf fire; knock it 99 times against the walls of Jerusalem, first found out by old Methusalem,[15] whose wife was sick and in great pain,
>I made her rise and walk again. She lived and bore children seven, and when she died she went to heaven. 40

(The Doctor rubs his patient with his wonderful liniment and pronounces in loud voice.)
>Rise! champion and act your part.

(St. George rises and assumes a warlike attitude, when he is challenged to mortal combat by the Turkish Knight.)

15 / i.e., Methuselah (Gen. v. 27).

Turkish Knight.
>Here come I, a Turkish Knight,
>Who learned in Turkish lands to fight;
>I'll fight this man with courage bold;
>If his blood's hot, it will soon run cold.

>*(St. George accepts the challenge, and they engage in deadly strife.)*

Enter Alexander, Czar of Russia.
>Here am I, Alexander, commander of the train;
>My noble deeds and great exploits have given me great fame;
>I made the lion to tremble, which did my name indict;
>Full fifty thousand soldiers – I put them all to flight.
>The Great Sham, the Great Mogul, with their dignity and splendor,   50
>Their honor and their opulence to me they did surrender.
>King George and Great Monsieur, I made quit the field,
>And Frederick Golloway unto me did yield.
>If any doubt my words, I say scratch up Bradley and boldly play.

>*(Music by Bradley) [the fiddler?].*

Enter Orson.
>Here am I, Orson, the wild man of the wood;
>I never feared danger, but slew all I could;
>First I was taken by a wondrous bear,
>And was fed by him for many a long year.
>Then I was taken by Prince Valentine,
>And little I thought he was a brother of mine.   60
>To prove the truth of what I say,
>My brother, Valentine, is here today.

Dan Donnelly.[16]
>Come all you heroes and men that would be witty,
>Come listen unto Donnelly, the wight of Dublin city;
>The Shamrock green I wear over my brow;
>And show me the man who dare oppose me now!
>No one! I do insist!
>For I have conquered nations with my mighty fist!

>(END OF THE TRAGEDY)

I have given a few of the 36 verses of this "powerful" tragedy; sufficient to show one of the good old customs prevailing in St. John's years ago.

16 / For Donnelly see above and n. 4.

II. *The Change Islands Play.* Date, c. 1900. Source, J. J. Peckford, the *Newfoundlander*, December, 1949, pp. 2-3.

[This version of the play] is from the memory of Mr. Peckford, who says that it was performed at Change Islands, Fogo District, when he was a boy of 10 or 12, about 50 years ago. Mr. Peckford never saw the words in print, but he believes his version from memory is pretty near the mark.

"It was," continues Mr. Peckford, "introduced to our young people by an English schoolmaster, Mr. Justinia [sic] Dowell[17] by name. "The soldiers, as we called them" – actors in the play – "would start St. Stephen's Day and visit all the houses in the town and would keep it up for several days. They would have quite a jolly time, and they looked very smart in their trimmed pants, white shirts and high hat with ribbons and tassles (they were dressed to kill!). They also carried swords made from birchwood, and made properly, too." Mr. Peckford's version of the old mummers' play follows:

SOLDIERS ACTING AT CHRISTMAS

Roomer (Introduction Officer).
   Room, room, gallant room, room required here tonight
   For some of my bold champions are coming forth to fight;
   Old act, new act, acts you never saw before,
   For I am the very champion that brings old Father
      Christmas to your door,
   And if you don't believe these words I say, step in Father
      Christmas and boldly declare thy way.

Father Christmas.
   Here comes I, old Father Christmas, welcome or welcome not,
   I hope old Father Christmas will never be forgot;
   Here comes I old Johnny Jack, my wife and family on my back,
   My wife so big and my children so small,
   Takes more than a crumb of bread to feed them all,   10
   And if you don't believe these words I say, step in
      King George and boldly declare thy way.

17 / This is Justinian Dowell, a teacher with the Anglican School Board in Fogo District towards the end of the nineteenth century. He was listed as a "Way" or postal official at Change Islands in 1887 (see *A Year Book and Almanac of Newfoundland 1887*, p. 61). Mr. Fred Kirby, the Anglican Superintendent of Education, has kindly informed us that Dowell's name occurs in departmental records from this district between 1887 and 1909.

King George.
>Here comes I, King George, from old England I did spring,
>Some of my victorious works I am going to bring;
>I fought the fiery dragon, I brought him to the slaughter,
>And by those very means I'll win fair Zebra,[18] King
>>of Egypt's daughter.
>
>And if you don't believe these words I say, step in King
>>of Egypt and boldly declare thy way.

King of Egypt.
>Here comes I, the King of Egypt, in uniform do appear;
>King George, King George, thy comrade is here;
>He is a man of courage bold, I am his armour-bearer
>To cut down his enemies if there are any of them here.   20
>And if you don't believe these words I say, step in
>>Valiant Soldier and boldly declare thy way.

Valiant Soldier.
>Here comes I, the Valiant Soldier, Slasher is my name,
>Sword and pistol by my side, I hope to end the game,
>One of my brothers I saw wounded, the other I saw slain.
>And by those very means I'll fight King George all on
>>the plain (*takes a step*).

Next scene, King George.
>Whist, whist, bold man, what thou art telling
>Apple dumplings thou are selling,
>Stand where thou are and call in Brother Turk to act
>>thy part.

(Valiant Soldier).
>Turk, Turk, come with speed, help in my time of need,
>Thy time of need I do implore, I was never in such
>>need before.   30

Turkish Knight.
>Here comes I, the Turkish Knight, come from the Turkish
>>land to fight;
>
>I'll fight King George with courage bold, if his blood
>>is hot I'll make it cold.

(King George again).
>Who art thou that speak so bold?

---

18 / i.e., Sabra. Chambers, *The English Folk Play*, discusses her appearance in both plays and chap-books.

(*Turkish Knight*).
>Haul out thy purse and pay for satisfaction I will
>>have before I go away.

(*King George*).
>No satisfaction thou shan't get, while I have strength
>>to stand,
>For I don't care for no Turk stands on this English land.

>(*They cross swords and both say*),
>>You and I the battle try, if you conquer I will die.

(*Turkish Knight*).
>I am cut down but not quite dead,
>It is only the pain lies in my head,
>If I once on my two legs stood,   40
>I'd fight King George to my knees in blood.

(*King George*).
>On the ground thou dost lie, and the truth I'll tell to thee,
>That if thou dost but rise again thy butcher I will be.

(*Turkish Knight*).
>Come, Valiant Soldier, be quick and smart,
>And with my sword I will pierce King George's heart.

(*Turkish Knight on his feet again, and continues*).
>I do not care for thee, King George, although thou art
>>a champion bold,
>I never saw that Englishman yet could make my blood run cold.

(*King George*).
>You Turkish dog, King George is here, happy for another
>>hour to come,
>I'll cut thee and I'll hew thee, I am bound to let thee
>>know,
>I am bold King George from England before I let thee go.   50

(*The two together with crossed swords*).
>You and I the battle try, if you conquer I will die.
>(*King George falls to the floor*)

(*Turkish Knight*).
>Now the battle I have won, thank God I am free,
>And if that man do rise again his butcher I will be.

(King George).
   (King George rises from the floor and strikes the Turk)
   I suppose you thought that I was dead, but yet alive remain,
   And go and tell the doctor the Turkishman is slain.

(Father Christmas and the Doctor).
   Doctor, doctor, come with speed,
   Help me in my time of need,
   My time of need I do implore,
   I was never in such need before.

   (Father Christmas then tries to revive the Turk himself, but with no success. He says)
   Is there a doctor to be found   60
   Can heal my son of his deadly wound?

(Doctor).
   Yes, there is a doctor to be found
   Can heal thy son of his deadly wound.

(Father Christmas).
   What is thy fee?

(Doctor).
   Fifty guineas is my fee, but if the money is paid down,
   I will do it for ten pond [pound].

(Father Christmas).
   What can you cure?

(Doctor).
   I can cure the hits, fits, palsy and the gout,
   If there is any evil spirit in this man I can sure
      drive it out.

(Father Christmas).
   What kind of medicine have you got?   70

(Doctor).
   I have a little bit of hare's grease and mare's grease,
   The wig of a weasel and the wool of a frog,
   And twenty-four ounces of September fog.

(Father Christmas).
   Where do you rub all this stuff?

(Doctor).
   I rub a little to his temple, and a little to the
     crack-bone of his heart,
   Arise, arise, bold champion, and boldly act thy part;
   Arise, arise, my lofty man, I long to see you stand,
   Open your eyes and look about, I will take you by the hand.
   (The man comes to his feet).

(Pickedy Wick).
   Here comes I, Pickedy Wick, put my hand in my pocket
     and pay what I thinks fit;
   Ladies and gentlemen, sit down to their ease,   80
   Put their hands in their pockets and pay what they please,
   And if you don't believe those words I say, step in
     Beelzebub and boldly clear thy way.

(Beelzebub).
   Here comes I, Beelzebub, under my arm I carries my club;
   In my hand I keeps my pan, I thinks myself a jolly fine man.
   Money I wants, money I crave, and money I'll have to
     carry me to my grave.
   And if you don't believe those words I say, step in
     bold Hercules and boldly clear thy way.

(Bold Hercules).
   Here comes I, bold Hercules, I boldly stem the weather,
   I took the rainbow from the skies and spliced both ends
     together,
   And if you don't believe those words I say, step in Jack
     Tar and boldly clear thy way.

(Jack Tar).
   Here comes I, Jack Tar, just returned from sea, sir,   90
   With the shiners on my breast, and what do you think
     of me, sir?
   I am a brisk young sailor and always on the sea,
   And now I am home, my heroes, I am full of life and glee;
   The battle will soon be over and now we will sing one song,
   And we will cheer our hardy comrades as we gladly march
     along.

(*All the company then form into a ring, with Father Christmas in the centre, and they sing the following ditty*).
The pig and the bug and the bumble-bee,
There is one more river to cross;
The pig and the bug and the bumble-bee,
There is one more river to cross.
One more river and that's the river of Jordan,   100
One more river, there is one more river to cross.

(THE END OF THE PLAY)

Mr. Peckford gives a description of the uniforms worn by the "mumming" actors: blue pants with red ship [*sic*] on the side seams, white shirt and a belt, with stars on their breast. Hats with stars on them and colored tassles. However, Father Christmas was dressed in Father Christmas style, the doctor in professional attire, and Jack Tar in a navy suit.

III.   *The Salvage Play*. Date, c. 1900. Source, Barney Moss,[19] the *Newfoundlander*, January, 1950, pp. 14–15.
"This is an account of the mumming play that was used on Christmas times in the early days by the first settlers in Newfoundland. They used to start out St. Stephen's Day and visit from house to house. They would keep it up for 12 days, everyone clad in war equipment that was required to do battle in those days. It's a great play, well worth resurrecting for the benefit of future generations. I have seen the old fellows at Christmas time acting it, all dressed in uniform. There's no play today can come up to the old-fashioned mumming play, because at Christmas times everyone is into it."
(Note: In all cases Mr. Moss spells Christmas in the old form of "X Mass.")

Beelzebub.
   Here comes I, Beelzebub, and on my shoulder carries my club,
   And in my hand a threepenny pan; ain't I a smart jolly old man.
   If you don't believe what I do say, step in Father
      Christmas and clear the way.

Father Christmas.
   Here comes I, old Father Christmas, all in my merry bloom,
   Come, gentlemen and ladies, come, give me little room;
   Room, room, brave gallant, room; give me room to rhyme

---

19 / Tape recordings of Mr. Barnabas Moss reciting the play were made in 1964 and again in 1965 by J. D. A. Widdowson.

And I will give you some revels to pass away old
   Christmas time.
Old activity, new activity, the like was never seen,
I pray you now Dim Dorthy step in.

Dim Dorthy.
   Here comes I, Dim Dorthy, with a fair face and a fat
      commarity,   10
   Although my commarity is but small, I'm the biggest
      bully of them all.
   If you don't believe what I do say, step in Sir Guy
      and clear the way.

Sir Guy.
   Here comes I, Sir Guy, a man of mighty strength,
   Who slew down Duncow, eighty feet in length;
   Is there anyone here holds King George a spleen,
   I'm resolved to conquer, it's for King George I'll die.
   If you don't believe what I do say, step in King
      George and clear the way.

King George.
   Here comes I, King George a man of courage bold,
   And with my glittering sword I won ten crowns of gold,
   I fought the fiery dragon till I brought him to great
      slaughter,   20
   And by those bloody means I won the Queen of Egypt's
      daughter.
   Close in a closet I was kept, then upon a table rack,
   And after that upon a rock of stone,
   'Twas there I sat and made my grievous moan.
   Then the Turkish Knight put his foot on land to fight;
   To fight I would even, if I was slain, till every drop
      of blood would quiver in his veins.
   If you don't believe what I do say, step in, Valiant
      Soldier, and clear thy way.

Valiant Soldier.
   Here comes I, the Valiant Soldier, bold, Slasher is my name,
   Sword and buckler by my side in hopes to win the game;
   My head is made of iron, my ribs are made of steel,   30
   I means to fight the Turkish Knight and slay him in
      the field.

King George.
  Hark, I hear a footstep.

Valiant Soldier.
  That may be the Grand Turk.

King George.
  If that be the Grand Turk, let him appear.

Grand Turk Enters.
  Here comes I, the Grand Turk, out of prison for to fight,
  To fight King George, that man by name, if I had him
    what dreadful work I make;
  I would cut him and slay him as small as dust,
  And send his body to the devil for a Christmas pie crust.

King George.

  Stop! Stop! Don't speak so hot,
  There's a man in this room thou knowest not,   40
  I'll cut thee and slay thee and when that is done,
  I will fight the bravest champion that's under the sun.

Grand Turk.
  Why, King George, did I ever do you any harm?

King George.
  Yes! therefore you deserve to be stabbed.

Grand Turk.
  Stab for stab, I will punch you to the ground,
  Where I mean to lay your body down.
  (*The battle is set in array between King George and the Grand Turk, King George slays the Grand Turk, his body lying dead on the ground. King George, sorry for his brother champion, calls for a doctor.*)
  Doctor, doctor, come with speed,
  And help me in my time of need;
  The time of need I never saw before
  Till I saw my brother champion lying dead upon the floor.   50
  Is there a doctor here to be found!

Doctor.
  Yes, there's a doctor here at hand
  Who can cure your brother champion
  Of his deadly wound and make him stand.

King George.
   What can you cure, noble doctor?

Doctor.
   I can cure all things: Itch, stitch, the 'pox, the
      palsy and the gout,
   And if the divil is in him I can root him out.

King George.
   How far have you travelled, noble sir?

Doctor.
   I've travelled from England through France and Spain,
   And always back to old England again.   60
   I have a little bottle in the waist band of my breeches
      pocket
   Called ice, some tice; some gold for lice; some, the
      wig of a weasel;
   The wool of a frog and eighteen inches last September's
      fog.
   Hold it over a slow turf-fire in a wooden saucepan.
   Mixed with a hen's tooth and a cat's feather;
   Three drops to his temple and one to his heart,
   Rise up, brother, and play your part.

(The dead Turk is brought to life by the doctor's medicine.
The Grand Turk cries out).
   Terrible! Terrible! The like was never seen,
   A man knocked out of seven senses into a hundred and
      nineteen;
   Not be bucks nor it by bears, one of the divil's
      whirligigs blowed me up in the air.   70
   If you don't believe what I do say, step in Turkish
      Knight and clear the way.

Turkish Knight.
   Here comes I, the Turkish Knight,
   All from the Turkish land to fight;
   To fight King George or the Valiant Soldier bold,
      Slasher is his name;
   Show me the man before me will stand,
   I'll cut him down with my courageous hand.

Valiant Soldier.
    I'm the man before you will stand
    And that you soon shall know,
    And if you do your worst or best
    I'll give you blow for blow.   80

Turkish Knight.
    I don't mind your words as figs.
    Neither your blows or bumps,
    If you cut me off my legs,
    I'll fight you on my stumps.

(The battle is on between the Turkish Knight and the Valiant Soldier. The Turk, wounded, falls to the ground).

Valiant Soldier.
    O, see, O, see, what I have done,
    I have cut him down like the fallen sun;
    Ten thousand more such men I'll fight,
    For to maintain King George's rights.

Turkish Knight.
    O stop, O stop your hand, there's one thing more I crave,
    If you spare me my sweet life I'll be your English slave.   90

Valiant Soldier.
    Arise, arise you Turkish dog, and to your country make your way,
    And tell unto your Turkish fleet what a champion old England bears today,
    Step in Oliver Cromwell and clear the way.

Oliver Cromwell.
    Here comes I, Oliver Cromwell, as you may suppose,
    I conquered many nations with my copper nose;
    I made the French to tremble, the Spanish to shake,
    I fought the jolly Dutchmen until I made their hearts ache.
    If you don't believe what I do say, step in the captain of the play.

The Captain and His Wife Appear.
    Here comes I, the captain of the play,
    And to my men I lead the way,   100
    As I stood on the pewter rock of fame,

And on the champion bear the blame.
I'm not like some of those Turkish dogs
That go out after night and disturb the people and
    make a noise,
Step in the wren and clear the way.

The Wren.
    The wren, the wren, the king of all birds,
    St. Stephen's Day I was caught in the firs;
    Although I am little my honor is great,
    Rise up, Skipper, and give us a treat;
    If you got no rum give us some cake.   110
    If you fills the plate of the small,
    It will not agree with those boys atall,
    But if you fills it of the best,
    We hope in Heaven your soul will rest.

(Song follows, sung by the crowd).
    Ye midwives and widows, come now pay attention
    To those few lines I'm now going to mention.
    Of a maid in distraction who is now going to wander,
    She relied upon George for the loss of her lover.
        (Chorus, after each verse)
    Broken-hearted I'll wander,
        For the loss of my lover,   120
    My bonnie light-horseman
        Was slain in the war.

    Three years and six months since I left England's shore,
    My bonnie light-horseman will I ever see more.
    She mounted on horseback, so gallant and brave,
    Amongst the whole regiment respected he was.

    If I had the wings of an eagle as swift as the dove
        I would fly
    I would cross the salt sea where my true love do lie,
    And with my fond lips I would bear on his grave,
    And kiss his pale cheeks so colder than clay.   130

    (END OF THE PLAY)

APPENDIX I Janneying in 'Coughlin Cove'

BY CLYDE E. WILLIAMS

EDITORIAL NOTE: Clyde Williams, then a student in an undergraduate folklore course, heard Melvin Firestone deliver his paper on "Mummers and Strangers in Northern Newfoundland," and decided to see what he could find out about the custom in his wife's home community of 'Coughlin Cove,' the pseudonym used here for a small village on the Avalon side of Trinity Bay. The paper describes the custom in an east coast community, and thus enables us to present a description of the mumming practice in an area not covered by the other papers.

'Coughlin Cove'[1] is a fishing community of about one thousand inhabitants in Trinity Bay. It lies northwest of Carbonear, and is accessible by a secondary road.

During the Christmas holidays, when all the men of the community are 'home from the water' (many of them are employed as seamen on freight and passenger vessels), groups of two or three men will make the rounds of the houses of their friends and neighbours. At each home they will have a drink or two of rum offered them. The groups tend to become larger as the visits progress. On the day before Christmas, or during the holiday evenings, the visits may be the occasion for impromptu parties at which beer and liquor flow freely; there will be singing, square-dancing, conversation, and horseplay.

From Christmas Eve until three or four days after Christmas (and

1 / Most of the information in this paper was elicited from my wife, born in 1939, who lived in 'Coughlin Cove' from the time she was six months old until she was fifteen. All quotations are hers. Although children in 'Coughlin Cove' go janneying, this paper is limited to the adult practice. I would like to express my thanks to Dr. Herbert Halpert for helpful criticism and suggestions.

only then) the adults of both sexes and all ages dress up or 'janney up.' To disguise their faces both men and women make 'false faces' from cardboard, paper bags, or cloth sacks. Holes are cut for the eyes, the mouth, and perhaps the nose; on the mask the features are emphasized with crayon or lipstick. When a cardboard mask is used, sheep's wool may be glued over the mouth to form a moustache.

In masking, the emphasis seems to be more on disguising one's self successfully than on creating a frightening appearance. Occasionally a janney may use a nylon stocking pulled down over the head, and then have the face painted up with lipstick, shoe polish, or soot.[2] Some janneys lay over the head a piece of mesh curtain which falls down to cover the face; a hat is then put on the head and pulled down to keep the veil in place. On one occasion a man used an old gas-mask to disguise his face. No one ever goes janneying without his face being covered.

To cover the rest of the body, janneys may dress in a pair of 'long-johns' – men's long underwear – pulled over their clothes. Or they may wear a woman's dressing-gown, usually one of a flowered pattern and made of cotton material, which reaches to the feet. A string or belt around the waist keeps the gown closed. Or a coat may be worn turned inside out. Other janneys may dress in 'oil clothes' – heavy, black rubber rain clothes habitually worn by fishermen at work: "The whole outfit – sou'wester, rubber pants and jacket, and 'long rubbers.' "[3] In fact, any old clothes which will create a strange and fantastic effect may be worn.

When 'janneying-up' women usually dress like men and men like women. Both sexes may carry walking sticks (to make believe they are crippled) and act like old men or women. Both men and women may also use pillows to create humps on backs or enormous stomachs. When using pillows for stomachs they will rub the area with mock pride and satisfaction, or complain of a pain, or pretend to be pregnant.

It is only more recently that such elaborate costumes have come into fashion among the janneys. Before that (c. 1949) "Quilts used to be all the rig-up." Quilts were the easiest to dress up in and are still used. "A nice one, a clean-looking one" would be chosen, "probably a flowered one – one of the nice ones," because people notice them and sometimes make comments on the quilts worn by the visiting janneys: "My that's a lovely quilt." Since quilts are only washed and hung out

2 / My wife remarked that it seemed strange to her that no one had ever disguised himself as a negro.
3 / Long rubbers are heavy rubber boots commonly worn by fishermen.

on the clothes-line about once a year, and since neighbours do not often enter the bedroom to see the quilts on the beds, the danger of its being recognized when worn by the janney would not be great. A quilt would be wrapped around the body and over the head so as to cover the face, except for a small opening for the wearer to peer out of. It would be tied around the waist, usually with a man's neck tie or a piece of string.

Along about seven-thirty in the evening of a week-day night[4] janneys set out from different houses in groups of two to six. Sometimes a few of the older people will 'take along music' – accordions, 'mouth organs' (harmonicas), and occasionally a guitar.

A person meeting janneys on the road would avoid an encounter with them if possible:

Outdoors you're more afraid of them than in the house – you never knows what they're gonna do. You try to keep away from 'em as much as you can. They'd say "Good-night" to you. You'd ignore them; you wouldn't carry on a conversation or anything. They might run after you or something like that. You don't mind 'em when you're dressed up yourself.

When the janneys come to a house they wish to visit, they open, without knocking, the storm-door, stick their heads inside the 'porch'[5] and 'sing out': "Any janneys in tonight?" in the high-pitched, squeaky voice that janneys always use – 'janney-talk.'[6] If the people who live in the house don't want the janneys to come in they reply, "No, no janneys tonight," and the janneys will go away grumbling, perhaps remarking, "She's afraid she'll get her house dirty."[7]

Some people will say, "How many of yez?" and the janneys will shout back, "Two or three," or however many there are. If there are janneys already in the house and the hosts are afraid that the situation will get out of hand, they will probably not allow the newcomers in.

4 / There are no janneying activities on Sundays, or after midnight on Saturdays. Sundays are strictly observed as the day of rest: "You're not supposed to go chopping wood or anything like that on Sundays – it's the day of rest." Janneys "wouldn't have it in their minds" (i.e., it wouldn't occur to them) to go janneying on Sundays.

5 / The 'porch' is a small room at the rear of the house used for storing wood, hanging coats, cooking utensils, and so on. A door, which is always kept closed, leads from the porch into the kitchen.

6 / 'Janney-talk' may sometimes be ingressive, that is, air is drawn into the lungs during speech instead of being exhaled as in normal talk. Some janneys are able to disguise their voices so successfully as to make it very difficult to determine whether a man or woman is speaking.

7 / If anyone had died within the past month or so within a certain house, the janneys will not visit that home.

The hosts fear that with too many present, the invariable horseplay may become too violent. Also, "Some people don't like it because janneys whisper to one another and probably are afraid because you never knows what they're gonna do. Probably Aunt Bertha might get Dad down and tickle him and do all sorts of things with him, you never knows." The janneys will never enter a house until they are invited in.

If, however, the owner of the house is ready for a lot of noise and horseplay ('carrying on'), the janneys are asked to enter with, "Yes, come in."

Once inside the kitchen – always the scene of household social activities – the janneys are offered a place to sit, or else they will look around and sit down without being asked since the invitation to enter implies an invitation to be seated. Or they may not take seats at all, but remain standing and move around the room. The hosts often keep their distance from the janneys until they get an idea how they are going to behave or who they are. "They're fearful – you never knows who's under a costume, sure."

If the janneys settle down enough for conversation, the talk is centred around establishing the true identity of the visitors. Some janneys, however, if they are not frequent visitors in the house, and therefore do not feel quite at home among the members of the host group, may not like attempts to be made to discover who they are and will make this known.

They won't answer any questions; they won't co-operate when you're guessing and asking 'em anything. They probably sit in a chair by themselves with their hands on their knees. They want to leave earlier and say to the other janneys, "Come on, let's go."

If this is the case the hosts will not continue guessing since they do not know who the janney is and do not wish to risk offending him.

Thus, with a single group of janneys, two types of behaviour may prevail. Some members of the group may remain quiet and withdrawn from the activity around them; others are active participants in the guessing, conversation, and horseplay. The guessing will continue with the latter and remarks may be made by members of the host group about the costumes of the janneys. This is done in order to get clues from the reactions of the janneys about their identity: "I believe I've seen that coat before"; "I think I saw that quilt hanging on Larna's clothes-line today"; "Isn't that Ed Seward's coat you got on there?"

If a guesser thinks he knows who the janney is, he may, to confirm his suspicions, ask the janney where his or her spouse is: "Where's Wallace tonight?" or "How come you ain't got Wallace with you tonight?" The hosts may also ask questions about supposed members of the janney's family: "Didn't see your father today;" or, "How many rabbits did your father get today?"

Always speaking in their 'janney-talk' the janneys reply with "all sorts of funny answers": "My father didn't go into the woods (which may or may not be true), you didn't see my father today," or, "I got neither father."

The janneys may also question members of the host group: "Ed, was you in the woods today?" Or they may give clues to their identity by hinting that they were present at a given time or place when one of the guessers was also present: "I saw you down in the shop this morning," or, "Didn't I see you at Joshua's house today?" The member of the host group will then try to recall who had been present at the time or place mentioned in order to make more accurate guesses.

Usually when the correct identity of the janney is guessed he will 'throw up,' that is, he will uncover his face.[8] However, some janneys do not 'throw up' when their identity is determined, especially if they happen to be persons who are not regular visitors in the home and do not feel quite at their ease.

As each janney is identified, the hosts continue guessing at the identity of those who are still covered. Since people know who the uncovered janney 'runs around with' (i.e., his friends), they will have a clue to the probable identity of the others.

If, just after entering the house, the male janneys begin 'carrying on' and indulging in buffoonery, they may sit down by the women and girls of the house (or any visiting girls who happen to be present) and pinch and squeeze their legs, put their arms around them and try to kiss them and otherwise tease and 'torment' them. Some of the women when in disguise are 'just as crazy' – they might also pinch and squeeze the men, or put their arms around them. On the only occasion that I have ever seen janneys,[9] two of them made unexpected grabs at the groins of one or two of the men in the household. The men, who took this behaviour quite in their stride, of course attempted to evade these thrusts and fended them off with much laughter and amusement.

8 / When a janney uncovers his face, he immediately resumes his everyday behaviour. But he will not give away the identities of his fellow janneys.

9 / Christmas 1963.

I was quite startled at this activity, and even more surprised to learn later from my wife that the two janneys were women of my acquaintance, both of whom were in their mid-forties and very respectable members of the community. Since the janneys' behaviour is to a very large extent governed by how well they know the members of the host group, this type of behaviour is rather an extreme.

On the other hand, if the hosts have a good idea who the janneys are, they may themselves be the aggressors, run after them, grab the janneys around the waist or even in the 'front of the pants' or in the seat of the pants. One woman used to chase after the janneys (if she were sure she knew a janney well) and, grabbing at his groin, say, "How's your old cock?" In most cases this ribaldry would be greeted with laughter by all present. Other people run after the janneys and try to get their veil or mask off and "Some folks try to haul the clothes off 'em." This, too, would only be done if the hosts were sure of the identity of the janney, and hence knew that he would not be offended.

Even if there is no music (i.e., no musical instruments), someone may ask the janneys to "Give us a jig." One or two of the janneys might get out on the floor and perform a 'step-dance.' Real step-dancing is a kind of soft-shoe tap dance performed in street shoes and to music. True step-dancers in 'Coughlin Cove' have learned their art from their fathers or grandfathers. A janney 'step-dance,' however, might be "Nothing, only jumpin' around – they don't know how to step-dance, they just get out and try to do it." If, of course, the janneys were good step-dancers, their performance would be greeted with approval and praise.

If the janneys are well known in the home, they may ask for a drink or a piece of Christmas cake: "Annie, got a bit of Christmas cake to give us?" "Got either little drop?" Making requests of this nature would only be done by janneys since normally a neighbour visiting the home would never ask for food or drink. The hosts are always willing to provide refreshments if the janneys will 'throw up' their veils or remove their masks. But most janneys will refuse to do this until they have been identified. They may say, "Name us first and we'll throw up." So the guessing may continue until the janneys are all named or have uncovered their faces. They are then served cake, and the man of the house may ask them if they would have a drink of rum, beer, or 'homebrew' (homemade beer).

A janney who has not been named may have to do without his bit of refreshment, unless he makes his identity known on his own initiative by throwing up his veil.

For the janneys to have refreshments in the course of their visit is the exception rather than the rule. They usually make their visits brief, rarely staying longer than three-quarters of an hour before moving on to the next house.

If the hosts do not succeed in identifying all the janneys, after ten or twenty minutes the janneys will probably take their leave. One of them may say, "Come on, janneys," and all will get up and leave at once with a "Good night" or "Merry Christmas" in janney-talk as they go out the door.

If the janneys have all been identified and have 'thrown up,' one may say to the others, "Come on, let's go to the next house," or, "Let's go over to (the name of a nearby neighbour's) house now." And all will go out together, bidding the hosts good night or Merry Christmas, either in their own voices or in janney-talk, as they don their masks again and resume the role of the janney.[10]

10 / Conversations with elderly residents, as well as with younger persons in 'Coughlin Cove,' indicate that the custom of janneying is not practised by as many as it was in the past. Only a few people nowadays, I am told, dress up at Christmas time and go janneying. The reason invariably given is that the various church organizations and the local fishermen's society always have frequent 'times' (square dances) and church socials (or 'Jiggs' feed,' a pork-and-cabbage supper) during the Christmas season, and these functions absorb people's attention to such a degree that janneying is 'going out.' My wife sums it up: "It's just gone out of style, that's all; people won't let 'em in and there's always some society having their times."

APPENDIX II   Mummering and Janneying:
                 Some Explanatory Notes

                              BY J. D. A. WIDDOWSON

The word 'mummering' is one of the two most common terms for the activities of disguised Christmas house-visitors in Newfoundland. This variant of 'mumming' is not recorded in the *Oxford English Dictionary*, Wright's *English Dialect Dictionary*, or such other dictionaries and glossaries as are available to us. It is, however, very precisely recorded three times from Ducklington, Oxfordshire, January 1884, in the Bodleian Library MS. Eng. Poet. c.17 (Falconer Madan MSS.);[2] and this suggests that further investigation by recorders of local speech in Great Britain may well supply supporting evidence for a British origin of this common Newfoundland usage. The usual printed form 'mumming' is occasionally also found in oral use in Newfoundland.

In many areas on the east and south coasts, 'mummering' is regarded as the normal, long-established term. (It is perhaps worth noting that there are a very few descriptions of mummers repeating simply "mum, mum, mum" when called upon to speak, rather than disguising their voices in other ways.)[3]

The noun 'mummer' [ˈmʌmɚ], [ˈmɔᶜmɚ] for the disguised visitor naturally has the same general distribution as 'mummering.' The current data in the Newfoundland Dictionary file at Memorial University suggests that the term is the most frequent one on the south coast and in the Bay St. George and Codroy Valley areas of the west coast.

1 / I wish to thank the editors of this volume, Dr. Herbert Halpert and Dr. G. M. Story, for advice and assistance in preparing this Appendix.
2 / This was noted and drawn to my attention by G. M. Story who uncovered the important Madan collection of play texts at Oxford in 1965.
3 / Cf. *OED* entries under *Mum, Mummer, Mumming*.

It is the one most commonly used in St. John's, and is found frequently elsewhere on the east coast where, with some exceptions, it is regarded as the "old" term. In some communities both 'mummering' and 'mummer' may be the only accepted terms.

'Janneying' and 'janney,' today common and widespread words used for the disguised figures (both male and female) of the Christmas season, seem to be peculiar to Newfoundland. So far as we know 'janneys' first appeared in print in 1896. Patterson[4] (who gives no specific locality) speaks of

... *old teaks* and *jannies*, boys and men who turn out in various disguises and carry on various pranks during the Christmas holidays, which last from 25th December to old Christmas day, 6th January....

Since then the words have appeared in various forms, chiefly in local newspapers. Extensive field recording and questionnaires since 1963 have demonstrated conclusively that they are known over much of the Island; however, despite our persistent inquiries, no one has been able to say where the word comes from.

'Janney' and 'janneying' appear to be the normally accepted terms on the west coast of the Great Northern Peninsula, where they bear the stamp of old established usage. Only in scattered areas on the east coast, for example, Harbour Grace, is 'janney' accepted as an old term, but in these few places it is often regarded as older than 'mummer.' Far more often, at least in the great majority of communities covered by our surveys, 'janney' and 'janneying' are said to have become popular about forty years ago. In communities where 'mummer' and 'janney' are found side by side, 'mummer' is most often regarded as the older and more established one.

At present we have insufficient evidence to make definitive historical assertions. We might, however, suggest tentatively that the uncertainty among informants about which term is the older reflects the relative isolation of many communities up to the recent past. This isolation may have led to the preservation of certain words in a given locality, from which they spread very slowly. 'Janney' and 'mummer' may even have existed independently in given communities and been diffused as communications improved. But one cannot ignore the possibility, however faint, that 'janney' may have been introduced to the east coast from the west coast.

It is also possible that in some communities 'mummer' was super-

---

4 / George Patterson, "Notes on the Dialect of the People of Newfoundland," *Journal of American Folklore*, IX (1896), 36.

seded at a fairly early date by 'janney,' and the older term 'mummer' forgotten, only to be reintroduced by increasing contact with other communities where it had never been lost.[5]

It is worth noting that those who act in the versions of the folk plays which we have recorded on the east coast may be referred to by several names besides mummers, but never as 'janneys.' In such communities 'janney' is frequently known, but today is often used pejoratively by the older people to distinguish younger disguised Christmas house-visitors from "the real mummers we used to have way back."

There is, however, no suggestion in the printed sources of any such distinction. Many of them, indeed, suggest that the terms are identical in meaning. Nevertheless, only mummers go mummering and only janneys go janneying. Moreover, janneys 'janney up,' but mummers 'rig out' or 'dress up.' One can be 'janneyed-up' (i.e., disguised as a janney), but mummers are usually said to be 'rigged up,' 'rigged out,' or merely 'dressed up.' This fine discrimination seems to be consistently observed.

Although the chosen spelling *janney* reflects the typical Newfoundland pronunciation [ˈjænɪ], the variants [ˈjɑnɪz] and [ˈjɛnɪz] are reflected in the *johnnies* and *jennies* listed by G. A. England.[6] The latter pronunciation is found especially in areas of predominantly Irish settlement. These variant pronunciations reflect the range of the phoneme /a/ in general Newfoundland usage. This wide vowel range through $/a/ > /a/ > /æ/ > /ɛ/$ (roughly from 'johnny' to 'jenny' in general Newfoundland pronunciation), complicates any attempted etymology. It obscures the fact that here we are undoubtedly dealing with a variant of the word *John(ny)*, which commonly appears in printed English West Country material as *Jan*.

The derivation of *janney* as a generic term for mummer has not been traced. It is not known in this sense, the competent authorities assure us, in the British Isles,[7] and (as noted above) no Newfoundland informant has been able to suggest its origin. But clearly the term, if not coined in Newfoundland, has taken root here, probably from some West Country source.

5 / A report from Harbour Grace suggests that 'janney' has been known there for about seventy years and is used by the older generation. Nonetheless, some of the older people as children remember their elders using 'mummers.'

6 / "Newfoundland Dialect Items," *Dialect Notes*, V (1925), 335.

7 / However, the term *janneying* [ˈjæniIn], meaning 'making a fool of oneself,' was recorded from Arnacton, Somerset, by Dr. Kirwin in 1966. His informant stated that children who were being ridiculous would be told to 'Stop *janneying* about.'

What follows is an attempt to explore some of the more plausible derivations of *janney*.

The derivation suggested by P. K. Devine,[8] though apparently unsupported, in a curious way reinforces a possible etymology. We suggest that *janney* may most plausibly be derived from a West Country pronunciation of *Johnny*, meaning: a man, a chap, fellow, country bumpkin, speaker of dialect.[9] The evidence may be presented concisely as follows:

Jan is a generic name for a Cornishman, and although comparatively few Newfoundland settlers came from Cornwall, the term may have been a direct borrowing/importation. The name *John* is commonly spelled *Jan* in West Country material (cf. *Transactions of the Devonshire Association,* LXXXV [1953], 105ff; *ibid.*, XCII, 128; *Jan* Ridd in *Lorna Doone*). Two Newfoundland instances, *Jan* Leck and *Jan* Baker, occur in George Patterson, "Notes on the Folk-lore of Newfoundland," *Journal of American Folklore,* VIII (1895), 288 and 289. More significant, however, is the use of the name *Jan* in Royal Navy slang as a "popular nickname, in lieu of proper Christian name, given to a seaman from the West Country (Somerset, Devon, etc.) e.g., *Jan* Pope, *Jan* Keddie etc." (private communication, Mr. V. Du Pree); and the use of *Janners* as a "group term for seamen hailing from the West Country" (same source). *Jan* as the nickname for a Devonian seaman is recorded by John Irving, *Royal Navalese* (1946), p. 100. (I am grateful to Dr. W. J. Kirwin for this and other valuable references.) These usages support the suggestion that *Jan* or *Janney*, already in use as nicknames for a regional group, may have been adopted locally in Newfoundland as specialised terms for *mummers*. This is further emphasised by the occurrence of *Jan* for Father Christmas, in several West Country mummers' play texts (see for example, J. S. Udal, *Folk-Lore Record*, III, pt. I. [1880], 98), and the appearance of characters called variously *Johnny Jack*, and so on, in West Country mummers' plays. It is especially interesting that in a Hampshire version of the play the entire group of mummers are called *Johnny*

8 / "Likely a variant of the old Anglo-Saxon word *zannies* meaning fools," Devine's *Folk Lore of Newfoundland* (1937), 29.

9 / For extensive evidence supporting the idea of *John/Johnny* in these and similar senses, see *OED*, *EDD*, the entries for *John/Johnny* in the indexes of *Notes and Queries* between 1859 and 1893, and *Johan, jônée, joanée, jouanneé,* and so on, in Arnold van Gennep, *Manuel de Folklore Français Contemporain*, I, part 4 (1949), 1788.

I am indebted to members of the Devonshire Association, especially Miss Theo Brown, Miss Gillian F. Moore and Mrs. Alison Wilson, for helpful suggestions on the possible derivation of *janney*.

Jacks. (See D. H. Moutray Read, "Hampshire Folklore," *Folklore*, XXII [1911], 328: "At Freefolk and Longstock the Mummers are known as 'Johnny Jacks,' and this was defined for me by the daughter of a local farmer as 'when the chaps go round dressed in gaudy paper clothes and tall hats acting the fool.'" See also the reference to Wiltshire mummers under *John Jack* in *EDD*.)

This reference to acting the fool brings us back full circle to Devine's etymology, for the *OED* derivation of *Zany* gives: a.F. *zani*, or its source It. *zani, zanni* name of servants who act as clowns in the 'Commedia dell' arte,' properly, the Venetian and Lombardic form of *Gianni = Giovanni* John.

This tendency to apply the name *John, Jack,* and so on, in a general sense is also apparent in the variants of the *Jonkanoo* figure of the West Indies (see F. G. Cassidy, *Jamaica Talk* (1961), chap. 12, pp. 256-63). This is illustrated in the following quotation from James Hooper in *Notes and Queries*, 9th Ser., I (May, 1898), 426: "'JONKANOO': 'JOHN CANOE' – In chap. VII, vol. II of Theodore Hook's 'Gilbert Gurney,' the rollicking Daly, speaking of a Lady Wolverhampton ('Dow Wolf'), says: 'I am her pet-plaything – a sort of Jonkanoo general for her dignity balls.' The curious word *Jonkanoo* is evidently a form of *John Canoe*, and, as we read in chap. x of Michael Scott's delightful 'Tom Cringle's Log,' a *John Canoe* is a negro Jack Pudding, and these John Canoes wore white false faces, and enormous shocks of horse hair fastened to their wooly pates. Their character hovers somewhere between that of a harlequin and a clown. John Canoe does not figure among the many Johns of Dr. Brewer's 'Phrase and Fable,' and probably it would be futile to seek the exact origin of the phrase."

One might well agree that it is futile to seek a definitive etymology of such phrases as *John Canoe*. Nevertheless there is an affinity between a number of these terms, which centres semantically around the idea of "a man/individual who (dresses up/disguises and) acts the fool." The widespread use of *John(ny), Jack,* and so on, as nicknames of a general or particular nature may be seen in the laborious notes on *Johnny Cake*, and so on. The variations in the pronunciation of such related terms as *Jonnock*, are also considerable. (See *Johnny Cake, Notes and Queries*, 3rd ser., XI [1867], 21, 146; *Jannock, ibid.,* 4th ser., I [1868], 28, 279; *ibid.*, 6th ser., VI [1882], 28, 95, 137, 213, 356; *ibid.*, 8th ser., IV [1893], 158, 376–77; *Jonnick, Somerset and Dorset Notes and Queries*, XXI [1934], 178; George Patterson, "Notes on the Dialect of the People of Newfoundland," *Journal of American Folklore*, VII [1895], 29.)

Other suggested etymological avenues explored include:
1. The possible connection with *January/Janus/Jan*. See also the reference to *Janivet* (or *Lanivet*) feast in Cornwall (Miss M. A. Courtney, "Cornish Feasts and 'Feasten' Customs," *Folk-Lore Journal*, IV [1886], 246). See also the references to *Jana, Janara, Jas*, or *Jans* in Violet Alford and Rodney Gallop, "Traces of a Dianic Cult from Catalonia to Portugal," *Folk-Lore*, XLVI (1935), 358–59.
2. Association with chattering and with birds which make chattering or similar noises. (See *Janner, Janny, Jaunder, Jannerer* in *EDD*; *Jaunder* in *OED*; *Janny* in R. Pearse Chope, "Devonshire Plant Names," *Report and Transactions of the Devonshire Association*, LXV [1933], 263; *Johnner* in *Old Cornwall*, V, no. 12 [1961], 533.)

From this inconclusive exploration (which could be infinitely prolonged and extended)[10] of the etymology of one term for Newfoundland mummers, we turn, finally, to other terms that have been recorded through fieldwork and questionnaire in addition to mummers and janneys.
1. 'Fools,' 'Old Fools,' 'Ribbon Fools.' Usually specialized terms denoting mummers as dancers (?), or accompanying those performing the play, sometimes bearing flag, sticks and bladders to clear the way.
2. 'Darbies.' Predominantly Southern Shore. Cf. *Johnnie/Johnny/Johnny Darby* in E. Partridge, *Dictionary of Slang and Unconventional English*.
3. 'Teaks,' 'Old Teaks.' Dr. J. Jordan draws my attention to *Tadhg*, in P. S. Dinneen, *Irish-English Dictionary*. The equation with "Tim Irishman" parallels John as a generalized appellative. 'Teak' has been recorded recently in St. John's in the jocular sense of 'a fool.'
4. 'Morgans.' Extremely rare (one report only).
5. 'Soldiers.' Term for the performers of the play (Change Islands).

Future investigations, through fieldwork, questionnaire, and analysis of printed sources can be expected to throw further light on the complex of terms associated with Christmas mumming in Newfoundland, their use and their derivation.

10 / See, for example: *Jan Jeaks, EDD; Jan Jake*, R. Morton Nance, *Word-Lore*, II (1927), 27; *John Jago*, R. Morton Nance, "Snail Lore," *Old Cornwall*, V (1957), 348; *Jan, OED; Janney, Dictionary of American Slang; Jandy-*Crowders, Charles H. Laycock, ed., *Report and Transactions of the Devonshire Association*, LVII (1925), 146; *Jandy-*Crowders, R. Pearse Chope, "Devonshire Plant Names," *ibid.*, LXIV (1932), 345; *Janney* (surname), *Notes and Queries*, 4th ser., VI (1870), 275; *Jan Kees, Notes and Queries*, 10th ser., V (1906), 15–16; *Jenkyn*, Little *John, ibid.*, 109, 155, 195.

APPENDIX III **The Newfoundland Distribution of the Mummers' Play and Christmas Disguising**

The information given here on the Newfoundland distribution of the Mummers' Play and Christmas disguising is derived principally from three sources: (*a*) fieldwork by contributors to this volume; (*b*) a postal questionnaire sent to informants throughout the Island in 1964, and questionnaires on Christmas customs and frightening figures administered to students at Memorial University in 1964 and 1966; (*c*) documentary references to Christmas customs in Newfoundland. In most cases, the identification of the custom in a given community from one of these sources was confirmed by another independent source.

We have no doubt that further investigation of the Christmas housevisit will reveal an even wider distribution than that represented by the more than three hundred communities listed in this appendix. Such investigation will enable us to know more precisely than is now possible the variation in the use of the terms 'mummers' and 'janneys'; the extent to which adult mumming is still practised; and perhaps further texts and fragments of the Mummers' Play will also come to light. In the meantime, the information collected here provides ample evidence of the very wide distribution of the custom of Christmas disguising throughout Newfoundland, its particular frequency in certain parts of the Island, and the lively and enduring impression it has left even in such places as St. John's, where it is now only a memory, and among the survivors of abandoned settlements (e.g., Brunette, Fair Island, Silver Fox Island).

The editors will welcome additional reports of the custom to add to our records. Material accumulated since Christmas 1966 (our arbitrary cut-off date for this appendix) is being processed for future publication.

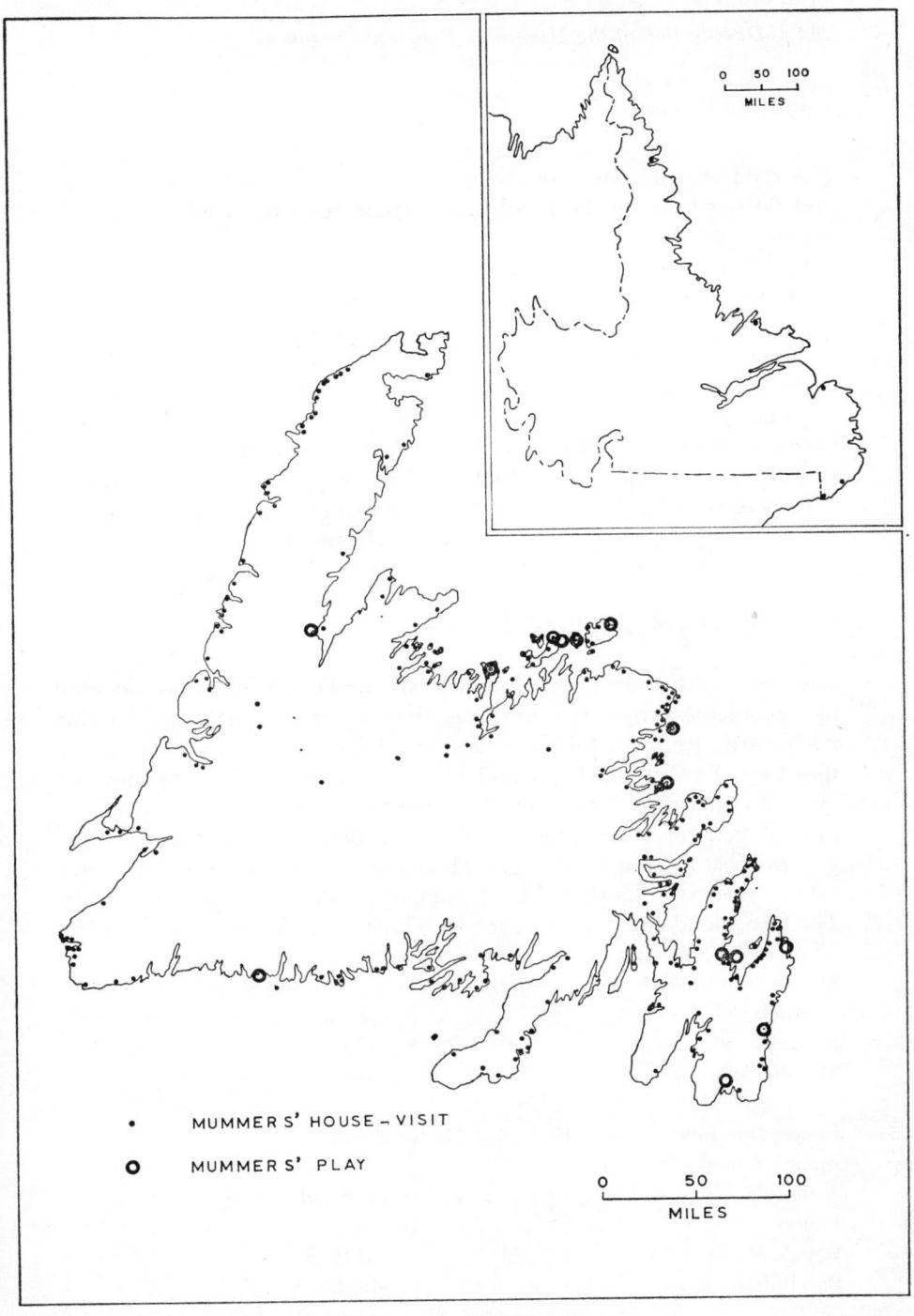

MUMMING AND THE MUMMER'S PLAY : A DISTRIBUTION MAP

A Distribution of the Mummers' Play

The data are presented in the alphabetical order of the communities and do not indicate the number of variant texts reported.

Brigus, Conception Bay (fragment)
Burgeo, south west coast (fragment)
Change Islands, north east coast (text)
Fortune Harbour, Notre Dame Bay (fragment)
Greenspond, Bonavista Bay (report)
Herring Neck, Twillingate Island (report)

North River, Conception Bay (report)
Renews, southern shore (text)
Salvage, Bonavista Bay (text)
Sop's Arm, White Bay (report)
St. John's (text)
Tilting, Fogo Island (text)
Trepassey, southern shore (text)
Vocksinge (Boxey, south coast?) (fragment)

B Distribution of Christmas Disguising

The communities are listed alphabetically under sub-headings provided by the major geographic areas as they occur on the map, working northwards from St. John's around the Island in a counter-clockwise direction. Except for Fogo and Change Islands, island communities are not separately listed but are included under the heading of the nearest general geographic feature. The definition of some of these general features (e.g., Straight Shore, south west coast) is to some extent arbitrary; they could, of course, be delimited in other ways. The few inland communities are placed separately at the end of the list.

St. John's and nearby communities (Cape Spear to Cape St. Francis)
Flatrock
Kilbride
Middle Cove
Pouch Cove
St. John's
Torbay

Conception Bay (Cape St. Francis to Grates Point)
Adam's Cove
Avondale
Bauline
Bay de Verde
Bay Roberts
Bell Island
Black Head
Brigus
Broad Cove
Caplin Cove

Carbonear
Chamberlains
Clarkes Beach
Coley's Point
Cupids
Dunville
Flat Rock
Grates Cove
Gull Island
Harbour Grace
Harbour Main
Hibb's Hole
Holyrood
Kelligrews
Kingston
Long Pond, Manuels

Northern Bay
North River
Ochre Pit Cove
Perry's Cove
Port-de-Grave
Portugal Cove
Red Head Cove
Salmon Cove
Spaniard's Bay
St. Phillips
Topsail
Upper Gullies
Upper Island Cove
Victoria
Western Bay

Trinity Bay (Grates Point to Cape Bonavista)

Butter Cove
Champney's East
Chance Cove
Chapel Arm
Daniel's Cove
Deer Harbour
Dildo South
Goobies
Gooseberry Cove
Grates Cove
Green's Harbour
Harcourt
Hatchet Cove
Hodge's Cove
Hopeall
Heart's Content
Ireland's Eye

Lady Cove
Loreburn
Monroe
Melrose
New Chelsea
New Melbourne
New Perlican
Old Perlican
Old Shop
Port Rexton
Port Union
Southport
Sunnyside
Trinity
Trouty
Winterton

Bonavista Bay (Cape Bonavista to Cape Freels)

Badger's Quay
Bonavista
Bragg's Island
Cape Island

Clark's Head
Dark Cove
Duntara
Eastport

Elliston
Fair Island
Flat Island
Fox Cove
Gambo
Glovertown
Gooseberry Island
Greenspond
Happy Adventure
Keels
King's Cove
Knights Cove
Newman's Cove
Newton
Pinchard's Island
Port Blandford
Portland

Pound Cove
Princeton
Safe Harbour
Salvage
Sandy Cove
Shambler's Cove
Silver Fox Island
St. Brendan's
St. Chad's
Summerville
Sweet Bay
Templeton
Tickle Cove
Trinity
Valleyfield
Wesleyville

Straight shore (Cape Freels to Farewell Head)
Cape Freels
Carmanville
Deadman's Bay
Frederickton

Ladle Cove
Lumsden North
Lumsden South
Musgrave Harbour

Fogo and Change Islands
Change Islands
Fogo
Indian Islands
Island Harbour

Joe Batt's Arm
Stag Harbour
Tilting

Notre Dame Bay (Farewell Head to Cape St. John)
Aspen Cove
Beaumont
Beaumont North
Beaumont South
Botwood, Bay of Exploits
Bridgeporte, New World Island
Cottrell's Cove
Crow Head, Twillingate Island
Dover
Durrell's Arm, Twillingate Island
Exploits, Bay of Exploits

Fortune Harbour
Herring Neck, New World Island
Hillgrade, New World Island
Horwood
Jackson's Cove, Green Bay
Leading Tickles
Lewisporte
Little Bay
Little Bay Islands
Little Burnt Bay
Long Island

Lushes Bight
Merritt Harbour, Twillingate Island
Moreton's Harbour, New World Island
Nipper's Harbour, Green Bay
Norris Arm, Bay of Exploits
Northern Arm, Botwood
Pilley's Island
Point Leamington
Port Anson
Quinton's Cove
Robert's Arm
Salt Harbour, New World Island
Seldom
South Brook
Southern Head Harbour
Springdale
Summerford, New World Island
Tilt Cove, Green Bay
Triton
Twillingate
Waldron's Cove, Bay of Exploits
Wellman's Cove, Green Bay
Wild Bight

Baie Verte Peninsula (Cape St. John to Partridge Point)
Baie Verte
Coachman's Cove
Silverdale

White Bay (Partridge Point to Harbour Deep)
Little Harbour Deep
Sop's Arm
Sop's Island

Great Northern Peninsula: east coast (Harbour Deep to Cape Bauld)
Roddickton, Canada Bay
Conche
St. Anthony

Great Northern Peninsula: west coast (Cape Bauld to Bonne Bay)
Anchor Point
Bear Cove
Belldowns Point
Blue Cove
Brig Bay
Cow Head
Daniel's Harbour
Eddy's Cove East
Flower's Cove
Gargamelle
Glenburnie
Green Isle Brook
Green Isle Cove
Hawke's Bay
Parson's Pond
Pine's Cove
Plum Point
Port au Choix
Portland Creek
Port Saunders
River of Ponds
Rocky Harbour
Rocky Harbour Cove
Sandy Cove
Savage Cove
Shoal Cove
St. Paul's
St. Paul's Inlet
Three Mile Rock
Trout River
Woody Point

228 Distribution of the Mummers' Play and Disguising

West coast (Bonne Bay to Cape Ray)
Aguathuna, Benoit's Cove, Bay of Islands
Bonne Bay
Cape Anguille
Codroy
Corner Brook, Bay of Islands
Curling, Bay of Islands
Doyles
Great Codroy
Highlands, Bay St. George
Kippens, Bay St. George
Millville
O'Regans
Picadilly
Sandy Point, Bay St. George
Searston
Shallop Cove, Bay St. George
St. Andrew's
St. George's, Bay St. George
Tompkins
Upper Ferry
Woodville

Southwest coast (Cape Ray to Pushthrough)
Burgeo
Burnt Islands
Cape Lahune
François
Grey River
Harbour Breton
Muddy Hole
New Harbour
Port-aux-Basques
Ramea
Rencontre
Richard's Harbour
Rose Blanche

Hermitage Bay (Pushthrough to Pass Island)
Gaultois
Hermitage
Pushthrough

Fortune Bay (Pass Island to Terrenceville)
Anderson's Cove
Belleoram
Brunette Island
English Harbour West
Little Bay East
Little Bay West
Pool's Cove
Terrenceville

Burin Peninsula (Terrenceville to Great Paradise)
Burin
Flat Island
Garnish
Grand Bank
Great Burin Island
Lawn
St. Lawrence

Placentia Bay (Great Paradise to Cape St. Mary)
Argentia
Baine Harbour
Burnt Island
Clattice Harbour

Fair Haven
Fox Cove
Freshwater
Harbour Buffett
High Beach
Isle Valen

Marystown
Petit Fort
Rock Harbour
Spencer's Cove
St. Joseph's

St. Mary's Bay (Cape St. Mary to St. Shotts)
Branch
Colinet
Gaskiers

St. Joseph's
St. Mary's
St. Vincent's

Trepassey and the southern shore (St. Shotts to Cape Spear)
Admiral's Cove
Bay Bulls
Brigus South
Calvert
Cappahayden
Ferryland

Petty Harbour
Portugal Cove South
Renews
Trepassey
Witless Bay

Inland communities
Badger, Central Nfld.
Bishop's Falls, Central Nfld.
Buchans, Central Nfld.
Cormack, Western Nfld.
Deer Lake, Western Nfld.

Gander, Central Nfld.
Grand Falls, Central Nfld.
Whitbourne, Eastern Nfld.
Windsor, Central Nfld.

Labrador
Cartwright
Makkovik

Red Bay

Select Bibliography

NEWFOUNDLAND

An Act to make further Provision for the Prevention of Nuisances, 24 & 25 Vic., c. 3, June 1861.

Anspach, Lewis. *A History of Newfoundland* (London, 1819).

Black, W. A. "The Labrador Floater Cod Fishery," *Annals of the Association of American Geographers*, I (1960), 267–93.

Bond, G. J. "Old Christmas Customs," in *The Book of Newfoundland*, ed. J. R. Smallwood (St. John's, 1937), II, 259.

Bonnycastle, Sir R. H. *Newfoundland in 1842* (London, 1842), 2 vols.

Brown, (Miss) Theo. "The Mummer's Play in Devon and Newfoundland," *Folk-Lore*, LXIII (1952), 30–34.

Browne, P. W. *Where the Fishers Go* (New York, 1909).

Bruemmer, Fred. "The Mummers," *The Beaver: Magazine of the North*, outfit 297 (Winter 1966), 24–25.

Burton, Sir Richard. *Ultima Thule; or a Summer in Iceland* (London, 1875), 2 vols.

Cartwright, George. *A Journal of Transactions and Events During a Residence of Sixteen Years on the Coast of Labrador* (Newark, Notts., 1792), 3 vols.

Cell, Gillian T. "Willoughby," in *The Dictionary of Canadian Biography* (Toronto, 1966), I, 670–71.

Census of Newfoundland, 1794–95 (manuscript).

Census of Newfoundland and Labrador, 1869 (St. John's, 1870).

"The Change Islands Play," in *The Newfoundlander*, XII, no. 7 (December 1949), 2–3.

Christmas Review (St. John's, 1892).

Select Bibliography

Cormack, W. E. *Narrative of a Journey across the Island of Newfoundland in 1822* (Edinburgh, 1836).

Daily News (St. John's), January 3, 1955; December 28, 1955; December 20, 1956; December 24, 1965.

Devine, P. K. *Devine's Folk Lore of Newfoundland in Old Words, Phrases and Expressions* (St. John's, 1937).

"Quaint Christmas Customs," *Christmas Bells*, no. 10 (St. John's, December 1901), 4.

Ye Olde St. John's (St. John's, 1936).

England, George Allan. "Newfoundland Dialect Items," *Dialect Notes*, v (1925), 322–46.

Vikings of the Ice: Being the Log of a Tenderfoot on the Great Newfoundland Seal Hunt (Garden City, N.Y., 1924).

Evening Telegram (St. John's), December 24, 1885; December 24, 1956; December 21, 1962; December 22, 1964.

Feltham, J. "The Development of the Fisherman's Protective Union in Newfoundland, 1908–1923," Unpublished Memorial University History thesis, 1959.

Fisherman's Advocate (Port Union), December 23, 1949.

Gosling, W. G. *Labrador: Its Discovery, Exploration, and Development* (London, 1910).

Gosse, Edmund. *Life of Philip Henry Gosse* (London, 1890).

Graham, William F. "The Star of the Sea Society," in *The Book of Newfoundland*, ed. J. R. Smallwood (St. John's, 1937), II, 196–97.

Gunn, Gertrude E. *The Political History of Newfoundland, 1832–1864* (Toronto, 1967).

Haie, Edward. "The Voyage of Sir Humphrey Gilbert" [Haie's *Report*], in Richard Hakluyt, *Voyages & Documents*, ed. Janet Hampden (Oxford, 1958), pp. 236–82.

Harrington, Michael Francis. "Newfoundland's Old-time Christmas," *The Atlantic Advocate*, XLVIII (1957), 22–23.

Hayman, Robert. *Quodlibets, lately come over from New Britaniola, Old Newfoundland ... Composed and done at Harbor-Grace* (London, 1628).

Howley, J. P. *A History of the Beothucks, or Red Indians* (Cambridge, 1915).

Innis, Harold A. *The Cod Fisheries: The History of an International Economy* rev. ed. (Toronto, 1954).

James, C. T. "The Society of United Fishermen," in *The Book of Newfoundland*, ed. J. R. Smallwood (St. John's, 1937), II, 192–95.
Jones, Gwyn. *The Norse Atlantic Saga: Being the Norse Voyages of Discovery and Settlement to Iceland, Greenland, America* (London, 1964).
Jukes, J. B. *Excursions in and about Newfoundland during the Years 1839 and 1840* (London, 1842), 2 vols.

Kirwin, William. "Lines, Coves, and Squares in Newfoundland Names," *American Speech*, XL (1965), 163–70.

Lench, Charles. *An Account of the Rise and Progress of Methodism on the Grand Bank and Fortune Circuits from 1816 to 1916* (St. John's, 1916).
Lench, Charles. *The Story of Methodism in Bonavista and of the Settlements visited by the Early Preachers*, 2nd ed. (St. John's, 1919).
Lind, Henry. The Diary of Rev. Henry Lind, 1857–1864 (manuscript).
Lodge, Sir Thomas. *Dictatorship in Newfoundland* (London, 1939).
Lounsbury, R. G. *The British Fishery in Newfoundland, 1634–1763* (New Haven, 1934).

McCrea, R. B. *Lost Amid the Fogs: Sketches of Life in Newfoundland* (London, 1869).
McLintock, A. H. *The Establishment of Constitutional Government in Newfoundland, 1783–1832: A Study of Retarded Colonisation*, Royal Empire Society Imperial Studies, no. 17 (London, 1941).
Melchen, Elizabeth V. " 'Janneying' in Newfoundland," *New York Folklore Quarterly*, VII (1951), 272–74.
Millais, J. G. *Newfoundland and its Untrodden Ways* (London, 1907).
Moreton, J. *Life and Work in Newfoundland* (London, 1863).
Mosdell, H. M. *When Was That? A Chronological Dictionary of Important Events in Newfoundland* (St. John's, 1923).
Mowat, Farley. *Westviking: The Ancient Norse in Greenland and North America* (Boston, 1965).
Mowat, Farley. "Will Ye Let the Mummers In?" *Weekend Magazine*, XVI, no. 52 (1966), 6–9.

Newfoundland Express (St. John's), December 29, 1863.

Oldmixon, John. *The British Empire in America*, 2nd ed. (London, 1741), pp. 1–19.

Parsons, A. A. "Memoirs of Christmas – How the Great Festival Used to be Celebrated," *Holly Leaves* (St. John's, 1917), 19–20.

Patterson, George. "Notes on the Dialect of the People of Newfoundland," *Journal of American Folklore*, IX (1896), 19–37.

Patterson, G. "Notes on the Dialect of the People of Newfoundland," *Transactions of the Nova Scotian Institute of Natural Science*, IX (1896), 44–78.

Pazdzior, E. "The Fishing Industry," in *Newfoundland and Labrador: The First Fifteen Years of Confederation*, ed. R. I. McAllister (St. John's, 1966), pp. 117–32.

Pedley, Charles. *The History of Newfoundland from the Earliest Times to the Year 1860* (London, 1863).

Perlin, A. B. *The Story of Newfoundland* (St. John's, 1959).

Perret, Robert. *La Géographie de Terre-Neuve* (Paris, 1913).

Prowse, D. W. *A History of Newfoundland from the English, Colonial, and Foreign Records* (London, 1895).

Public Ledger (St. John's), June 9, 1835.

Report of the Newfoundland Royal Commission (London, 1933).

Richards, Rev. Canon J. T. "The First Settlers on the French Shore," *Newfoundland Quarterly*, LII, no. 3 (1953), 17–19, 44; ibid., LII, no. 4 (1953), 15–16, 23.

Rogers, J. D. *A Historical Geography of the British Colonies*, v, part 4: *Newfoundland* (Oxford, 1911).

Rothney, G. O. "The Denominational Basis of Representation in the Newfoundland Assembly," *Canadian Journal of Economic and Political Science*, XXVIII (1962), 557–70.

Rothney, G. O. *Newfoundland: from International Fishery to Canadian Province*, The Canadian Historical Association Booklets no. 10 (Ottawa, 1959).

Rowe, F. W. *The Development of Education in Newfoundland* (Toronto, 1964).

The Salvage Play, in *The Newfoundlander*, XII, no. 8 (January 1950), 14–15.

Seary, E. R. *Toponymy of the Island of Newfoundland*, Check-list no. 2, Names: 1, *The Northern Peninsula* (St. John's [Memorial University of Newfoundland] 1959).

Senior, (Mrs.) E. "The Origin and Political Activities of the Orange Order in Newfoundland, 1863–1890," Unpublished M.A. thesis, Memorial University of Newfoundland, 1960.

Smallwood, J. R. ed. *The Book of Newfoundland* (St. John's, 1937), 2 vols.

Smallwood, J. R. *Newfoundland 1941: Hand Book, Gazetteer and Almanac* (St. John's, 1941).

Smith, Nicholas. *Fifty-two Years at the Labrador Fishery* (London, 1936).

The St. John's Play, in "Rambling Thoughts about Christmas," by William Whittle, *Evening Telegram*, Christmas number, December 21, 1885; reprinted in *Evening Telegram*, December 21, 1962, pp. 22–23.
Stansford, Joshua. *Fifty Years of My Life* (London, 1950).
Stearns, Winfrid Alden. *Labrador: A Sketch of its People, its Industries and its Natural History* (Boston, Mass., 1884).
Story, G. M. "The Dialects of Newfoundland," in *The Book of Newfoundland*, ed. J. R. Smallwood (St. John's, 1967), III, 559–63.

Telegraph (St. John's), February 9, 1861.
Thompson, Frederic F. *The French Shore Problem in Newfoundland* (Toronto, 1961).
Times (St. John's), December 22, 1860.
Toque, Philip. *Newfoundland: As it was, and as it is in 1877* (Toronto, 1878).

W., J. T. "An Old-time Christmas," *Christmas Greeting* (St. John's, 1893), 17–20.
Whitbourne, Sir Richard. *A Discourse and Discovery of Newfoundland* (London, 1620).
Williamson, James A. *The Cabot Voyages and Bristol Discovery Under Henry VII*, Hakluyt Society, 2nd ser., no. CXX (Cambridge, 1962).
Wilson, William. *Newfoundland and Its Missionaries* (Cambridge, Mass., 1866).
Wix, Edward. *Six Months of a Newfoundland Missionary's Journal, from February to August, 1835* (London, 1836).

A Year Book and Almanac of Newfoundland for 1887 (St. John's, 1887).
Yonge, James. *The Journal of James Yonge, Plymouth Surgeon, 1647–1721*, ed. F. N. L. Poynter (London, 1963).

OTHER WORKS

Abbott, G. F. *Macedonian Folklore* (Cambridge, 1903).
Alford, Violet. *Sword Dance and Drama* (London, 1962).
Ashton, John. *Chap-Books of the Eighteenth Century* (London, 1882).
Ashton, John. *A righte Merrie Christmasse* (London and New York, n.d.).
Atteridg, Louise Van Nederynen. "Dutch Lore in Holland and at Castleton, N.Y.," *New York Folklore Quarterly*, X (1954), 245–65.

Balch, E. E. "In a Wiltshire Village: Some Old Songs and Customs," *The Antiquary*, n.s., IV (1908), 379–82.
Barrett, William Alexander. *English Folk-Songs* (London and New York, n.d. [1891?]).
Beattie, John. "Understanding and Explanation in Social Anthropology," *British Journal of Sociology*, X (1959), 45–60.
Bede, Cuthbert [Rev. Henry Bradley]. "Christmas at Exeter in 1737," *Notes and Queries*, 2nd ser., X (December 15, 1860), 464–65.
Boas, Franz. "The Central Eskimo," *6th Annual Report of the Bureau of [American] Ethnology, 1884–85* (Washington, 1888), 399–669.
Bonser, Wilfrid. *A Bibliography of Folklore*, Publications of the Folk-Lore Society, CXI (London, 1961).
Bunzel, Ruth L. "Zuñi Katcinas," *47th Annual Report of the Bureau of American Ethnology, 1929–1930* (Washington, 1932), 837–1086.
Burne, Charlotte Sophia, and Jackson, Georgina F. *Shropshire Folk-Lore* (London, 1883).

Campbell, Donald T. "The Mutual Methodological Relevance of Anthropology and Psychology," in *Psychological Anthropology: Approaches to Culture and Personality*, ed. F. L. K. Hsu (Homewood, Illinois, 1961), pp. 333–52.
Cawte, E. C., Helm, Alex, and Peacock, N. *English Ritual Drama*, Publications of the Folk-Lore Society, CXXVII (London, 1967).
Cawte, E. C., Helm, Alex, et al., "A Geographical Index of the Ceremonial Dance in Great Britain," Part One, *Journal of the English Folk Dance and Song Society*, IX, no. 1 (1960), 1–41.
Chambers, E. K. *The English Folk-Play* (Oxford, 1933).
Chambers, E. K. *The Mediaeval Stage* (Oxford, 1903), 2 vols.
Clark, William Smith. *The Early Irish Stage. The Beginnings to 1720* (Oxford, 1955).
Cline, Ruth H. "Belsnickles and Shanghais," *Journal of American Folklore*, LXXI (1958), 164–65.
Courtney (Miss) M. A. "Cornish Feasts and 'Feasten' Customs," *Folk-Lore Journal*, IV (1886), 109–32.
Courtney, (Miss) M. A. *Cornish Feasts and Folk-Lore* (Penzance, 1890).
Creighton, Helen. *Folklore of Lunenburg County, Nova Scotia*, National Museum of Canada, Bulletin no. 117 (Ottawa, 1950).
Creighton, Helen. *Songs and Ballads from Nova Scotia* (Toronto and Vancouver, 1933).
Cross, Tom Peete. *Motif-Index of Early Irish Literature*, Indiana University Publications, Folklore Series, no. 7 (Bloomington, Indiana, 1952).

Dacombe, Marianne R., ed. *Dorset Up Along and Down Along* (Gillingham, Dorset [1936]).
Dawkins, R. M. "The Modern Carnival in Thrace and the Cult of Dionysus," *Journal of Hellenic Studies*, xxvi (1906), 191–206.
Dawkins, R. M. "A Visit to Skyros," *The Annual of the British School at Athens*, xi (1904–1905), 72–80.
Dean-Smith, Margaret. "The Life-Cycle Play or Folk Play: Some Conclusions Following the Examination of the Ordish Papers and Other Sources," *Folklore*, lxix (1958), 237–53.
Durkheim, E. *Elementary Forms of the Religious Life* (London, 1915).

Elworthy, Frederick Thomas. *Horns of Honour* (London, 1900).
English Dialect Dictionary, cited as *EDD*.

Fergusson, R. Menzies. *Rambles in the Far North*, 2nd ed., (Paisley and London, 1884).
Foster, George M. "Community Development and the Image of the Static Economy," *Community Development Bulletin*, xii (1961), 124–28.
Foster, George M. "The Dyadic Contract: a Model for the Social Structure of a Mexican Peasant Village," *American Anthropologist*, lxiii (1961), 1173–92.
Foster, Jeanne Cooper. *Ulster Folklore* (Belfast, 1951).

Gailey, Alan. "The Folk-Play in Ireland," *Studia Hibernica*, vi (1966), 113–54.
van Gennep, Arnold, *The Rites of Passage* (Chicago, 1960).
Gillham, C. E. *Medicine Men of Hooper Bay* (London, 1955).
Gluckman, Max. *Custom and Conflict in Africa* (Glencoe, 1959).
  Essays on the Ritual of Social Relations (Manchester, 1961).
  Rituals of Rebellion in South-East Africa (Manchester, 1954).
Goffman, Erving. *Presentation of Self in Everyday Life* (New York, 1959).
Goody, Jack. *Death, Property and the Ancestors* (Stanford, 1959).
Green, E. R. R. "Christmas Rhymers and Mummers," *Ulster Journal of Archaeology*, 3rd ser., ix (1946), 3–21.

Hardwick, Charles. *Traditions, Superstitions, and Folk-Lore* (Manchester and London, 1872).
Hardy, Thomas. *The Return of the Native* (London, 1878).
Helm, Alex. "In Comes I, St. George," *Folklore*, lxxvi (1965), 118–36.
Hoggan, Frances. "Notes on Welsh Folk-Lore," *Folk-Lore*, iv (1893), 122–23.
Howison, Daniel, and Bentley, Bernard. "The North-West Morris: A General

Survey," *Journal of the English Folk Dance and Song Society*, IX, no. 1 (1960), 42–55.
Hunt, Robert. *Popular Romances of the West of England* (London, 1865), 2 series.

James, E. O. *Seasonal Feasts and Festivals* (London, 1961).
Johnson, L. G. "Laurence Williamson," *Scottish Studies*, VI (1962), 49–59.
Jones, Edward. *Musical and Poetical Relicks of the Welsh Bards*, 2nd ed. (London, 1794).

Kennedy, Douglas. *English Folk Dancing, Today and Yesterday* (London, 1964).
Kennedy, Patrick. *The Banks of the Boro: A Chronicle of the County of Wexford* (London and Dublin, 1867).
Kennedy, Patrick. "Hibernian Country Pastimes and Festivals Fifty Years Since," *Dublin University Magazine*, LXVII (1863), 581–88.
Kidson, Frank. *English Peasant Songs*, ed. Ethel Kidson (London, 1929).
Kittredge, G. L. [Note] *Journal of American Folklore*, XXII (1909), 394.
Kluckhohn, Clyde. "Navaho Witchcraft," *Papers of the Museum of American Archaeology and Ethnology, Harvard University*, XXII, no. 2 (Cambridge, 1944); also reprinted as *Navaho Witchcraft* (Boston, 1962).

Lawson, J. C. "A Beast-Dance in Scyros," *The Annual of the British School at Athens*, VI (1899–1900), 125–27.
Lawson, John Cuthbert. *Modern Greek Folklore and Ancient Greek Religion* (1910; reprinted New Hyde Park, N.Y., 1964).
Leach, E. R. *Rethinking Anthropology*, London School of Economics Monographs in Social Anthropology, no. 22 (London, 1961).

Madan Collection: Bodleian Library MS. Eng. Poet. c.17.
Martin, E. W. *The Shearers and the Shorn: A Study of Life in a Devon Community* (London, 1965).
Megas, George A. *Greek Calendar Customs*, 2nd ed. (Athens, 1963).
Miles, Clement A. *Christmas in Ritual and Tradition*, 2nd ed. (London and Leipsic, 1913).
Mok, Paul. "Folklore of the Netherlands," *New York Folklore Quarterly*, VI (1950), 221–33.
Moss, Fletcher. *Didisburye in the '45* (Manchester, 1891).

Needham, Joseph. "The Geographical Distribution of English Ceremonial Dance Traditions," *Journal of the English Folk Dance and Song Society*, III, no. 1 (1936), 1–45.

Norbeck, Edward. "African Rituals of Conflict," *American Anthropologist*, LXV (1963), 1254–79.

O'Conor, Manus. *Irish Com-All-Ye's* (New York, 1901).
Oinas, Felix J. "Spirits, Devils, and Fugitive Soldiers," *Journal of American Folklore*, LXXVI (1963), 225–30.
O'Keefe, Daniel. *The First Book of Irish Ballads*, 4th ed. (Cork, 1965).
O Lochlainn, Colm. *Irish Street Ballads* (Dublin and London, 1939).
The Oxford English Dictionary, cited as *OED*.

Parsons, Elsie Clews. "The Zuñi A' doshlĕ and Suukĕ," *American Anthropologist*, n.s., XVIII (1916), 338–47.
Paynter, S. Freda. "Guise-dancing at Quito," *Old Cornwall*, II, no. 9 (Summer 1935), 19.
Pearse, Andrew. "Carnival in Nineteenth Century Trinidad," *Caribbean Quarterly*, IV (1956), 175–93.
Percy, Thomas. *Reliques of Ancient English Poetry*, ed. Henry B. Wheatley (London, 1887), 3 vols.
Petrie, George. *The Complete Collection of Irish Music*, ed. Charles Villiers Stanford (London, 1905).
Pitt-Rivers, J. A. *The People of the Sierra* (London, 1954).
Plotnicov, Leonard. "Fixed Membership Groups: the Locus of Culture Processes," *American Anthropologist*, LXIV (1962), 97–103.

Radford, Cecily. "Three Centuries of Playgoing in Exeter," *Report and Transactions of the Devonshire Association*, LXXXII (1950), 241–69.
Rasmussen, Knut, and Worster, W. *Eskimo Folk-Tales* (London, 1921).
Rink, Henry. *Tales and Traditions of the Eskimo* (Edinburgh and London, 1875).

S., J. B. "Waits and Mummers," *Notes and Queries*, 6th ser., XII (December 19, 1885), 489.
Shoemaker, Alfred L. *Christmas in Pennsylvania: A Folk-Cultural Study* (Kutztown, Pennsylvania, 1959).
Simmons, Leo W., ed. *Sun Chief: The Autobiography of a Hopi Indian* (New Haven, 1942).
Simpkins, John Ewart, ed. *Examples of Printed Folk-Lore Concerning Fife*, Publications of the Folk-Lore Society, LXXI (London, 1914).
Spiro, Melford E. "An Overview and Suggested Reorientation," in *Psychological Anthropology*, ed. F. L. K. Hsu (Homewood, Illinois, 1961), pp. 459–92.

Spiro, Melford E. "Social Systems, Personality, and Functional Analysis," in *Studying Personality Cross-Culturally*, ed. Bert Kaplan (Evanston, 1961).

Stephenson, C. H. "King Christmas," *Notes and Queries*, 4th ser., VIII (December 23, 1871), 525.

Sternberg, Thomas. *The Dialect and Folk-Lore of Northamptonshire* (London and Northampton, 1851).

Stewart, Alexander. *Reminiscences of Dunfermline and Neighbourhood*, 2nd ed. (Edinburgh, 1889).

Tolstoy, Leo. *War and Peace*, trans. Louise and Aylmer Maude (New York, 1938), 2 vols.

Wace, A. J. B. "Mumming Plays in the Southern Balkans," *The Annual of the British School at Athens*, XIX (1912–1913), 248–65.

Wace, A. J. B. "North Greek Festivals and the Worship of Dionysos," *The Annual of the British School at Athens*, XVI (1909–1910), 232–53.

[Wehman Bros.] *Six Hundred and Seventeen Irish Songs and Ballads* (New York, n.d.).

Wehman's Irish Song Book, no. 1 (New York, 1887).

Welch, Charles E., Jr. " 'Oh, Dem Golden Slippers': The Philadelphia Mummers Parade," *Journal of American Folklore*, LXXIX (1966), 523–36.

Welch, Charles E., Jr. "Some Early Phases of the Philadelphia Mummers' Parade," *Pennsylvania Folklife*, IX (Winter 1957–58), 25–27.

Welsford, Enid. *The Court Masque* (Cambridge, 1927).

Withington, Robert. *English Pageantry, An Historical Outline* (Cambridge [Mass.], 1918), 2 vols.

Wood-Martin, W. G. *Traces of the Elder Faiths of Ireland* (London, New York and Bombay, 1902), 2 vols.

Wright, A. R., and Lones, T. E. *British Calendar Customs: England*, Publications of The Folk-Lore Society, XCVII, CII, CVI (London, 1936–1940), 3 vols.

Index

Acadian French, 20
Aguanthuna, 151
Albania, 57
Alexander, 185
Alexander, Czar of Russia, 172, 188, 194, 196
Alexander, Sir. 188
Alexander the Great, 171, 188–89
Anchor Point, 68
Anspach, L. A., 169, 176
Antrim, North, 52
Austria, 35, 43
Avalon Peninsula, 9, 12, 19, 26, 28, 29, 179, 182, 209
Avondale, 160, 163

Badger's Quay, 149, 156
Baine Harbour, 151
Balkans, 57
Bay Bulls, 155
Bay Roberts, 25, 169, 178
Bear Cove, 64, 69
Beelzebub, 59, 190, 201, 202
Bell Island, 31
belsnickles, 35, 39, 40, 41, 43
Beothic Indians, 21, 134
Big Brook, 68
Black Man, 138
Black Peter, 36, 43
Blanc Sablon, 183
Bonavista, 25
Bonavista Bay, 19, 184
Bond, Rev. G. J., 175–76

Bonne Bay, 68
Bonnycastle, Sir Richard, 171
Boo Man, 72
Booth, Edwin, 193
Boston, Mass., 19, 52–53, 193
Bradley the fiddler, 189, 194, 196
Brigus, 169, 181
British Isles, 9, 28, 29, 184
Buchans, 31
Bulgaria, 57
Burgeo, 20, 24, 183, 184
Burin, 24
Burnt Islands, 153

Cabot, John, 10
Calvert, Sir George, 12
Campbell, Donald T., 73–74
Cape Bonavista, 13
Cape Breton Island, 105
Cape Freels, 19
Cape Norman, 64
Cape Race, 13
Cape Ray, 20
Cape St. John, 20
Captain, 206
Captain's Wife, 206
Carbonear, 25, 27, 29, 209
carolers, 36
Carson, William, 26
Carter, Mr. Justice, 178
Carter, "Munn," 174
Cartwright, George, 168–69
'Cat Harbour,' 19, 129–44

242 Index

Catalina, 161
Cawte, E. C., 38, 56
Chambers, E. K., 51, 55, 57, 176
Change Islands, 20, 160, 184, 197
Change Islands Play, 187, 189–90, 192, 197–202
chap-books, 189, 190
Cheshire, 190
China, Emperor of, 189
Christmas bull, 5, 43, 46
Christmas Guisers, 56
Christmas holidays, see Newfoundland
Christmas Rhymers, 56
Coachman's Cove, 148, 157, 159, 162, 163
Coaker, Sir William, 30
Codroy Valley, 216
Cody, Bill, 175
collectors, 36, 37, 38, 39
Conception Bay, 26, 27, 30, 31, 134, 169, 170, 176, 178
Conche, 153, 156, 160
Cooks Harbour, 68
Cooper the pugilist, 189
Cork, 26, 177
Cormack, W. E., 21
Corner Brook, 31, 68, 69
Cornwall, 16, 45, 46, 219
'Coughlin Cove,' 209–15
Courtney (Miss), M.A., 46
Cromwell, Oliver, 14, 59, 191, 206
Cupids, 12

Daley, Bob, 193
Dame Dorothy, 190
Darbies, 221
Davis Strait, 10
'Deep Harbour,' 20, 44, 77–103
Deer Lake, 68
Devil, 59, 72, 73, 138, 139, 154, 180
Devine, P. K., 185, 219
Devonshire 16, 56, 172, 219
Dim Dorthy, 190, 203
Doctor, the, 58, 188, 189, 190, 191, 193–94, 195, 200, 201 204 205
Donegal, 191
Donnelly, Dan, 189, 194, 196
Dorset, 16, 46, 56, 189
Dowell, Justinian M., 190, 197

Dreeling, Mickel, 193
drinking, 67, 84–88, 109, 111, 113, 114, 126, 127, 214
Dublin, 189, 196
Ducklington, Oxfordshire, 216
Dun Cow, 191, 203
Durkheim, Emile, 113

Eastport, 156, 163
Ecuador, 39, 41, 43, 44
Eddies Cove East, 68
England, 35, 38, 39, 44, 199, 207
Eskimos, 14, 36, 121–27 129
Exploits 162

Father Christmas, 175, 189, 190, 194, 197, 200, 202, 219
Feild, Bishop Edward 178
Ferolle, 68
Ferryland, 12, 13
fishermen, European, 10, 12, 15, 17, 20, 63, 134, 168
Fishermen's Protective Union, 30
fishery, see Newfoundland
Flowers Cove, 64, 72
Fogo, 20, 135, 197
Foley, Davey, 174
folk play, 35, 36, 51, 52, 56–61, 171, 172, 182, 184, 185, 187–207, 224
'fools,' 45, 171, 173, 174, 175, 176, 177, 183, 194, 221
Fortune, 24
Fortune Bay, 19, 30
Fortune Harbour, 151, 152, 153, 156, 158, 161, 162, 163
France, 21, 46
Frazer, Sir James, 35
French Shore, 63
Freud, Sigmund, 118

Galatians, 188
Galloway, Frederick, 189, 196
Gander, 141
George, 207
George's Bank, 23
Germany, 43
Gilbert, Sir Humphrey, 167–68
Glovertown, 148, 149, 150, 152
Gluckman, Max, 117

Gosse, Philip Henry, 27, 29
Graham, John, 55
Grand Bank, 24, 25
Grand Banks, 10, 23, 32
Grand Falls, 31, 153
Grand Turk, 191, 204, 205
Great Britain, 13, 32, 38, 216
Great Mogul, 196
Great Monsieur, 196
Great Sham, 196
Greece, Northern, 57
Green, E. R. R., 191
Greenland, 14
Green's Harbour, 158
Greenspond, 135
Guisers, 38, 39, 41, 45, 46, 56
Gulf of St. Lawrence, 9, 105, 183
Guy, John, 12
Guy (of Warwick), 191, 203

Hallowe'en, 39, 40, 89, 112, 148, 153, 161
Hamilton, Marquis of, 13
Hampshire, 219
Harbour Grace, 12, 18, 25, 27, 135, 152, 169, 177, 180, 217
Harbour Le Cou, 158
Hardy, Thomas, 60
Harrington, M. F., 185
Harvey, Sir John, 193
Heart's Content, 152
Hebron, 121, 126
Hector, 185
Helm, Alex, 56, 60, 187, 188, 189, 192
Helston Flora (or Furry) Dance, 36
Hercules, 190, 201
Hereford, 189
Hermitage Bay, 19
Hero-combat Play, 36, 56, 57–61, 171, 172, 187–207
Herring Neck, 184
hobby horse, 5, 43, 46–47, 66, 167, 175, 193
Hogmanay, 39
Holland, 43
Horwood, Harold, 183
Hunt, Robert, 45
Hunting the Wren, 5, 191, 192

Iceland, 9, 12

India, Emperor of, 189, 196
Indians, 20, 21, 43, 75, 105, 134
inquisitors, visitation by, 36, 42–43
Institute of Social and Economic Research: publications, 4n
Ireland, 13, 16, 28, 38, 56, 57, 188, 191, 192
Irish, 16, 26, 28, 29, 172, 177, 189, 221
Italy, 46

Jack Tar, 190, 201, 202
Jamaica, 12
Jan, 219, 221
janivet, 221
janner, 221
jannerer, 221
Janners, 219
janney, etymology and usage, 217–21
jannneying, 217–21
janny, 221
Janus, 221
jaunder, 221
jennies, 218
Jerusalem, 195
Joe Batts Arm, 149, 161
John, 219, 220
John Canoe, 220
Johnny, 219
Johnny Jack, 189, 197, 219, 220
jonnock, 220
Jordan, river, 202
Jukes, J. B., 28, 170–71

Kennedy, Patrick, 49
Kennoway (Scotland), 39
Kentucky, 190, 191
Kildare, the Curragh of, 189
Kilkenny, 177
King George, 189, 190, 191, 196, 197, 198, 199, 203, 204, 205
King of Egypt, 190, 198
King's Cove, B.B., 170
Kirke, Sir David, 13
Kluckhohn, Clyde, 75
Labrador, 9, 10, 20, 24, 63, 121–27, 147, 168, 181, 183
Labrador Current, 10
LeMarchant, Sir Gaspard, 193
Leach, E. R., 142

Lind, Rev. Henry, 183
Louis XIV, 189, 196
Louisiana, 46
Lunenburg, 40

Main Brook, 68
Makkovik, 121–27
Man, Isle of, 189
Mardi Gras, New Orleans, 35, 53–54
Maritimes, 10
May-boys, 49–51
mayers, 36
Mediterranean, 24
Mercer, Isaac, 178
Methuselah, 195
Micmac Indians, 20, 21
Millais, J. G., 14
Moakler, Leo, 187
Moravian missions, 20, 121, 125, 126
Morgans, 221
Morris Dance, 36, 55
Morris, Patrick, 26
Moss, Barney, 202
mummer, etymology and usage, 216–17
mummering, 216–17
Mummers
    bans: London, 176; Newfoundland, 51, 178, 179; New Orleans, 54; Philadelphia, 53–54; Trinidad, 53
    dance procession, 36, 47, 48
    disguise, 37, 58, 59, 63, 65–67, 82, 88–90, 110, 122, 130, 131, 147–64, 173, 174, 176, 177, 182, 210, 211
    groups, 37, 90–102, 110, 111, 114, 115, 122, 130
    guessing identities, 37, 38, 42, 67, 90–102, 110, 111, 113, 114, 115, 132, 212–15
    history of in Newfoundland, 166–85
    "house-visit," 4, 5, 35, 36, 37, 38, 39, 41, 42, 44, 67, 68, 80–102, 109, 112–14, 123–25, 131–33, 211–15, 184
    Newfoundland Mummers' play text, 5, 56, 59, 60, 61, 171, 172, 184, 185, 187, 188, 189, 192, 193–96, 197–207, 224
    parade, 36, 47–55; Philadelphia, 35, 53, 54; St. John's, 48, 171, 174, 175, 176
    violence, 44–47, 51–55, 67, 68, 73, 116, 117, 124, 125, 126, 132, 176, 180, 183, 213, 214
Murphy, Masey, 174
"My Bonny Light Horseman," 192, 207

'naluyuks,' 36, 44, 45, 121–27, 129
Nameless Cove, 64
Natashquan, 183
Navaho Indians, 75
Nelson, Horatio Lord, 171
New England, 9, 13, 21
Newfoundland: American bases, 31, 106;
    Christmas holidays, 22, 67, 80–83, 102, 103, 109, 148, 168–85, 209
    condition of settlers, 10–33 *passim*, 168
    Confederation, 20, 31, 106
    early colonies, 12–13, 15
    early literature, 12
    fisheries, 10–13
    geographical data, 9–10
    hunters, hunting, 9, 14
    origin of settlers, 16, 56, 105, 134
    population, 15, 16, 24, 25
    provenance of Mummers' Play, 56, 172, 189, 191, 192
    railway, 31
    religious violence, 27–28, 135, 177
    seal hunt, 14, 22, 23
    spread of settlements, 19–21
    truck system, 22, 31
New Orleans, 35, 53, 54, 55
New Perlican, 148
Nipper's Harbour, 149, 151, 156, 159, 162
Norfolk, 49
Norsemen, 10, 14
North America, 39, 43
North Pole, 67, 158
North Sydney, 105
Northern Peninsula, 9, 20, 63, 68, 158, 217
Northumberland, 16
Notre Dame Bay, 19, 25, 184
Nova Scotia, 9, 20, 21, 28, 35, 40, 43, 105

Old Fools, 221
Old Nick, 138, 153
Old Perlican, 153, 156
Old Teaks, 221
Old Tup, 43
"One more river to cross," 202
'oonchooks,' 49, 51, 174, 176
Orson, 189, 194, 196
Ottawa, 158

Pace Egg Play, 56, 190
pace-eggers, 38
Paddy Whack, 190
pageants, 35, 48
Parsons, A. A., 175
Peckford, J. J., 197, 202
Pennsylvania, 35, 41, 43
perchtenlauf, 35
Petit Nord, 63
Philadelphia, 35, 53–54, 55
Pickedy Wick, 190, 201
Pickle Herring, 190
Placentia Bay, 19, 26
Plough Jacks, 56
Plough Monday Play, 56
Plough or Wooing Play, 36, 56, 57, 59
Plymouth, 167
popular plays, 55
Port Blandford, 148, 158, 163
Port Union, 182
Portland Creek, 153
Priam, King, 185
Prowse, D. W., 170, 177–78
Pueblo Indians, 43

Quebec, 183–84
Queen of Egypt, 203

Renaissance dumb-show, 36, 55
Renaissance masque, 35, 36, 55
Revesby Play, 190
Ribbon Fools, 221
Room, 189
Roomer, 189, 197
'Ross,' 20, 105–18, 129
"Runaway, The," 69, 71
Russia, 41–42, 43, 44
Russia, Czar of, 172, 188
Ryan, Daniel, 170

Sabra, 198
St. Anthony, 69, 71, 153
St. Dennis, 59
St. George, 185, 187, 188, 194, 195, 196, 198
"St. George, Tragedy of," 56
St. George's, 154, 157
St. George's Bay, 216
St. John's, 22, 24–25, 27, 30, 47, 48, 51, 70, 135, 141, 148, 151, 152, 168, 169, 170, 171, 172, 178, 179, 184, 187, 193, 196, 217
St. John's Play, 187, 188–89, 192, 193–96
St. Joseph's, P.B., 151, 153, 154, 160
St. Mary's, 149, 150, 152
St. Michael, 185
St. Michael, feast of, 46
St. Nicholas, 36, 43
St. Patrick, 59, 185, 188, 189, 194, 195
St. Stephen's Day, 5, 35, 53, 182, 191–92, 197, 202, 207
Salvage, 149, 152, 153, 157, 160
Salvage Play, 187, 190–91, 192, 202–07
Sandy Cove, 64, 66, 67
Sandy Point, 183
Santa Claus, 72, 109, 122, 136–37
Savage Cove, 63–64, 66, 72
Scotland, 14, 20, 35, 39, 40, 43, 56
Shallop Cove, 154, 159
Sharp, Cecil, 55
Shetland, 35, 39, 40
Shrove Tuesday, 41
skaklers, 35, 39, 40
Skipper, 207
Slasher, 190, 198, 203, 205
Smith, Nicholas, 181
Soldiers, 221
"Soldiers Acting at Christmas," 56
Somerset, 16, 46, 56, 219
Sop's Island, 150, 157, 159
Soulers, 36, 38, 56
Souling Play, 56
Spiro, Melford E., 75
step-dancing, 67, 83, 87, 98, 133, 214
Stephenville, 106
Straits of Belle Isle, 63, 65, 129, 140
strangers, 68–75, 133–41, 144
Stubbes, Philip, 167

Sword Dance, 35, 36, 55
Sword Dance Play, 36, 56
Sword Dancers, 56

Teaks, 221
Thomas, Noah, 178
Thrace, 35
Tipperary, 177
Tipteerers, 56
Tolstoy, Leo, 39, 41–42
Toole, Mick, 178
Trepassey, 12
Trinidad, 40, 43, 53, 55
Trinidad Carnival Parade, 53
Trinity, 182
Trinity Bay, 19, 30, 182, 209
Turk, 200
Turkish Knight, 59, 188, 190, 191, 194, 195, 196, 198, 199, 203, 206
Twillingate, 20, 25, 184
Tyrone, 192

Ulster, 28
United States, 48, 68

Valentine, 189, 194, 196
Valiant Soldier, 190, 191, 198, 199, 203, 204, 205, 206
Vaughan, Sir William, 12

Virginia, 13, 35, 40, 43
"Vocksinge" (Boxey?), 185

Wales, 46
Waterford, 26, 177
Wellington, Duke of, 171
Welsford, Enid, 55
Wesleyville, 152, 153, 161
West Country, 13, 14, 16, 17, 23, 25, 26, 56, 57, 59, 135, 171, 189, 190, 218, 219
West Indies, 24, 46
West Virginia, 35, 40, 41
Wexford, 49, 177, 188
White Boys, 56
Whittle, William, 173–75, 176, 179, 188, 192, 193
Winterton, 153, 158, 159, 160
Winton, Henry, 27, 177
witchcraft, 137, 138, 141
Wix, Edward, 20, 30
Wooing Play, see Plough Play
Wren, the, 191, 207
Wren-boys, 35, 36, 38

Yonge, James, 15
Yugoslavia, 57

zany, 220
Zebra, 198

This book

was designed by

ANTJE LINGNER

under the direction of

ALLAN FLEMING

and was printed by

University of

Toronto

Press